Barbara Korte, Doris Lechner (eds.)
History and Humour

**Historische Lebenswelten in populären Wissenskulturen**
**History in Popular Cultures** | Volume II

**Editorial**

The series **Historische Lebenswelten in populären Wissenskulturen | History in Popular Cultures** provides analyses of popular representations of history from specific and interdisciplinary perspectives (history, literature and media studies, social anthropology, and sociology). The studies focus on the contents, media, genres, as well as functions of contemporary and past historical cultures.

The series is edited by Barbara Korte and Sylvia Paletschek (executives), Hans-Joachim Gehrke, Wolfgang Hochbruck, Sven Kommer and Judith Schlehe.

Barbara Korte, Doris Lechner (eds.)
# History and Humour
**British and American Perspectives**

[transcript]

Printed with the support of the German Research Foundation (DFG).

**Bibliographic Information published by the Deutsche Nationalbibliothek**
The Deutsche Nationalbibliothek lists this publication in the Deutsche Nationalbibliografie; detailed bibliographic data are available in the Internet at http://dnb.d-nb.de

**© 2013 transcript Verlag, Bielefeld**

All rights reserved. No part of this book may be reprinted or reproduced or utilized in any form or by any electronic, mechanical, or other means, now known or hereafter invented, including photocopying and recording, or in any information storage or retrieval system, without permission in writing from the publisher.

Cover concept: Kordula Röckenhaus, Bielefeld
Cover illustration: Detail from wrapper design for *Punch* in
   M.H. Spielmann (1895): *The History of Punch*, London: Cassell and Company,
   p. 48, kindly provided by Sandra Martina Schwab.
Typeset by Katja Bay, Freiburg
Printed by Majuskel Medienproduktion GmbH, Wetzlar
ISBN 978-3-8376-2593-6

# Contents

**History and Humour: Charting the Field**
Barbara Korte and Doris Lechner | 7

**The Persistent Regency: The Presence of the Past in Victorian Illustrated Comic Literature**
Brian Maidment | 21

**Richard Doyle's Comic Histories: A Victorian Look at the Middle Ages**
Sandra Martina Schwab | 47

**History ›from below‹: Stanley Holloway's Monologues for the Variety Stage**
Stefanie Lethbridge | 69

**Merrying the Monarch: Charles II in Historical Comedies (1800 to the Present)**
Dorothea Flothow | 87

**On Boots, Beef, and *Blackadder*: The Comic Historiography of the Duke of Wellington**
Ulrike Zimmermann | 111

**We ARE Amused! The Comical Uses and Historical Abuses of Queen Victoria's Infamous Reproach ›We are not amused‹**
Duncan Marks | 133

The Old World and the New: Negotiating Past,
Present, and Future in Anglo-American
Humour, 1880-1900
Bob Nicholson | 151

›There Wont Be Inny Show Tonite‹: Humoring the
Returns of Scopic Violence in
Suzan-Lori Parks's *Venus*
Irvin J. Hunt | 171

Geoff Hurst's Ball: Popular Tabloids and
Humour on the Dark Side
Martin Conboy | 193

List of Contributors | 211

Index | 215

# History and Humour
## Charting the Field

BARBARA KORTE AND DORIS LECHNER

The series in which this book is published is concerned with ›popular‹ ways in which historical knowledge is generated, communicated and used in society.[1] Popular history is intended to appeal, and to appear relevant to those who are not professionally concerned with the past – the so-called ›general‹ audience who encounter history in their everyday lives because they want to be educated, because they are looking for orientation, or because they want to be entertained. Humorous representations of history are of obvious importance to such interests, and there are more of them than one might expect, even though history tends to be associated with serious modes of presentation (academic, heroic, tragic) rather than with comic ones. Yet Clio also smiles and laughs out loud: Humorous renderings of historical events and figures have made a significant contribution to ›popular‹ history since around 1800. We find them in many cultures and in a wide range of texts, images and performances, in styles both coarse and refined. This is unsurprising in so far as, although one can identify cultural variation, a sense of humour seems to be a common human trait that permeates all our various lifeworlds and the ways we try to make sense of them. Humour can be aggressive and scathing, but it may also be pleasant and entertaining. A

---

[1] We would like to thank Katja Bay for her invaluable help in preparing this volume. Our thanks also go to Malena Klocke for her help in indexing as well as Natalie Churn for proofreading.

dose of humour can make the most serious situations and subjects more bearable, as in gallows humour, and this translates to our confrontation with history. Even some of the darkest and tragic episodes of history have been presented in humorous modes: The Nazis have been the subject of biting satire in films such as Charlie Chaplin's *The Great Dictator* (1940), Mel Brooks's *The Producers* (1968) or Quentin Tarantino's *Inglourious Basterds* (2009). As Roberto Benigni's Oscar-winning *Life is Beautiful* (1997) has impressively shown, even the horror of concentration camps can be conveyed with tragi-comic humour. More examples of humorous perspectives on history from film and television suggest themselves: *Blackadder* (BBC, 1983-1989) is world-famous for its relentless view of British history which systematically debunks those in power through wit as well as slapstick. *M.A.S.H.*, both the original film (1970, dir. Robert Altman) and its television spin-off (CBS, 1972-1983), has amused world-wide audiences with an equally black-humoured perspective on the Americans at war in Korea. And the end of the GDR has been the subject of one the most successful German film comedies of recent years, *Good-Bye Lenin* (2003, dir. Wolfgang Becker).

Print culture has produced its own classics of humorous history, such as the French *Asterix* series whose inglorious Romans may have had more impact on the historical imagination of generations of readers all over the globe than any history book. Especially in Britain, with which the present book is particularly concerned, the history spoof has a long tradition. Sellar and Yeatman's *1066 and All That*, first published in 1930, not only continued a nineteenth-century tradition of comic historiography but also set the tone for later products such as the comprehensive *Horrible Histories* series, which was originally written for children but is also popular with adult readers in the English-speaking world and beyond (Terry Deary, 1993-present). As Jerome de Groot notes: »The books play on children's fascination with goriness, selling themselves as ›history with the nasty bits left in‹. The books are mischievous, irreverent and iconoclastic, appealing to a child audience's desire for silly jokes, presenting history as something tactile and simple.« (de Groot 2009: 39)

These few examples already demonstrate that humorous representations of history have a strong potential to attract audiences, and that they often remain in the public memory for a considerable period of time. While entertaining, they also provide knowledge and, most significantly, may give rise to historiographical awareness and a critical attitude towards the authoritative narratives which history books tend to offer. This was exploited, for instance, in *The Comic History of England* by Gilbert Abbott A'Beckett, who was on the original staff of the satirical magazine *Punch*. The *Comic History* was first published in 1847/8 but remained available in the twentieth century. It was intended to »demolish« the »romance of history« (A'Beckett 1907 [1847/8]: vi), and A'Beckett writes in his preface:

»Though the original design of this History was only to place facts in an amusing light, without a sacrifice of fidelity, it is humbly presumed that truth has rather gained than lost by the mode of treatment that has been adopted. Persons and things, events and characters, have been deprived of their false colouring, by the plain and matter-of-fact spirit in which they have been approached by the writer of the ›Comic History of England.‹ He has never scrupled to take the liberty of tearing off the masks and fancy dresses of all who have hitherto been presented in disguise to the notice of posterity. Motives are treated in these page as unceremoniously as men; and as the human disposition was much the same in former times as it is in the present day, it has been judged by the rules of common sense, which are alike at every period.« (Ibid.: v-vi)

Not only history is the butt of humour, then, but also those who write and teach history. Indeed, *1066 and All That* is, above all, a spoof of eminent historiography: With barely more than one hundred pages, the book is conspicuously slim for its subject (the history of Britain, after all), undermines ›serious‹ facts with nonsense and trivia,[2] has a ridiculous errata page, and ends with a parody of the history school book, giving a list of absurd questions for student essays. Similarly, the *Horrible History* series is not just funny but, as de Groot observes, »a challenge to traditional, institutionalised forms of knowledge as represented in history classes« (de Groot 2009: 39). The series' *Barmy British Empire* (Deary 2002), for instance, certainly makes us laugh, but it can also alert young readers to the ›nasty bits‹ of im-

---

2   »Napoleon ought never to be confused with Nelson, in spite of their hats being so alike; they can most easily be distinguished from one another by the fact that Nelson always stood with his arm like this, while Napoleon always stood with his arm like that« (Sellar/Yeatman 1999 [1930]: 97).

perial rule that are now in the focus of postcolonial historiography but may not yet have entered their history classroom.

Humorous representations have also been used as source material for historical study (without being historically themed themselves) and for popularisations of history since the nineteenth century. Thomas Wright's *Caricature History of the Georges, or, Annals of the House of Hanover, Compiled from the Squibs, Broadsides, Window Pictures, Lampoons, and Pictorial Caricatures of the Time* (1867, first ed. 1848) is a remarkable example from Victorian Britain. Wright here made the effort to collect caricatures and satirical songs from the previous century, complaining in his preface how little trouble had been taken to collect and preserve this material. The result of his dedicated work was a monumental and attractively illustrated book intended not only for further use by historians, but also for general readers interested in the previous century, which is presented to them as an entertaining mix of serious historical information, as well as notes on cultural tastes and fashions that appeared ludicrous to a more sober age.

Humour and history, then, appear to make good bedfellows, as the contributions to this volume indicate from different angles, for different periods and with different kinds of material. But how is humour to be defined? ›Humour‹ and related concepts – such as ›the comic‹, ›wit‹, or ›laughter‹ – have given rise to a daunting number of studies from philosophy, psychology, literary and media studies; other studies have their background in sociology and cultural history, as well as gender and postcolonial studies.[3] There are several classics in the field to which scholars today return, notably Freud's studies on laughter (1917 [1905]), Bergson's *Le rire* (1911 [1900]) and Bakhtin's exposition of the carnivalesque (1984 [1940]). Most recent scholarly work takes humour »seriously«[4] and approaches it so scrupulously at times that its categories become intimidating, bewildering and, taken together, quite contradictory.[5] Not even the key terms appear to be

---

3   Cf. the survey article by Stefan Horlacher (2009); as well as Morreall (1987); Powell/Paton (1988); Cameron (1993); Fietz/Fichte/Ludwig (1996); Berger (1997); Bremmer/Roodenburg (1997); Pfister (2002); Reichl/Stein (2005); Pailer et al. (2009).

4   Cf. Palmer's (1994) title *Taking Humour Seriously*. To Palmer, arguing »that some comedy is art is to take it very seriously indeed« (1994: 1).

5   Cf. Morreall (1987: 4-5) on the difficulty of defining humour, laughter and amusement also in light of the changing understanding of these concepts across time;

used with fixed meanings or in a stable relationship with their conceptual neighbours. Some theorists distinguish between humour and the comic, others draw a line between humour and wit, or both and laughter. It seems pragmatic in our context to follow those who use ›humour‹ as an umbrella term for all occasions that give rise to the bodily phenomenon of laughter or the mental state of amusement (cf. Morreall 1987: 4). The sociologist Anton Zijderveld in his *Sociology of Humour and Laughter* (1983) employs humour as »an overarching concept, covering such phenomena as wit, mirth and the comic« (2).[6] Similarly, Bremmer and Roodenburg in their cultural history of humour define the latter as a »message – transmitted in action, speech, writing, images or music – intended to produce a smile or a laugh« (1997: 1). Not only do such definitions include the wide range of media and genres in which humour manifests itself. They also comprise the wide span of humorous modes from gross, undignified physicality to intellectual satire and refined verbal play.

Research on humour and its functions is diverse, but it is possible to identify three major converging lines of thought – the *structural*, *psychological* and *social* functions of humour,[7] which also underlie the case studies in this volume. These three functions operate on different levels: first, regarding the context and content of a humorous reference; second, the emotions it reacts to or which are evoked by it; and thirdly, processes of identity formation or demarcation. The functions are not strictly separate from each other but interlinked.

The *structural* function concerns the conditions under which humour is perceived and/or produced. To Simon Critchley, the »comic world« is one »with its causal chains broken, its social practices turned inside out, and common sense rationality left in tatters« (2002: 1). There is widespread agreement across scholarly disciplines that humorous effects depend essentially on the perception of *incongruity*: Humour is generated by and/or perceived as an incompatibility of frames of reference or expectations. It de-

---

Palmer (1994: 5-7) addresses the problem of defining and demarcating terms for ›funnyness‹; cf. also Neale/Krutnik (1990: Chapters 1 and 4).

6  This coincides with one of the definitions given in the *Oxford English Dictionary*: »That quality of action, speech or writing, which excites amusement; oddity, jocularity, facetiousness, comicality, fun« (»humour | humor, n.«. 2013: 7.a.).

7  Cf. for instance Morreall (1987); Palmer (1994); Berger (1997).

stabilises ›normal‹ and ›expected‹ ways of seeing, it provokes dominant frames of reference; it creates zones of transgression and subversion; it creates surprise; it undermines certainties and causality– which can also be established through a transgression of or play with literary genres.[8]

Viewed *psychologically*, humour can create relief in situations of stress and fear, or demonstrate a person's emotional control over a situation, but it can also be used to ridicule and humiliate others. As Zijderveld concludes,

»A considerable part of humour consists of deviations from, and playful banter with, the institutionalized patterns of our emotions. [...] By erasing the boundaries between the couth and uncouth, the proper and the improper, the decent and the indecent, the civilised and the uncivilised, etc., black humour at first hurts our feelings, until laughter covers up the embarrassment.« (Zijderveld 1983: 15)

That humour at times »mercilessly violates« taboos (ibid.: 15) is obvious also from Peter L Berger's assertion of humour's aggressive as well as defensive functions: While a »common occasion for comic laughter has to do with belittling, humiliating, or debunking an individual or entire group of people« and humour, hence, »can be used as a weapon« (Berger 1997: 51),[9] it can also »help manage fears associated with any threat, no matter what the case«, as it then »functions to contain terror deriving from events that are threatening in actual fact« (ibid.: 58). Similarly, Zijderveld points to the »*liberating effect* of humour and laughter – as relief from psychological, social and even political pressures« (1983: 38). Humour's special powers seem to lie in the fact that it has both cognitive and affective sides.

Arguably, the *social* nature of humour is of the utmost relevance to our topic. As Henri Bergson wrote pertinently in *Le rire*: »To understand laughter, we must put it back into its natural environment, which is society, and above all we must determine the utility of its function, which is a social one.« (1911 [1900]: 7-8) To Bergson, laughter is a corrective when life becomes rigid, mechanical and ceremonial: »Any individual is comic who automatically goes his own way without troubling himself about getting into touch with the rest of his fellow-beings. It is the part of laughter to reprove his absentmindedness and wake him out of his dream.« (Ibid.: 134)

---

8   Cf. Berger (1997: 84); Neale/Krutnik (1990: 3).
9   On the aggressive function cf. also Zijderveld (1983: 38-42).

The function of the carnivalesque in Bakhtin's sense also has an eminently social function in that it can help to articulate and at the same time contain subversive trends in society.[10] Zijderveld has diagnosed a mirror function of humour: It distorts and simultaneously illuminates society by creating a distanced, defamiliarising view. To Zijderveld, »the humorist is able to disturb our definitions of reality, causing the emergence of doubt as to the value of daily routines and giving rise to some confusion as to the very foundations of reality« (1983: 9). And he also notes: »This may be humour's most important function: it often works as a de-ideologizing and disillusioning force. A socially accepted and traditional structure of meaning is exposed to a totally different structure of meaning, while the former is, as it were, looked at from the perspective of the latter.« (Ibid.: 58) Berger agrees with Zijderveld in many respects. In *Redeeming Laughter* (1997), he states that »A good cartoon or a good joke can often be more revealing of a particular social reality than any number of social-scientific treatises. Thus the comic can often be understood as a comic sociology.« (Berger 1997: 70) While emphasising the subversive functions of the comic, Berger points out that it can also play a stabilising role, by trying to keep excess at bay and society in balance: »Comedy ridicules those who think that they are richer, stronger, more handsome, or more intelligent than in fact they are, and the audience enjoys these discrepancies.« (Ibid.: 17-18) To Berger, »Humor functions sociopositively by enhancing group cohesion. [...] Almost inevitably, though, humor also has socionegative aspects. It draws the boundaries of the group and ipso facto defines the outsider.« (Ibid.: 57) Similarly, Powell and Paton hint at »the use of humour by social actors as a means of social control or resistance to such control« (Powell/Paton 1988: xiii), and Palmer looks into »the extent to which the social identity of occasions and participants determines the existence of humour« (Palmer, 1994: 12). Humour can thus play an important role in constituting identity, and in turn, it is a good marker of identities, for instance distinctive national and ethnic ones.

How can such insights about humour be related to history, and popular history in particular? The debunking function of humour seems of obvious

---

10 Also cf. Bremmer/Roodenburg: carnival etc. »can temporarily dissolve the rigid social rules with which we all have to comply, although often with low rather than high humour« (1997: 2).

significance here: Humour – in its function of »playing with institutionalized meanings« (Zijderveld 1983: 8) – can deflate the myths that have been woven around historical events and their players; it reduces greatness and glory to a human scale and can thus throw a light on power relations. Humour reveals the inequality of power and questions the principles through which power is legitimised. Humorous renderings may explicitly counter historical master narratives, question dominant interpretations, and undermine the ideal that history follows plans and always has a cause.[11]

Humour may also help an audience to come to grips with a traumatic history. The fact that history involves trauma, however, raises an ethical issue involved in the relieving and entertaining potential of humour: Is it permissible, or when is it permissible, to laugh about certain episodes of history? Who may produce humorous representations, and who is authorised to laugh about them? Hitler, the Third Reich and World War II generally are a case in point. While British and American culture have produced great satirical work on this chapter of history, its comic rendering in a German context is still received far more controversially.[12] The recent satirical novel *Er ist wieder da* (2012) about Hitler by the German writer Timur Vermes even raised the attention of the British media. The *Daily Mail Online*, for instance, dedicated an article to the controversy around its bestseller status in Germany:

»A former journalist with a German mother and Hungarian father, Vermes has helped to stoke a debate over rising neo-Nazism, disillusion with a failing currency

---

11 On the combination of history and humour cf. also the volume by Salmi on *Historical Comedy on Screen* (2011), which in its introduction (9-30) identifies anachronism, a play with genre conventions as well as the otherness of the past as main sources for historical humour.

12 A few years ago, the German director Dani Levy produced a farcical comedy entitled *My Führer: The Truly Truest Truth About Adolf Hitler* (2007), in which the title role was played by a well-known comedian. The film proved to be rather insignificant and disappeared quickly from the cinemas, but it caused a major discussion when it was released – while serious German films about the Nazi period and even Hitler (cf. *Der Untergang*, 2004, dir. Oliver Hirschbiegel) have been acclaimed world-wide. On transcultural dimensions of humour cf. Dunphy/Emig (2010).

and fears of inflation – the same toxic mix which enabled Hitler to come to power in the 1930s. Some have seen its success as proof that the guilt-ridden postwar generation has given way to one able to laugh at the monster who still haunts them. The book hit the hardcover number one slot in fiction, beating Ken Follet's Winter Of The World into second place, after being released in September. Reviewers are divided between whether readers are laughing at Hitler, with him – or at themselves. So far 17 foreign licences for it have been issued and Vermes is likely to become a millionaire out of his parody on a subject unthinkable for Germans just a few short years ago; treating the architect of WW2 and the Jewish Holocaust as a figure of fun.« (Hall 2013)

As this example indicates, some humorous approaches to history hence are transcultural, while in other respects it is tied more closely to nationally specific tastes and sensitivities. In cultural comparison, it appears that the Anglo(-American) traditions of humour are comparatively robust in their take on various facets of history.

The chapters in this collection are case studies on the use of humour in Britain and the US from 1800 up to the present, depicting historical topics, actors and events from the Middle Ages up to the recent past in a variety of genres and media. All of these case studies underline the fruitful interaction of humour's structural, psychological and social functions with popular history's ability »to sate a diverse range of desires: for historical education and entertainment, for relaxation and distraction, for identity and orientation, for adventure and exoticism, for new experiences and environments, or to escape from everyday life into a past that appears simple and less complex than the present« (Korte/Paletschek 2009: 9; our translation).[13]

The first two chapters are dedicated to nineteenth-century caricatures, though they treat history at different levels: BRIAN MAIDMENT looks at the reappropriation of historical caricatures, while SANDRA MARTINA SCHWAB analyses caricatures with historical topics. In a book-historical approach,

---

13 »Wie nie zuvor ist Geschichte in den Alltag eingedrungen und scheint dabei verschiedenste Bedürfnisse zu befriedigen: nach historischer Bildung und Unterhaltung, nach Entspannung und Zerstreuung, nach Identität und Orientierung, nach Abenteuer und Exotismus, nach neuen Erfahrungen und Erlebniswelten oder auch nach einer Flucht aus dem Alltag in eine Vergangenheit, die Überschaubarer und weniger komplex erscheint als die Gegenwart« (Korte/Paletschek 2009: 9).

Maidment traces the afterlife of caricatures from the Regency period throughout mid- and late-Victorian reissues and discusses their recontextualisation. The popularity of these caricatures from the early nineteenth century throughout Queen Victoria's reign shows a sense of nostalgia, a yearning for a time in which social structures were allegedly still in order. The relief provided through nostalgic humour hence served as an attempt to reaffirm traditional social identities while distracting from contemporary Victorian anxieties. Schwab's analysis of Richard Doyle's caricatures on historical topics, by contrast, demonstrates above all a critique of contemporary society. Doyle's satire of medieval sources criticised the contemporary glorification of the Middle Ages and at the same time commented on current issues of public debate; furthermore, it paralleled historic and current topics in French-British relations. Schwab hence shows how multifaceted the combination of history and humour can be: Doyle's humorous historical accounts operate on a variety of levels such as meta-historical reflection, social comment, entertainment, as well as the demarcation of national identities.

The next two chapters are concerned with humorous representations of history on stage. STEFANIE LETHBRIDGE presents a look at history ›from below‹ in Stanley Holloway's monologues produced for the music hall. While these short comic pieces use history and humour to affirm a working-class identity, for instance by emphasising the importance of common soldiers in historical events such as the Napoleonic Wars, they do not contradict mainstream historical narratives; and while ›Great Men‹ such as Wellington may be depicted as unheroic and become a source *for* humour, »they are not normally made ridiculous«, as Lethbridge notes. Holloway's monologues on historical topics thus indicate a moderate use of humour as resistance to established hierarchies. DOROTHEA FLOTHOW's analysis of historical comedies on Charles II continues this idea of humorous depictions of ›Great Men‹ as unheroic. Charles II, as a king with whom the monarchy was restored in 1660 after the English Civil War and the Republic but whose lifestyle also gained him the epithet of the ›merry monarch‹, appears to invite humorous treatment through the incongruity already inscribed in his historical image. As Flothow shows, a vast corpus of comedies from 1800 to the present exemplifies a common regress to stereotypical characters and plots, whose popularity with the audience can be explained through the dramatic irony added by the knowledge of the historical king's real identity as well as an escapist, exotic presentation of the past as a frivolous – or carnivalesque – other.

How ›Great Men‹ – or ›Great Women‹ – have long seemed to lend themselves to humorous appropriation can also be seen in ULRIKE ZIMMERMANN's and DUNCAN MARKS's chapters. Both analyse, across various genres and media, the long-lasting comic afterlife of the Duke of Wellington and Queen Victoria respectively. Zimmermann looks at caricatures, films and everyday material objects which satirise the Duke and show how he invited caricature through the »comic irritation« of his two conflicting images: the »dashing war hero and the elderly politician«. Even during his lifetime, the friction between his earlier military and later political career resulted in humorous depictions in order to deflate the threat which Wellington's political presence might have induced. While Wellington seems to have embraced the comic treatment of his character (up to a certain extent), a quotation ascribed to Queen Victoria is rather taken to illustrate a presumed lack of humour. Marks analyses the afterlife of the famous »We are not amused« (WANA). Tracing its reappropriations through different media such as books, plays, films up to the internet and social media, Marks observes an increasing detachment of the phrase from its historical context and presumed royal enunciator. He concludes that the phrase now rather serves to affirm or criticise a national or social identity, as it is often used to express Britishness or an ironisation of a British or posh attitude.

The use of history and humour to negotiate identities plays a central role in the last three chapters, which all reach across national borders by regarding issues of identity and alterity. BOB NICHOLSON, in a transatlantic comparison of late-Victorian usage of history in newspaper joke columns and comic novels, observes a struggle on the part of Britain to come to terms with America's increasing economic and cultural superiority. Thus, joke writers and literary humorists tended to »juxtapose images of the American future with those of an idealised British past« and emphasised the »centrality of history to British national identity at a time when the country's future was beginning to look increasingly uncertain«. This uncertainty may also be observed in the fact that British humorists turned to the past in the attempt to reaffirm British superiority, yet the popular reception of transatlantic humour at the same time indicates an acceptance of modern American culture in Britain. While the humorous use of history here serves to come to terms with a present threat, humour can also help to deal with a traumatic past. IRVIN J. HUNT analyses Suzan-Lori Parks's absurdist play *Venus* (1997) which depicts the traumatic history of an African woman, Sarah Bartman, who was exhibited in Victorian freak shows across Europe. As Hunt concludes, Parks uses humour not in order to produce distance from the violence of a colonial past. Rather, her way of presenting Bartman's history within the genre of an absurd comedy is meant to lead to self-reflection in that it helps the audience to immerse themselves into Bartman's trauma via the »unbearable lightness of Parks's humor«. Finally, MARTIN CONBOY considers »Humour on the Dark Side« by looking at the British tabloids' press campaign during the 1999 World Cup final between England and Germany, which drew its humour from populist World War II imagery. Thus, Conboy concludes that the humour created in the tabloids through a questionable repetition of national stereotypes does not serve as a »key to unlocking the past« but »is an acceptable way of maintaining populist prejudices in the present«.

The case studies assembled here attest to the many ways in which history and humour have intersected in past and present cultural production. Taken together, they illustrate how humour can function to project nostalgic and benign views of history, but also how its main function appears to lie in more or less gentle critique of history and the ways in which history has been presented.

## WORKS CITED

A'Beckett, Gilbert Abbott (1907 [1847/8]): *The Comic History of England*, London: George Routledge & Sons.
Bakhtin, M.M. (1984 [1940]): *Rabelais and His World*, Bloomington: Indiana UP.
Berger, Peter L. (1997): *Redeeming Laughter: The Comic Dimension of Human Experience*, Berlin: de Gruyter.
Bergson, Henri (1911 [1900]): *Laughter: An Essay on the Meaning of the Comic*, London: Macmillan. [*Le Rire: Essai sur la signification du comique*, Paris: Presses Universitaires de France, 1900.]
Bremmer, Jan/Herman Roodenburg (eds.) (1997): *A Cultural History of Humour: From Antiquity to the Present Day*, Cambridge: Polity Press.
Cameron, Keith (ed.) (1993): *Humour and History*, Oxford: Intellect.

Critchley, Simon (2002): *On Humour*, London: Routledge.
de Groot, Jerome (2009): *Consuming History: Historians and Heritage in Contemporary Popular Culture*, London: Routledge.
Deary, Terry (2002): *The Barmy British Empire*, London: Scholastic.
Dunphy, Graeme/Rainer Emig (eds.) (2010): *Hybrid Humour: Comedy in Transcultural Perspectives*, Amsterdam: Rodopi.
Fietz, Lothar/Joerg O. Fichte/Hans-Werner Ludwig (eds.) (1996): *Semiotik, Rhetorik und Soziologie des Lachens: Vergleichende Studien zum Funktionswandel des Lachens vom Mittelalter zur Gegenwart*, Tübingen: Niemeyer.
Freud, Sigmund (1917 [1905]): *Wit and Its Relation to the Unconscious*, New York: Moffat, Yard, and Co. [*Der Witz und seine Beziehung zum Unbewußten*, Frankfurt/Main: Fischer.]
Hall, Allan (2013): »Hitler Novel Tops German Chart: Comic Novel Follows the Nazi Leader as He Falls Asleep in 1945 and Wakes Up in 2011«. In: *Daily Mail Online* 6 January 2013 (www.dailymail.co.uk/news/article-2258178/Hitler-novel-tops-German-chart-Comic-novel-follows-Nazi-leader-falls-asleep-1945-wakes-2011.html). Accessed 27 May 2013.
Horlacher, Stefan (2009): »A Short Introduction to Theories of Humour, the Comic, and Laughter«. In: Gabi Pailer et al. (eds.), *Gender and Laughter: Comic Affirmation and Subversion in Traditional and Modern Media*, Amsterdam: Rodopi, 17-47.
»humour I humor, n.« (2013): In: *OED Online* [March 2013], Oxford: OUP (www.oed.com). Accessed 27 May 2013.
Korte, Barbara/Sylvia Paletschek (eds.) (2009): *History Goes Pop: Zur Repräsentation von Geschichte in populären Medien und Genres*, Bielefeld: transcript.
Morreall, John (ed.) (1987): *The Philosophy of Laughter and Humour*, Albany: State U of New York P.
Neale, Steve/Frank Krutnik (1990): *Popular Film and Television Comedy*, London: Routledge.
Pailer, Gaby et al. (eds.) (2009): *Gender and Laughter: Comic Affirmation and Subversion in Traditional and Modern Media*, Amsterdam: Rodopi.
Palmer, Jerry (1994): *Taking Humour Seriously*, London: Routledge.
Pfister, Manfred (ed.) (2002): *A History of English Laughter: Laughter from Beowulf to Beckett and Beyond*, Amsterdam: Rodopi.

Powell, Chris/George E.C. Paton (eds.) (1988): *Humour in Society: Resistance and Control*, Basingstoke: Macmillan.

Reichl, Susanne/Mark Stein (eds.) (2005): *Cheeky Fictions: Laughter and the Postcolonial*, Amsterdam: Rodopi.

Salmi, Hannu (ed.) (2011): *Historical Comedy on Screen: Subverting History with Humour*, Bristol: Intellect.

Sellar, W.C./R.J. Yeatman (1999 [1930]): *1066 and All That*, London: Methuen.

Wright, Thomas (1867 [1848]): *Caricature History of the Georges, or, Annals of the House of Hanover, Compiled from the Squibs, Broadsides, Window Pictures, Lampoons, and Pictorial Caricatures of the Time*, London: John Camden Hotten.

Zijderveld, Anton C. (1983): *Sociology of Humour and Laughter* [*Current Sociology – La sociologie contemporaine* 30.3], London: Sage.

# The Persistent Regency

The Presence of the Past in Victorian Illustrated Comic Literature

BRIAN MAIDMENT

## THE VICTORIAN REAPPROPRIATION OF REGENCY CARICATURE

The after-life of Regency and early Victorian caricature through the later nineteenth century forms both a bibliographical spectacle and an extremely interesting study in cultural influence and continuity. In particular, analysis of the ways in which ›texts‹ originally published solely as images were overlaid by successive ›layers of textuality‹ offers an important insight into Victorian dependence on the explicatory powers of the verbal to ensure the proper understanding of the visual. This chapter seeks first to outline the considerable extent of the presence throughout the later Victorian period of a range of caricatures and other forms of comic graphic images originally issued during the Regency and early Victorian periods between 1820 and 1845. This is essentially an exercise in book history,[1] and provides, along

---

1   In this instance book history is used as a mechanism for tracing a sequence of editions of books and other printed material first issued in the first half of the nineteenth century on through the later nineteenth century and for showing the ways in which successive editions altered and extended the publication for later readers. Ideas of humour changed radically through the nineteenth century, with

with much other information, an interesting gloss on the cheap republication of sophisticated illustrated books that might have seemed beyond the reach of the mid-Victorian common reader. Second, and more difficult both to quantify and explain, I want to consider some of the ways in which early nineteenth-century graphic comedy was *re-made* for the Victorian reading public, an issue that brings together the consideration of both popular taste and the commercial opportunism of later nineteenth-century mass publishing. The textual accretions gathered by some images from Robert Seymour's *Sketches*, originally published in the mid-1830s, but extensively reissued in differing formats through the mid- and later nineteenth century, will be adopted as a mechanism for undertaking such an investigation into the Victorian appropriation of Regency caricature – an appropriation that used ›historical‹ and ›humorous‹ visuals to comment on some of its own cultural concerns: social change and urban life. Third, I therefore want to ask what drew later Victorian sensibilities to the comic visual spectacle offered by Regency and early Victorian caricature and comic art despite its use of an unfamiliar visual language, the localised topicality of the images and the anachronistic depiction of elements of a society that had long vanished.

Such a discussion needs to be situated in the broader context of changing modes of comic image making, publishing and distribution that characterised the first half of the nineteenth century. Most commentators have deplored the fading away of a vigorous political caricature tradition inherited from the late eighteenth century during these years, and have regarded the comic art of the 1820s, 1830s and 1840s as a moment of chaotic experimentation only resolved by the emergence of Victorian black and white illustration. At the conclusion to her magnificent contribution to the study of caricature as a characteristically British socio-political phenomenon, the *British Museum Catalogue of Political and Personal Satires*, for example, Dorothy George, by training a social historian, was looking for explanations for the decline, indeed the demise, of a great satirical tradition of political caricature, manifested largely in the form of single-plate engravings and etchings (cf. Stephens/George 1874-1950: XI, xiii-xvii). David Kunzle, in the course of another ambitious multi-volume project, a history of the comic strip in Europe and America, was pursuing an argument that saw the comic strip as

> wit and burlesque (especially shown in wordplay and puns) giving way to whimsy and ›fun‹.

a new and widespread medium that emerged in the 1840s in response to the emptiness and triviality of the visual images commercially produced in the 1830s (cf. Kunzle 1990: 20-21). Both analyses stressed that the 1820s and 1830s were a moment when one rich and genteel tradition of comic art faltered, became decadent, and was only slowly replaced by dynamic new media in the 1840s. Both commentators presented a narrative of decline and regeneration that linked aesthetic failure to the emergence of a massively extended consumer base. They both argued that the decline in quality in visual culture in the 1820s and 1830s was an inevitable and depressing consequence of attempts to broaden and/or democratise the market for caricature, and finally put an end to a complex and aesthetically successful caricature tradition in the 1830s. The aesthetic failure of caricature in the 1830s can be directly related to the poor taste and lust for visual diversion of a new audience/market for visual culture cynically and thoughtlessly supplied by entrepreneurial and commercially opportunistic publishers and their artists.

It is not the purpose of this essay to engage with these arguments in detail, although I have done so elsewhere (cf. Maidment 2013: Chapters 1-3), but rather to suggest that the Victorian public did not share the disdain for the comic art of the 1820s and 1830s suggested by Kunzle and George. Indeed the opposite is true – Victorian readers continued to buy Regency caricature, and cared enough about it to the extent of re-publishing large quantities of its products. They were also engaged in an important process of re-thinking Regency attitudes in ways that were relevant to their own social experience. In particular, Victorian comic artists and writers, presumably well aware of the attitudes and interests of their readers, began to abandon the picaresque and carnivalesque elements of Regency comedy – its sustained interest in the grotesque body, for example – in favour of a more naturalistic graphic account of contemporary life. It is that process of re-thinking that this essay seeks to discuss.

## THE SURVIVAL OF REGENCY CARICATURE IN VICTORIAN PRINT CULTURE: A SURVEY

Book history offers a useful method for quantifying the influence of Regency caricature in the Victorian period. Many of the best-known caricature publications from the 1820s and 1830s were persistently re-issued long into the nineteenth century, as the following survey of the survival of some Regency caricaturists' works shows. George Cruikshank's ›sketch-books‹, for instance, were reappropriated in various formats throughout the century.[2] *Scraps and Sketches*, which was first issued in four parts between 1828 and 1832, was reprinted in 1834, again in part in 1854, and then in a number of late-Victorian re-issues running at least on into the 1880s (cf. Cohn 1924: 57-58). *Illustrations of Time*, belonging initially to 1827, re-appeared under the imprint of Frederick Arnold in 1874 (cf. ibid.: 57). *My Sketch Book*, from 1834, had, as Cohn witheringly states, »often been reprinted in inferior style« (ibid.: 58-59). The nineteen annual volumes of *The Comic Almanac*, which spanned the years between 1835 and 1853 and which boasted Cruikshank's full-page etchings and tiny wood-engraved vignettes as a major attraction, were initially re-issued close to their original publication date in volumes that gathered several years together, but there were also, again to use Cohn's contemptuous speech on behalf of serious book collectors, »many later re-issues in volume form of the whole set. They are of little value« (ibid.: 63). Even without recourse to re-issues of individual publication, the late-Victorian enthusiast for even the sketchiest of Cruikshank's comic output could buy Simpkin Marshall's shoddily produced and undated late nineteenth-century reprint of *Four Hundred Humorous Illustrations by George Cruikshank* which threw together murky versions of much of the artist's occasional work, most of it over fifty years old. The volume was part of a series which included reprints of the work of several *Punch* artists. Cruikshank's hasty sketches and vignettes, then, were ever available throughout the nineteenth century, albeit often in poorly reproduced formats and, in the case of the re-issued oblong folios, surrounded with advertisements. As the above remarks from Cohn suggest, many believed such re-prints to be a vulgarisation and aesthetic betrayal of the original images. Sustained popularity, certainly for Cohn, came at a price.

Perhaps the most persistent Regency text of all throughout the nineteenth century, albeit in many guises, was Pierce Egan's novel *Life in London*. It was originally published in expensive serial form with aquatint illustrations

---

2 George Cruikshank (1792-1878) was the pre-eminent and commercially most successful British comic artist of the early Victorian period, best known for his work in Dickens's early novels. He also forms an important bridge between the Regency caricature and Victorian illustration.

by George and Robert Cruikshank in 1821 (fig. 1), but then spread far into mass and popular culture: through many theatrical adaptations with their accompanying trail of print culture in the form of play-bills, song books and play-texts; through cheap reprints of the novel with crude wood-engraved or photo-reproduced illustrations based on the originals (fig. 2 and 3); and even through commemorative printed handkerchiefs and ceramic figurines.

*Fig. 1: George and Robert Cruikshank's aquatint illustration for Pierce Egan's* Life in London *(1821).*

*Fig. 2: Title page with anonymous wood-engraved vignette for the Dicks edition of Pierce Egan's* Life in London *here renamed* Tom and Jerry *(n.d.).*

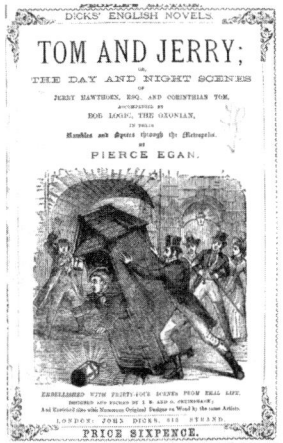

*Fig. 3: Double-page spread from* Tom and Jerry *(J. Dicks, n.d.) with both a full-page and a vignette wood engraving.*

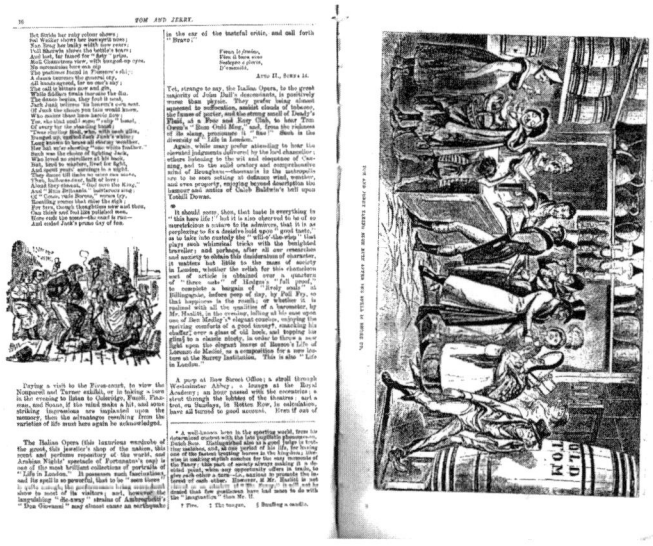

*Fig. 4:* The Literary Dustman. *Anonymous and undated wood engraving.*

Just to suggest the rich trail of cultural allusions, both high and low, accumulated by *Life in London* here is an anonymous wood engraved caricature with appended verses, which has interested a number of scholars of Regency popular culture (fig. 4).³ Despite its apparent crudity of rendition, this image draws together an entire tradition of jokes about a ›world turned upside down‹ by the ›march of intellect‹ – a world in which a dustman, one of the most degraded, visceral and contaminated of all urban tradesmen, reclines on a chaise longue smoking a cheroot and reading *The Penny Magazine* while his son hammers out an operatic rendition on a forte-piano. The presiding spirit here is Dusty Bob, the theatrical hero of many stage versions of *Life in London* (he had been a coal-heaver in the original novel), evoked by the portrait in the caricature's background of Bob and his invariable partner, African Sal. Such crucial comic tropes as this in which dramatic social change is visualised and managed through laughter, formed an important Regency legacy which allowed Victorian society to manage high levels of their own social anxiety through the varied modes of visual comedy (cf. Maidment 2007). In particular, the development of an urban society, which foregrounded the presence of the labouring classes and led to the emergence of a professional middle class, resulted in both a heightened level of social proximity and the emergence of culturally ambitious and economically significant artisans. Such changes are widely reflected in comic art at this time, which shifts focus from political themes to an interest in socio-economic change, and especially the increasingly obvious social presence of the labouring classes.

Another important and widely known book with its origins in visual culture but with an added interpretative text that ordered a sequence of graphic images into something with more narrative drive and social explication, Douglas Jerrold's and Kenny Meadows's *Heads of the People*, was first published with its full text in 1838, but repeatedly reprinted – its afterlife can be traced to the late 1870s with at least one Routledge edition dating from 1878 (cf. Lauster 2007). Interestingly in this case the original plates (fig. 5), intended as Dickensian illustrations, were given tremendous added gravitas by being turned into urban ›types‹ by the addition of commissioned essays (fig. 6) – another example of the way in which later Vic-

---

3   Cf. James (1976: 148-150); Hancher (2000: 97); Maidment (1996: 81-90).

*Fig. 5: Wood-engraved title page for the part-issue of Kenny Meadows's* Heads from Nicholas Nickleby *(William Tyas, n.d.).*

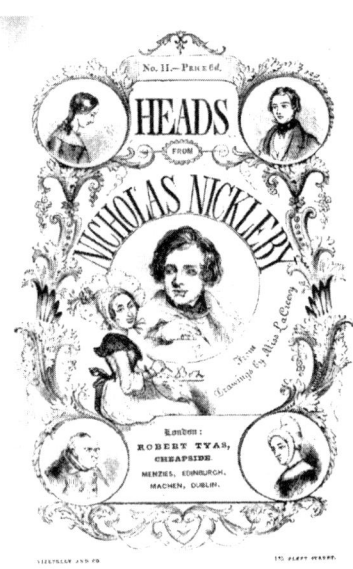

*Fig. 6: Double-page spread from Kenny Meadows's* Heads of the People *(David Bryce 1838).*

torian literary culture stressed the importance of the verbal in annotating and explaining the visual response to urban culture.

The key antiquarian and scholar Charles Hindley assembled a reprint *Gallery of Comicalities* for Reeves and Turner (n.d.) which drew together images by the Cruikshanks and Seymour originally published in *Bell's Life in London* and *Mornings at Bow Street*. Edward Moxon did a similar job in 1870 for Thomas Hood with *Whimsicalities, A Periodical Gathering*, although Hood himself and his son had already proved adept at reprinting and re-issuing much of the author's graphic work – and, indeed, the *Whimsicalities* itself had been re-issued by Henry Colburn as early as 1846 under the somewhat deceptive title of *The Comic Annual for 1846*. In these cases, anthologising formed a key process through which scattered and ephemeral images could be recovered from relatively obscure sources made cheaply available to a mass readership. Such volumes were also important in creating a ›canon‹ of early nineteenth-century comic art out of publications that had originally been published in expensive or ephemeral forms.

As well as reprinting, other modes of production and consumption, most obviously the compilation of scrapbooks and albums and the enduring popularity of illustrated fiction from the 1830s and 1840s, ensured the longevity of Regency caricature. Some of the reasons for the continuing presence of an earlier mode of humour on into the mainstream of Victorian popular consciousness were of course commercial. Reprint publishers like Thomas Tegg and Charles Tilt were well aware of the value of the copyrights they had acquired, and used every occasion to exploit them. Enterprising publishers and authors realised that they could add new texts to extant sequences of illustrations so that several massively successful books that had originated as predominantly visual sequences were re-packaged for the early Victorian reading public as texts – and of course *The Pickwick Papers* offers an important case study in re-packaging the visual as the verbal with illustrations.[4] Even philanthropy played a part: The work of both Seymour (fig. 7) and Thomas Hood, who had both endured financial hard-

---

4   The *Pickwick Papers* was originally conceived as a series of sporting illustrations by Seymour with some accompanying text. Working with the publishers, Charles Dickens transformed the project into an extended work of fiction thus relegating Seymour's plates to a subsidiary role and asserting the primacy of word over image that characterises the shape of the Victorian novel.

*Fig. 7: Cover for the re-issue of* Seymour's Sketches »*for the widow*« *(n.d., c.1837).*

ship, was extensively re-issued to support their families and dependents, with, as already suggested, Hood's work in particular endlessly reappearing in new guises. Moxon's chosen sub-title for *Hood's Own* – »being former runnings of his comic vein, with an infusion of new blood for general circulation« (Hood 1856) – managed to announce the book as a reprint in exactly the macabre way that Hood's work demanded. The 1861 Moxon reprint even showed as a frontispiece a plump and sybaritic wood sprite chuckling over a volume of *Hood's Comic Annual,* suggesting that somehow the good humour of the Regency comic writers and artists was connected to a mythical source from centuries before. By the early years of the twentieth century, Regency picaresque illustrated books had become exotic enough to inspire popular antiquarian interest, as the extensive series of the *Illustrated Pocket Library of Plain and Coloured Books* published by Methuen suggests. The series, published mainly between 1904 and 1905, included a volume by way of a descriptive commentary on Regency coloured plate books (cf. Paston 1905). For the first time, this pocket-sized series brought Pierce Egan, Robert Smith Surtees and other Regency sporting writers into the hands of a mass readership even if the original hand-coloured plates were reduced to garish mechanical reproductions, and formed the first stage in developing and sustaining a twentieth-century collectors' market in Regency colour-plate books (cf. Tooley 1954; Abbey 1972; Hardie 1990 [1906]).

## THE VICTORIANISATION OF SEYMOUR'S *SKETCHES*

Other illustrated humorous books that enjoyed a complex voyage through later Victorian print culture would include Gilbert Abbott A'Beckett's *Comic History of England,* with the hand-coloured plates by John Leech from the first serialised edition later reproduced as crude wood engravings in a long line of cheap mass circulation versions. But Seymour's *Sketches* is the book that provides the most spectacular Victorian survival of an urban picaresque derived from the eighteenth-century caricature tradition (cf. Maidment 2013: 162-169). At risk of over-simplifying an extremely complex publishing history, it can be said that there were essentially three versions of Seymour's *Sketches*.[5] The ›original‹ version comprised 180 images published in various ways without textual commentary first by Henry Wallis between 1834 and 1836 and then reprinted in five volumes by G.S. Tregear. These images pictured both farcical sporting adventures and urban incidents and formed, along with the same artist's *New Readings of Old Authors*, one of the defining visual accounts of just Victorian London. After Seymour's death, Wallis had 86 of the plates re-drawn on steel, and brought in ›Crowquill‹ (Alfred Forrester) to write a connecting narrative for the new sequence of plates, and re-issued the resulting volume as *Seymour's Humorous Sketches* in 1841. It was this version of Seymour's plates, with an emphasis on the narrative potential of the adventures of a gauche urbanite at large in the countryside playing at pursuits such as fishing and shooting,

---

5   In order to abbreviate what would be a lengthy discussion of various editions, consulting the entry for the *Sketches* in Brian Maidment's »Draft List« (2011) would provide a more complete account of its publishing history.

that continued to please later Victorian readers. Henry Bohn re-issued a second edition of this book in 1841, and later Bohn editions (from 1866 on) added in a descriptive list of the plates and a brief biography of Seymour, thus adding further layers of mediating textuality to an originally entirely visual project. The Bohn version of the book was then reprinted successively in (at least) 1866, 1872, 1878, 1880 and 1888, and even right at the end of the century some of the plates were to be found in the stock book of a Bristol printer.

The third distinct version of the *Sketches* with a completely different text to accompany Seymour's images was written by R.B. Peake, a well-established professional hack writer best known for theatrical adaptations and contributions to various humorous journals. Versions of the *Sketches* using Peake's text were issued under various titles in the 1840s, in at least three variant editions. The ›authorised‹ version seems to have been *Seymour's Humorous Sketches comprising ninety two caricature etchings illustrated in prose by R.B. Peake*, published by George Routledge in 1846. But the same year also saw the appearance of *An Evening's Amusement of the Adventures of a Cockney Sportsman, by R.B. Peake, Esq.*, and *Snobson's Seasons, Being Annuals of Cockney Sports* was published by M.A. Nattali around the same time. These disparate titles offer differing emphases, the first stressing Seymour's plates as the main attraction, the other two marketing the book largely through the appeal of hapless cockney encounters with the unfamiliar world of country sports and pastimes, suggesting not just a town/country clash of values but also, to some extent, a class one with the urban oik seeking the pleasures of the rural gentry and yeomen. In both the dated copies, the text remains the same, but the plates are different, and many of the same plates are printed at slightly different moments within the text. The various R.B. Peake editions all use more plates than the Crowquill ones, although both only use half of the images available in the original issues. In this R.B. Peake edition, the transformation of Seymour's original series of plates into something far more Pickwickian than Seymour had initially imagined was complete.

One late edition of the *Sketches,* published by Frederick Bentley (n.d., c.1880), offers ninety-seven caricature etchings »for the first time offered to the public free from the incumbrances of letter press«. This assertion was of course not true – Bentley here returns Seymour's project to its original form, although using only a selection of the images available in the series.

The publisher further notes in his Preface that »the conceptions of this famous Artist so speak for themselves, that they produce a hearty and spontaneous laugh [...]. [A]ny laboured description is a stumbling block rather than an advantage to them« (Bentley [c.1888]: Preface). In this Bentley edition, the images have also been organised into two sequences, with sporting images forming the first half of the book followed by images of urban incident for the remainder. Thus this late edition acknowledged the two strands of Seymour's interests in drawing the original *Sketches*, something that the additional texts by Crowquill and Peake had largely subordinated in their added narratives.

The publishing history of Seymour's *Sketches* thus suggests an important strand in the Victorian re-making of Regency caricature that was carried out by means of the physical transformation of (humorous) images into books, complete with text, and a whole variety of prefatory and para-textual material. Such material and textual re-makings were, as already suggested, not uncommon in the second half of the nineteenth century. Less easy to assess are the transformations in fields of reference, available allusions and the construction of meanings that undoubtedly took place as a consequence of the material changes to Seymour's ›book‹. In particular, later Victorian editions of the *Sketches* had to mediate between the traditional ascription of the tagline of ›sporting artists‹ to Seymour and a recognition of his considerable body of work concerned with socio-cultural change. One particular theme that recurred throughout Seymour's varied output was a delighted and occasionally caustic interest in the ›march of intellect‹, i.e. that series of revolutionary developments that established, among many technological, economic and cultural triumphs, mass literacy and widespread access to print culture for even poorly educated consumers. Seymour represented the march of intellect through a wide range of caricature modes and genres including large and complex detailed etchings and multi-panel gatherings of small vignettes organised by their thematic similarity (cf. Maidment 2007; Maidment 2013: 177-208). The *Sketches* included a good number of march-of-intellect images, several of them re-workings of the familiar tropes of the lower classes mimicking the manners and pretentions of the newly wealthy and irrupting noisily into the genteel havens of bourgeois respectability. In this world turned upside down figures such as the sweep, the dustman and the scavenger act out the wider implications of class contiguity and social change in the metropolis, with the socio-cultural ambitions of the lower classes opened up to sometimes uneasy mockery and the pretensions of the middle classes equally vulnerable to the caricaturist's eye.

The original publication of Seymour's *Sketches* was based on the assumption that the visual elements of the images together with their brief captions would provide – through their iconography, compositional tropes, cultural allusions and inherited graphic language – more than adequate information to allow the viewer access to both their humour and their sociocultural terms of reference. Yet the graphic language of caricature is so firmly based in the historical moment of its use that later interpretation, even a few years later, becomes challenging. This can, for instance, be seen in Peake's reappropriation of Seymour's sketches »Look, Papa, our dancing master says I do this as well as Taglioni« and »What shall I have the honor Gentlemen of selecting for your Evening studies«. Both appeared in the original *Sketches* published by Carlisle between 1834 and 1836 and were subsequently re-issued by Tregear. They are brought together and re-appear back to back in Peake's 1846 ›novelisation‹ of the *Sketches* in order to provide an occasion for a brief textual meditation on the march of intellect (fig. 8 and 9). Peake recast the two images, originally a conventional satirical commentary on working-class aspirations, as an occasion for a quite detailed investigation of the social locale, finances, domestic habits and world view of the dustman. In order to use these images as a prompt for social investigation rather than humorous commentary, Peake has to find a literary device that allows his narrator access to the lives of the poor. In this instance, in a writerly manoeuvre that acknowledges the picaresque rather than naturalism, Snobson, an invented narrative persona whose name suggests an upwardly mobile figure, has become the rent collector for a row of cottages let out to representatives of urban working, or rather *sometimes* working classes – dustmen, costermongers, sweeps and ›cab-drivers off work‹. In this role, Snobson is free to offer his scornful analysis of the march of intellect. At a moment »when times are so wonderfully improved and refined among our tenants« (Peake 1846: 48), the dustman Ben Dobie's daughter has begun ballet lessons at Mr. Paddletoe's academy. Despite Snobson's view, expressed in the Regency humorous tradition of sustained punning, that Miss Sally Dobie »ought to be scouring steps instead of dancing on them«, nevertheless she »attitudinises to the music of her father's pipe«.

*Fig. 8: »Look, Papa« from the R.B. Peake 1846 edition of* Seymour's Sketches.

*Fig. 9: »What shall I have the honour...« from the R.B. Peake 1846 edition of* Seymour's Sketches.

But Peake is interested enough in the domestic circumstances of Ben Dobie to sustain a quite lengthy analysis of his social circumstances and imagined attitudes. He notes that Sally commenced her dancing classes immediately after Boxing-day, a crucial moment in the financial well-being of the dustman trade, and continues to describe Ben Dobie's membership of the »Bagnigge Wells, and North Eastern, Back Road, Pentonville, Literary and Scientific Institute«, a membership justified in Ben's own words, by a vision of working-class social progress through education. Such a vision had also prompted Ben – whose »own learning vos neglected«, and who »can only sign his name with a criss-cross« – to seek an education for his son. In giving Ben Dobie a voice, admittedly a somewhat confrontational and self-defensive one, Peake nonetheless allows Snobson to segue into some conventional early Victorian platitudes about social mobility and the worth of self-education as an alternative to the gin palace. The annotation of Seymour's image through such a discussion of the cultural implications of working-class social ambition and the politics of literacy is here plausibly managed through the fictional conventions deployed. The image becomes the site of discussion through the transparently picaresque device of the narrator's role as rent collector. Yet alongside the picaresque improbabilities that allow the images from the *Sketches* to be given narrative continuity, there is also a naturalistic impulse here towards a closer investigation of life and habits of urban tradesmen – their social ambitions, their relative affluence, their participation in increased opportunities for social mobility. Before the twists of the heavily contrived narrative slide away on to Ben Dobie's interest in dog-fancying, the reader is confronted with a second image, this time of a dustman and his son irrupting into a bastion of gentility, the bookshop, and asking for something »wot's short and not werry dry«. A more conventionally mocking image, nonetheless, given the detailed account of the cultural activities of the massed Dobies on the opposite page, it comes as no surprise that a dustman might be found trespassing so far into the traditional enclaves of cultural privilege. And, as if to authenticate the presence of the dustman as a significant economic as well as social presence, Snobson's narrative finds time to offer important detail of the scale and nature of the trade in dust – »His [Ben Dobie's] master is the eminent contractor; he did not only private dust but public mud« (Peake 1846: 50). Ben, however, showed little interest in what he did, except to note the recent legislation that had prevented him from ringing his bell, with the consequence that the shouting involved in advertising his trade required ample supplies of beer to keep his throat in order.

In these ways, then, Regency visual tropes have been recast in the language and conceptual framework of early Victorian cultural politics, and burdened with a weight of socio-cultural explanation not required by the audience for the original image. It is important to stress that Peake's main interest in his novelisation of the *Sketches* was to re-assert Seymour's reputation as a sporting artist, but he was increasingly forced to rely on the many images of urban incident to be found in the original publication to give narrative variety to his text. Most of the chapter on »Summer« is given over to the social events of the metropolis rather than the country adventures of cockney sportsmen, thus retaining at least something of Seymour's satirical awareness of urban manners.

Peake's attempt to construct a continuous narrative, however warped by the non-sequential twists of his picaresque structure, was not a guiding principle for the Crowquill editions of the *Sketches*, which were constructed as a series of unrelated short narratives, anecdotes or verses attached to each of the chosen images thus freeing the text from any need to aspire to coherence. Crowquill, himself a caricaturist and comic writer with his roots in Regency humour, was an author much closer in sensibility to Seymour than Peake, and more interested in exploiting the conventions of Seymour's illustrations than in assimilating them into early Victorian social values. Nonetheless, Crowquill's tone is significantly different from Seymour's replacing the comic delight of the earlier artist with a more facetious, even sneering, attitude. His textual additions to Seymour's march-of-intellect images, for example, centre on a sustained exercise in sarcasm, a sarcasm focussed on the ignorance and pretentiousness of London lower-class tradesmen. The commentary on »You shall have the paper directly, Sir…« is a characteristic re-visiting of a widespread Regency caricature trope frequently used to represent the march of intellect – there are at least three versions of this image in circulation in the early 1830s, and Seymour himself re-worked the image, published as no. 10 of the first volume of the Carlisle and Tregear editions, elsewhere in the *Sketches* (fig. 10). The image has a fairly lengthy caption to emphasise the central ›joke‹. One dustman looks up from his paper to say »You shall have the paper directly, Sir, but really the Debates are so very interesting« to which his companion replies »Oh pray don't hurry Sir, it is only the scientific notes I care about«, thus gently suggesting the absurdity of a genteel and civilised exchange over cultural values taking place between two traditionally vulgar, filthy and ignorant urban labourers comfortably (if improbably) seated within a chop house or coffee shop, a bastion of urban leisure. Built out of notions of irruption and incongruity, Seymour's image is nonetheless a very gentle comedy of role reversal and cultural aspirations.

*Fig. 10: »You shall have the paper directly, Sir« from the G.S. Tregear edition of* Seymour's Sketches *(c.1834).*

Crowquill's text, however, imports a condescension entirely lacking in Seymour's original image. His commentary begins with assertive facetiousness – »What a thrill of pleasure pervades the philanthropic breast on beholding the rapid march of Intellect!« (Crowquill 1841: n. pag.) – and then introduces a rather laboured series of the puns that had come to characterise Regency humour before detailing, with a semi-mocking sense of affront, the ways in which the »interesting individuals« are surveying reports of political events »with as much interest as the farmer does the crows in his corn-field!« Crowquill stresses the dustmen's ›familiarity‹ in referring to politicians. Clearly, he regards this response as an act of ›overfamiliarity‹, an unjustified assumption of intimacy with political events inappropriate to the social standing and intellectual powers of working men. To further denigrate the cultural ambitions of the dustmen, Crowquill records their continuing conversation which is characterised by a series of inadvertent puns and allusions to their dirty trade – the Irish Member had *kicked up the dust* in the House, but his speech was *a heap of rubbish* they aver, and decide to turn Conservative because »my Sal says as how it's so genteel« (Crowquill 1841). With a parting exchange on the nature of the liberty of the press which confuses liberty with taking liberties, the men »down with the dust« (that is, pay their bill) and leave the coffee house.

The above reading of some of Seymour's prints from *Sketches* and their mediation into competing mid-Victorian versions of his Regency social vision perhaps permits wider generalisations about the ›re-makings‹ of his work. Seymour's urban vision, an essentially visual apprehension of the world, expressed through traditional caricature tropes of transgression and reversal – the would-be urban sophisticate unmanned and unmannered by the alien threats of a misunderstood countryside – was mediated into later Victorian consciousness through incremental levels of textuality. Crowquill's re-writing of this image of the trespass of the vulgar into the domains of the genteel – the world of leisure, print culture and the exchange of (perhaps) informed opinions – is, in contrast to Peake's commentary, centrally characterised by anxiety and class hostility. Crowquill is sarcastic and superior where Peake is curious, or even empathetic. In both cases, the original images, produced in unannotated form for an informed audience of readers well used to the tropes, conventions and visual language of Regency caricature, have been transmitted, through additional levels of textuality, into early Victorian culture by means of an extended commentary that ascribes them to new socio-political and ideological contexts.

The addition of texts that were beginning to emphasise naturalistic accounts of the urban scene rather than maintain the picaresque mode of Regency comic versions of the city provided a first step in the ›Victorianising‹ of Seymour's *Sketches*, and suggest the importance of the ›fictionalising‹ or ›narrativising‹ of graphic images as a mechanism for the ideological transformation of cultural meanings. But ultimately it was Bohn's explanatory notes to the plates (suggesting that their immediate visual meaning was likely to be obscure to later readers) and biography of Seymour in Bohn's 1866 edition that changed the meaning of the *Sketches* on into an interesting antique survival of a lost era rather than a living and immediate response to Regency London. Central to these later issues of the Bohn edition – containing Crowquill's textualisation of the images, and both Bohn's notes on the plates and his biographical memoir of Seymour –, an edition that was, reprinted again and again in the later Victorian period despite the deteriorating condition of the steel plates and the sustained facetiousness of Crowquill's text, was the belief that Seymour should be understood as essentially a sporting artist, whose main interest was to be found in his vision of would-be urban sportsmen laid low by their exposure to the practices and perils of rural life. Accordingly, the version of the *Sketches* that was remade for mid-Victorian consumption shows a yearning for a lost innocence, a world of comic outings into unfamiliar and transgressive urban and rural pleasure, in which accident, nuisance and misadventure, rather than urban crisis, were the dominant ideas. In order to construct this particular book, the publishers, first Wallis and then Bohn, reduced Seymour's original stock of 180 plates to 86, largely eliminating images of urban meetings and street culture in favour of the comic sportsmen through which Seymour had built his reputation. Indeed, reading the original Tregear edition which offered only plates, a very different London emerges – a teeming world of street collisions and urban presences – scavengers, dustmen, sweeps, draymen and the like – largely rendered through grotesque caricature modes, and, increasing, depicting a domestic as well as a street culture. It is this world of sometimes claustrophobic urban-ness that Seymour counterposed against the country adventures of his less than sophisticated urban escapees and seekers of rural delight in his original version of the *Sketches*.

In the tangled history of this illustrated text, then, we can see a struggle between competing meanings in Seymour's images, with Victorian awareness of the marketplace for visual comedy insisting that the urban grotesque should give way to a more gentle humour of reversal, out-of-placeness, and mutual incomprehension between the city and the country. Yet even in the Bohn version some lingering sense of a caricature version of the city emerges, as the detailed reading of the march-of-intellect images above suggests. In Seymour's urban images, the metropolis is constructed out of accidents, collisions, inconveniences and nuisances, mainly experienced on the streets but with an increasing interest in the domestic and cultural lives of the relatively poor. Such a city is also theatrical, visually stimulating, characterised by grotesque yet engaging physicality, and essentially benign. This picturesque and picaresque city imagined by the caricaturists of the 1820s and 1830s, despite the level of mediation that often accompanied its presence in later nineteenth-century visual culture, was startlingly available to later Victorian consumers.

## THE PERSISTENCE OF REGENCY COMEDY: SOME EXPLANATIONS

All the above discussions have been carried out under the implicit assumption that the mid- and late-Victorian re-making of Regency caricature was essentially a vulgarisation or cheapening of earlier publications aimed at bringing in a much wider range of buyers and readers. Such a process as this might be called, positively, a ›democratisation‹ of the text or, negatively, using a phrase drawn from Walter Benjamin, an assault on the text's ›aura‹. Thus genteel hand-coloured aquatints and etchings were turned into tonally crude wood engravings, and the expressive line of the satirical tradition gave way to the clumsy linearity of the mass-reproduced image. As already suggested, this is very much the analysis adpoted by two of the most influential accounts of comic art in the Regency period, those written by Dorothy George and David Kunzle. As well as her dismal picture of a vastly increased production of inferior and degraded images, George also saw the shift to a safer, more accommodated comic graphic tradition taking place. The mass production of satirical images, brought about by

»revolutionary changes in the modes of production and discourses for caricature in the 1830s, resulted in a slackening of aesthetic achievement and a loss of precise, if satirical, political engagement. While comic image making began to move towards safer, less scatological, less personal bourgeois forms and genres it was at the expense of comic art.« (Stephens/George 1874-1950: XI, xvii)

Kunzle formulated a similar narrative, describing the period as »a satirical hiatus, the social impasse of a larger, less well educated audience that sought diversion rather than enlightenment, leaving the caricaturist free to say anything – or nothing at all«. The result comprises »inchoate miscellanies and whimsical ephemera [...] frivolous, disjointed [...], flowing in no foreseeable direction [...], graphic bric a brac [...] of a metropolitan culture spewing and sprawling itself abroad« (Kunzle 1990: 20-21). It is interesting to note how far Kunzle's sense of aesthetic outrage leads him to desert all historiographical sense – how would it be possible for a discourse as complex as comic art to say »nothing at all«?

Are there other ways of thinking about the influence of Regency caricature on the Victorian imagination in the light of the discussion of Seymour's *Sketches* undertaken above that deny George's and Kunzle's sense of loss and decline? It is evident that Regency and early Victorian comic art remained popular throughout the nineteenth century, and, as this essay has suggested, there was a considerable trade in reprinting and re-formatting images for succeeding generations of book-buyers. The continuing popularity of the Cruikshanks, Seymour, the Heaths and their contemporaries throughout the Victorian period can perhaps be more positively explained, using the kinds of models of popular culture employed by Stallybrass and White (1986), in terms of a consistent bourgeois longing for a masculinised urban ›other‹ of cross-class and hence transgressive sociability that was nostalgically ascribed to Regency London.

William Makepeace Thackeray's essays about comic art and his childhood reading perhaps express this powerful yearning most fully.[6] His essay on Cruikshank centres on a profound sense of a loss. The comic energy that constructed a collective air of goodwill in the Regency had, Thackeray claimed, been lost under an early Victorian cloud of respectability and decorum that had descended on London:

»Knight's, in Sweeting Alley; Fairburn's, in a court off Ludgate Hill; Hone's, in Fleet Street – bright, enchanted palaces, which George Cruikshank used to people

---

6  Thackeray was himself of course an aspiring comic artist. His lengthy essay on George Cruikshank appeared in the *Westminster Review* in June 1840, and was reprinted in the same year by Henry Hooper in a pamphlet form containing additional illustration. Thackeray's study of John Leech, which contains a great deal about his own youthful interest in comic illustration, was published in the *Quarterly Review* in December 1854.

with grinning, fantastical imps, and merry, harmless sprites, – where are they? Fairburn's shop knows him no more; not only has Knight's disappeared from Sweeting's Alley, but as we are given to understand, Sweeting's Alley has disappeared from the face of the globe. Slop, the atrocious Castlereagh, the sainted Caroline (in a tight pelisse, with feathers in her head), the ›Dandy of Sixty‹, who used to glance at us from Hone's friendly window – where are they? […] and there make one at his ›charming gratis‹ exhibition. There used to be a crowd round the window in those days, of grinning, good-natured mechanics, who spelt the songs, and spoke them out for the benefit of the company, and who received the points of humour with a general sympathising roar. Where are these people now? You never hear any laughing at HB.; his pictures are a great deal too genteel for that – polite points of wit, which strike one as exceedingly clever and pretty, and cause one to smile in a quiet, gentle-man like kind of way.« (Thackeray 1902 [1840]: 287-288)

Thackeray has here summarised a central narrative that was, and sometimes still is, frequently used to describe the caricature tradition as it evolved, or, as most argue, declined in the period between 1820 and 1850. Outspoken, or, in Thackeray's terms, »bright, enchanted« caricature in the Regency period, he argues, brought people together round the print shop window, democratised humour for the barely literate masses, and reflected a society in which social and gender distinction was acknowledged, but assimilated into a vision of necessary and largely peaceable urban contiguity. In this world of »grinning, good-natured mechanics« caricature was a force for social harmony and shared vision – Cruikshank's grotesques were »harmless« and »fantastical«, the radical and politically active Hone was »friendly«, and the print shops presented a »charming« comic vision. Yet the energy, goodwill and street contiguity engendered by such a tradition had, Thackeray argued, dissipated in the middle years of the century into something »polite«, »clever«, and »pretty« – a damning sequence of terms that suggests an anodyne respectability that denies the robust masculinised give and take represented in Regency caricature.

Thackeray's sense of emotional and, indeed, ideological loss needs to be posited against the vastly increased level of commercialisation, adaptation and re-imagining that ran through the trade in prints, and especially caricatures and other forms of comic visual in the early Victorian period, and which sustained a version of Regency graphic satire on into the mid-Victorian period. Rather than suggesting a total loss of aesthetic and political energy, comic images in this period enact an entrepreneurial and artistic vigour focussed substantially in subject matter on social relationships, which had begun to become a major theme of single-plate caricature in the first two decades of the nineteenth century. Yet Thackeray may well have been right to identify satirical visual culture in this period as poised between the abusiveness and outspokenness of eighteenth-century political caricature and the debilitating gentility and whimsicality of Victorian graphic humour. In order to maintain an interest in the potentially destabilising world of carnivalesque streets, grotesque human shapes and the cultural challenges of social proximity that Thackeray here identifies as characteristic of the print trade, early Victorian artists re-worked and re-formulated their Regency comic inheritance in a number of important ways, often by imposing firm narrative shape on a social vision that had previously proceeded from a primarily picaresque mode of social comprehension. The dominant new graphic medium of the small-scale wood engraving, despite its size, tonal monotony and linear simplifications, began to evolve beyond an inherited repertoire of caricature tropes into a more naturalistic manner in which it is possible to identify the origins of social reportage. Yet, despite these developments and re-imaginings, the social vision of *Life in London,* of *Seymour's Sketches* and of a whole range of Regency graphic artists, a vision in which social difference was both acknowledged and accommodated within the rumbustuous communal life of the streets, in which urban proximity and contiguity seldom lapsed into threat or anxiety, and in which the picturesque and the picaresque still dominated over narratives of danger and contamination, still captivated many Victorian visions of the city. For the readers of *Bleak House, Mary Barton* and George Gissing, Seymour's London remained a visual fantasy of a cultural moment worth preserving and savouring.

## WORKS CITED

Abbey, J.R. (1972): *Life in London in Aquatint and Lithography 1770-1860*, London: Dawsons of Pall Mall.
Bentley, Frederick (n.d. [c.1888]): *Seymour's Humorous Sketches*, London: Frederick Bentley.
Bohn, Henry (ed.) (1866): *Sketches by Seymour*, London: Henry Bohn.

Cohn, Albert M. (1924): *George Cruikshank: A Catalogue Raisonne*, London: The Bookman's Journal.

»Crowquill, A.« [Forrester, A.] (1841): *Seymour's Humorous Sketches*, London: H.Wallis.

Hancher, Michael (2000): »From Street Ballad to Penny Magazine: ›March of Intellect in the Butchering Line‹«. In: Laurel Brake/Bill Bell/David Finkelstein (eds.), *Nineteenth Century Media and the Construction of Identities*, Basingstoke: Palgrave, 93-103.

Hardie, Martin (1990 [1906]): *English Coloured Books*, London: Fitzhouse Books.

Hood, Thomas (1859): *Hood's Own: Or, Laughter From Year to Year*, 2 vols., London: Moxon.

James, Louis (1976): *Print and the People*, London: Alan Lane.

Kunzle, David (1990): *The History of the Comic Strip: The Nineteenth Century*, Berkeley: U of California P.

Lauster, Martina (2007): *Sketches of the Nineteenth Century: European Journalism and its Physiologies 1830-1850*, Basingstoke: Palgrave Macmillan.

Maidment, Brian (1996): *Reading Popular Prints 1790-1870*, Manchester: Manchester UP.

Maidment, Brian (2007): *Dusty Bob: A Cultural History of Dustmen 1780-1870*, Manchester: Manchester UP.

Maidment, Brian (2011): »A Draft List of Published Book and Periodical Contributions by Robert Seymour«. *Victorian Institute Journal* 38, Digital Annex. In: *NINES Nineteenth-Century Scholarship Online* (www.nines.org/exhibits/Robert_Seymour). Accessed 29 May 2013.

Maidment, Brian (2013): *Comedy, Caricature and the Social Order 1820-1850*, Manchester: Manchester UP.

Paston, George (1905): *Old Coloured Books*, London: Methuen.

Peake, R.B. (1846): *Seymour's Humorous Sketches comprising ninety two caricature etchings illustrated in prose by R.B. Peake*, London: George Routledge.

Stallybrass, Peter/Allon White (1986): *The Politics and Poetics of Transgression*, Ithaca/NY: Cornell UP.

Stephens, F.G./M.D. George (1874-1950): *British Museum Catalogue of Political and Personal Satires*, 11 vols., London: British Museum.

Thackeray, W.M. (1902 [1840]): »An Essay on the Genius of George Cruikshank«. In: *Ballads and Miscellanies in the Biographical Edition of Thackeray's Works*, London: Smith Elder, vol. XIII, 287-288.

Tooley, R.V. (1954): *English Books with Coloured Plates 1790 to 1860 – A Bibliographical Account*, London: B.T. Batsford.

# Richard Doyle's Comic Histories
## A Victorian Look at the Middle Ages

SANDRA MARTINA SCHWAB

## INTRODUCTION

Richard Doyle was one of the leading and one of the most beloved illustrators of the early Victorian period. When he died, quite unexpectedly, in December 1883 at age fifty-nine, *The Musical World* called him »one of the most accomplished and delightful draughtsmen of modern times« (»Death of Mr. Richard Doyle« 1883: 788). Similarly, *The Pall Mall Gazette* wrote of him as »the most skilful caricaturist of the nineteenth century« (»One of Mr. Doyle's Bird's-Eye Views« 1883: 11). However, the obituaries and appreciations that appeared in large numbers in British magazines and newspapers during those December weeks also made it obvious that Doyle's fame had started to wane already during his lifetime. Indeed, in the decades following his death, his name nearly sank into obscurity. To the journalists of the 1880s, he already belonged to »a generation now passing away or growing old« (»Deaths of Note« 1883: 10). He had, it was felt, done his best work in his youth, long ago, when he was working for *Punch*. As *The Preston Guardian* put it, »[u]nluckily, the promise of his career was never wholly fulfilled. Of late years he has been comparatively unknown [...]« (»Stray Notes« 1883: n. pag.). Then as now Doyle was, and is, chiefly remembered for designing the famous *Punch* cover showing Mr. Punch and his dog Toby surrounded by a host of little fairies and mannikins that are so typical of Doyle's work. In 1902 Lewis Lusk described it as »one of the best decorative designs ever placed upon a magazine which stares the British Empire in the face every week« (1983 [1902]: 248).[1] The illustration (fig. 1) is a good example of Doyle's whimsical style and his particular brand of gentle humour, for it shows Mr. Punch doing a sketch of the so-called large cut, the central one-page political cartoon in each weekly issue

Fig. 1: Richard Doyle: Wrapper design for Punch (Spielmann 1895: 48).

of *Punch*: He is »using his dog Toby as a model for the British lion, with a crown upon its head« (Leary 2010: 36). Such whimsy and what *The Preston Guardian* called »charming fancy« (»Stray Notes« 1883: n. pag.) were characteristic of ›Dicky‹ Doyle's humour. As this chapter will show, this humour

---

1  Indeed, beginning in 1849, the year Doyle created the final version of his wrapper design, the cover stared the British Empire – and then the Commonwealth – in the face for over a hundred years before it was finally replaced in the mid-1950s by what the makers of *Punch* then considered trendier designs (cf. *Punch Then and Now* 1970: 18). One cannot help but feel that Lusk probably would have disagreed with their logic. After all, Doyle's cover had become the face of the magazine and embodied the iconic status *Punch* had achieved.

was often devoted to historical subjects – and thus a general interest of Victorian culture.

Among his *Punch* colleagues Doyle quickly became known as the »Professor of Mediæval Design« (Spielmann 1895: 455) because he excelled at caricatures of little knights – like the initial letter to the fifth installment of »Punch on the Constitution«, dealing with the reign of Henry VII after »[t]he Roses hav[e] ›ceased to blow‹ – or at all events to inflict their blows upon each other« (»Punch on the Constitution« 1848: 179). The mannikins in Doyle's initial letter, however, have not yet ceased their blows: Sitting on two roses, they continue to enact the Wars of the Roses (fig. 2). This interest in historical subjects as well as Doyle's often irreverent treatment of history – and his own contemporary culture – is evident already in his juvenilia and spans his whole career. In the pages to follow we shall look at some of Doyle's comic histories and historical parodies, ranging from his adolescent sketches to his work for *Punch* in the 1840s, his book illustrations in the 1850s, and finally, to his fairy paintings in his later career.

Fig. 2: Richard Doyle: Initial letter for »Punch on the Constitution« (1848).

## AN EARLY ENGAGEMENT WITH MEDIEVALISM

Young Doyle's love for tales of knights and times past becomes apparent in the journal which he kept in 1840 and which was published posthumously in 1885. Historical novels were read aloud in the family circle, and in March Richard Doyle began work on a large painting inspired by Sir Walter Scott's novel *Quentin Durward* (cf. Doyle 1885b: 32). Together with his brother James he also did a series of »Histories of ...« for the family's weekly show on Sunday, when the children would display their work of the past week for their father John Doyle, the caricaturist »HB«. On Sunday, 25 April, Richard Doyle presented his progress on his Quentin Durward (fig. 3), but his diary entry reveals how eager he was to continue with the histories, especially as he and James had received ample motivation from their father: »I happen at the present moment to be particularly anxious to go on with our new series of histories, which James and I are going to do and which anxiety is not materially lessened by Papa's having promised to get them bound when finished to the number of thirty« (Doyle 1885b: 51).

*Fig. 3: Richard Doyle: Illustration in* A Journal Kept by Richard Doyle in the Year 1840 *(Doyle 1885b: 51).*

»Papa« also seems to have been responsible for getting his son's *The Tournament, or The Days of Chivalry Revived* printed, a series of caricatures of the infamous Eglinton Tournament of 1839. This tournament, organised by Lord Eglinton as a contribution to the contemporary vogue of medievalism, invited caricature. Ian Anstruther has called it »the greatest folly of the century« (1963: 12), and it ended in torrential rain and much ridicule for the unfortunate Lord Eglinton. Fifty copies of Doyle's book arrived on 3 March 1840, much to his delight (cf. Doyle 1885b: 30). Doyle's caricatures illustrate the progress of Lord Eglinton's medieval re-enactment from the practice sessions (Plates 1 and 2) to the procession to the tilting ground in the rain (Plate 3), the melée (Plate 4), the tilting (Plate 5), and finally, the crowning of the victorious knight by the Queen of Beauty (Plate 6). Each plate has borders made up of tilting lances and little mannikins in fool's caps – parodies of the gothic borders so popular at the time. The people in the main illustrations are mostly rendered realistically. Much of the humour derives from the exalted postures and expressions of the knights as well as from an exaggerated depiction of what one contemporary has referred to as »the *impedimenta* of chivalry« (qtd. in Martin 1962: 95): On Plate 1, for example, two knights fight with overly large swords that make them look like children, and during the melée and the tilting the helmets with lowered visors resemble monstrous faces and reflect their wearer's emotions. Additionally, many of the helmets sport cute animals such as the little dogs on Plate 5. These animals parody the elegant or ferocious heraldic animals on medieval helmets and on those worn by the modern knights taking part in the Eglinton Tournament. The details on Plates 1 and 2 suggest that young Doyle attended the rehearsal of the Eglinton knights in the garden behind the Eyre Arms, a pub near Regent's Park, in June 1839: One of the illustrations on Plate 1 shows what was called the »Railway Knight«, namely, »a dummy knight perched on a wooden horse on wheels which rocketed down a pair of grooves towards the barrier and which, therefore might be used as an opponent« (Anstruther 1963: 154). Another piece of equipment from the rehearsal, the quintain, is depicted on Plate 2:

»This gadget for training mounted spearmen [...] resembles a man's torso with arms outstretched and was so fixed to an upright pole that it twirled freely like a weathervane. If it was struck on the chest exactly square by the charging knight, it caused his lance to shiver; if it was hit on the right or left breast it spun about and whacked his head as he passed it.« (Ibid.)

In contrast to the real dummies used during the rehearsal, Doyle's versions have the faces of living men. Thus, his Railway Knight looks like a man sitting on an enlarged toy horse, and his mustachioed quintain wears an alarmed expression as one of the knights gallops towards him. A much happier quintain appears in the border of Plate 3. Given that the illustration on this plate depicts the procession, with the knights and the spectators huddling miserably under large umbrellas, one cannot help but feel the quintain is grinning so broadly because he delights in the misfortune of the men who have pummelled him about earlier on.

Caricatures of the Eglinton Tournament also appear in Doyle's journal. On page 4 a fat knight stands grimly in the rain, his spindly legs a curious contrast to his large belly; and page 10 features a sketch of the melée amidst great clouds of dust, which lend the scene a look of utter chaos (fig. 4). The knights are all slightly too large for their horses, and in one case we only get to see a most unflattering back view of a knight, dominated by his and his steed's very round bottoms.

*Fig. 4: Richard Doyle: Illustration in* A Journal Kept by Richard Doyle in the Year 1840 *(Doyle 1885b: 10).*

The role of the caricaturist seems to have suited Richard Doyle particularly well because after having done the series of »Histories of ...« with his brother in 1840, in 1841 he decided to do a burlesque version (cf. »Introduction« 1885: n. pag.). The result were the *Comic English Histories*, published posthumously – first as a *Pall Mall Gazette* »Christmas Extra« in 1885 and then, a year later, in book form. The *Comic Histories* consist of twelve plates showing scenes from English history, for example »Edward the First Presenting His Son as Prince of Wales« (fig. 5): Here a comic contrast is created by the juxtaposition of the smug King Edward and the long-haired, barbarous Welshmen, grinning toothily. Moreover, Edward's royal poise is much diminished by the fact that he has to stand on tiptoe in order to reach over the balustrade – a detail that adds to the humour of the caricature.

*Fig. 5: Richard Doyle: from* Dick Doyle's Comic Histories with *The Startling Story of Tommy and the Lion (Doyle 1885a: n. pag.).*

## MEDIEVAL PARODY IN *PUNCH*

It was this gently deflating humour that made Richard Doyle ideally suited for his work with *Punch*. He joined the staff of the magazine in 1843, and his illustrations quickly gained popularity with the readership. For his initial letters Doyle often used chivalric caricatures to comment on and satirise issues of the day: For instance, the initial for the article »The Late Fight between the Premier and Young Ben« from 1845 shows two knights tilting (fig. 6). They display all the characteristics of typical Doyle knights: They are too large for their horses; one of the helmets seems to leer at his opponent; and both helmets are adorned by cute animals. The article itself deals with a series of parliamentary aggression between Robert Peel and Benjamin Disraeli, which it describes in the manner of a boxing match between ›Bob‹ and ›Ben‹.[2] Thus, the House of Commons becomes »the Parliamentary

---

2   The row was triggered by the debate on 20 February 1845 about whether or not the government was allowed to have letters opened, an issue that first came up during the debate on 14 June 1844, when a petition was presented from »W.J.

Ring«, and the verbal argument is turned into a physical fight, with »Pawky Bob« coming »down with a topper on the nob of his ›candid friend‹«. In the »Third Round [...] BEN [is] again on his legs, having recovered his wind and his senses. [...] BEN, regularly going in for mischief, planted a stunner on his *os frontis* [...]. PEEL floored. The Young Englander followed up his advantage with a lunge on the breadbasket« (»The Late Fight« 1845: 163). As can be seen from these examples, the article is liberally laced with boxing cant,[3] while terms such as *The Young Englander* as well as Doyle's tilting knights refer to Disraeli's connection with the Young England movement and Young England's idealisation of the past.

*Fig. 6: Richard Doyle: Initial for »The Late Fight between the Premier and Young Ben« (1845).*

---

Linton, Joseph Mazzini, and others, resident in London, complaining of the detention and opening of their letters at the General Post office« (»Postscript« 1844: 378). When the issue was discussed in the Commons in February 1845, Disraeli launched a personal attack on Peel by saying that Peel occasionally acted »the choleric gentleman« (»Imperial Parliament« 1845: 4).

3   *Nob* means »head«, and *breadbasket* stands for »stomach«. The translations are taken from *The 1811 Dictionary of the Vulgar Tongue*.

Three years later, in 1848, Doyle developed his most elaborate parody of history for *Punch*, in the context of the French invasion scare. Throughout the 1840s the relations between France and Britain were strained due to a number of troublesome or outright aggressive incidents (cf. Saville 1990: 53). The most prominent of these was the publication of a pamphlet in May 1844 on the state of the French naval forces. The authorship of the pamphlet soon became known. It had been written by the son of Louis Philippe, the Prince de Joinville, who had a post of high command in the French navy (cf. ibid.: 53). In the pamphlet he not only pointed out what he regarded as weaknesses in the French naval forces, but he also suggested that with the help of the steam engine the naval power of the British could be broken. Indeed, he went so far as to say »that had Napoleon I possessed a few steamers he might have been able to land 15,000 to 20,000 troops on British soil in 1805« (ibid.: 54). The British were outraged. Furthermore, there were serious concerns about the possibility of a French invasion, which in turn led to a discussion about the British defences, namely, whether they would be strong enough to withstand the French coming across the Channel with conquest in mind. In 1848 these worries were renewed when, as Joseph Barker reports in *The Reformer's Almanac*, the Duke of Wellington wrote »a great long letter, to warn the people against a French invasion, and to urge them to expend vast sums of money in fortifying the coast of the kingdom« (1848: 50).

On the whole, Mr. Punch maintained a rather sceptical stance on the matter and treated the worries in a satirical manner. Thus, he presented Charles Barry, the architect who was building the new Houses of Parliament in neo-gothic style, with »Our Barry-eux Tapestry« and wrote:

»Sir, – Allow me to offer you a contribution to the decoration of the House of Lords. It is a series of designs for Tapestry, commemorating the invasion which is to come off shortly. The designs are my own. The tapestry [...] will be strictly in character with the building, ›brandnew and intensely old.‹ It is also, like the building, a copy, in general character if not in detail. My original is the well-known Bayeux Tapestry, which commemorates the first French invasion of these islands, under William the Conqueror. [...] I trust my designs and my verses will be found in strict harmony with your noble modern-antique Houses of Parliament, and be leave to subscribe myself,

Your servant and admirer,
PUNCH«. (1848: 33)

With this article, the accompanying poem, and the illustrations by Doyle, Mr. Punch obviously intended to kill two, if not three or even four, birds with one stone. First of all »Our Barry-eux Tapestry« is a satirical thrust against Barry's Houses of Parliament and the historicising style of decoration that was used within and without. In addition, it makes fun of both Wellington's letter and Joinville's pamphlet; and lastly, it is an explicit parody of the Bayeux Tapestry.

The illustrations are done in the same naïve outline style that Doyle would later use for, and make wildly popular with, his series »The Manners and Customs of ye Englyshe in 1849«. As Richard D. Altick has pointed out, »Doyle's comic stylization was primarily a *reductio ad absurdum* of the medieval practice«: He exaggerated the characteristics of medieval art, i.e., »flat linearity (no shading or molding), absence of perspective, and, on the part of the figures, lack of individuality, stiff unnatural poses, and faces delineated either in sharp profile or frontally« (Altick 1997: 166). These are also the artistic features of the Bayeux Tapestry. Doyle's parody must be seen in the context of the nineteenth-century fascination with that venerable piece of embroidery. The tapestry had come to prominence in the early 1800s:

»Almost unknown during the first eight hundred years of its existence, and disappearing entirely from view at the end of the fifteenth century, [the tapestry] was discovered by Napoleon in the course of his preparations for the invasion of England, and exhibited for the first time outside Bayeux in 1803 [...]. It was the enthusiasm of British Gothicists which led to the tapestry's second migration and its return, in the form of imitation and print, to the country where it had originally been embroidered, and whose history it purported to tell.« (Samuel 2012: 32)

Thus, in 1816, the Society of Antiquaries of London sent Charles Stothard to France in order to copy the complete tapestry. He presented his finished work, hand-coloured engravings, to the Society in 1819, and the engravings were published by the Society in the early 1820s (cf. Society of Antiquaries). In subsequent years Stothard's drawings as well as the tapestry itself were much discussed in contemporary periodicals. Given the interest of the Doyle family in history and given Stothard's prominence as a historical draftsman, it can be assumed that not only John Doyle, but also his sons knew of and had seen a copy of the engravings of the Bayeux Tapestry. Indeed, the illustrations for »Our Barry-eux Tapestry« reveal that Richard

Doyle must have closely studied his model, for he copied the overall structure of the illustrations – a broad middle frieze framed by borders along the upper and lower edges – as well as certain textual features: Words are separated by dots; capital letters are used throughout; V replaces U; and a small horizontal line adorns the pointy top of the A, like this: Ā.

In contrast to the medieval model, however, Mr. Punch's »Barry-eux Tapestry« does not celebrate a French victory, though at first it looks as if the Prince de Joinville's scheme might be successful: As proposed in his pamphlet of 1844, the French troops cross the Channel on steamships in the first panel (fig. 7), which is clearly based on the depiction of William the Conqueror's fleet from the Bayeux Tapestry. Yet Doyle renders this threatening scenario ridiculous not only by using a flat, almost childish style of

Fig. 7: Richard Doyle: Illustration for »Our Barry-eux Tapestry« (1848: 33).

illustration, but also by making the French soldiers look extremely miserable and seasick. Some of them even fall off their ship, and in addition, they are accompanied by a boat-load of (French) poodles. As on the original Bayeux Tapestry, the explanatory text identifies key events and key figures like Joinville. Several of the explanations are scribbled into the illustrations in a similar manner as the explanations on the original tapestry are embroidered between the pictures. However, in a double parody Doyle pokes fun at the medieval identifications, for in his first panel, he also points out the gulls (»YE GVLLES«) and the poodles (»HERE·ARE·POODLES«).

The second illustration shows the French »LANDYNGE« on the English coast in Brighton and marching past bathing machines (and their occupants), while the Duke of Wellington, who is easily recognisable by his hawk-nosed profile, is »ON·YE·LOOKE·OVTE« in the wrong place. The power of steam once again plays an important role in the next stage of the French advance, as they use »AN·EĀRLYE·TRAINE« to reach the capital, much to the astonishment of »Y$^E$RVSTICS·AND·DOMESTICK·ĀNIMALES«. This panel, too, seems to be loosely based on a specific scene from the Bayeux Tapestry, namely the advance of the Norman foraging party after the arrival of William's fleet on the British shore. Between the soldiers on horseback and the man identified as Wadard, the embroidery shows two empty Anglo-Saxon houses in the background and men with animals in the foreground. These figures are typically taken to be Normans slaughtering the livestock they have found (cf. Wilson 1995: 186; Bridgeford 2006: 129), but Doyle seems to have used them as models for his rustics: Joinville's train rushes past a countryside scene with a house (not empty), several people and several farmyard animals, among them a cow. With its bent legs it is almost exactly a mirror image of the tapestry's cow.

The topic of the next picture is the »ADVANCE·OF·YE TROOPES·AND·POODLE·DOGES« into London (fig. 8). While at least one of the

*Fig. 8: Richard Doyle: Illustration for »Our Barry-eux Tapestry« (1848: 36).*

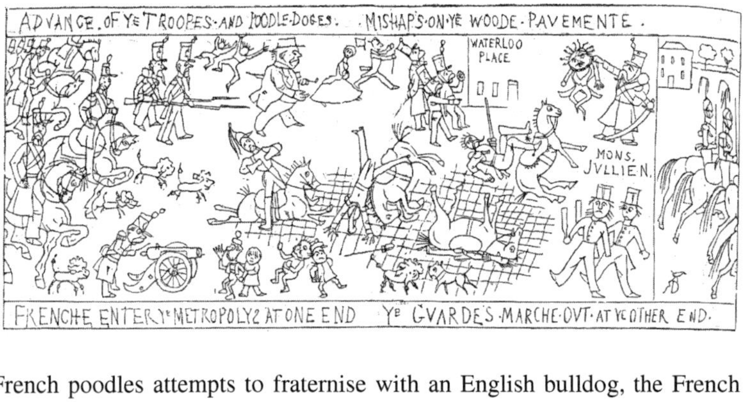

French poodles attempts to fraternise with an English bulldog, the French cavalry meets with »MISHAPS·ON·YE WOODE·PAVEMENTE«. These mishaps form the central part of the illustration and parody an episode on the Bayeux Tapestry titled »*Hic ceciderunt simul Angli et Franci in prelio*« (»Here at the same time English and French fell in battle«) (transl. Wilson 1985: 173). For two of Doyle's fallen horses – the horse which throws its rider over its head and the horse whose hindlegs have slipped – equivalents can be found on the tapestry. They thus present further evidence that Doyle must have closely studied his medieval model and carefully selected scenes and figures to use for his parody.

Apart from the historical humour, the panel also includes topical jokes and contemporary satire. One of the French soldiers has captured Monsieur Jullien, the eccentric musical director of Drury Lane, and the slippery wooden pavement that becomes part of London's defence system gives us a notion of a contemporary nuisance and a serious danger. In an earlier issue that year *Punch* had already poked fun at the slippery pavement in London and recommended »Go-carts for Adults« (1848: 24) to prevent pedestrian accidents. Reports about accidents in other period periodicals reveal how serious the issue was. For example, in April 1845 *The Examiner* ran the following story:

»The Hon. Colonel Cavendish, of the 1st Life Guards, met with rather a severe accident last week when driving down Regent street, by his horse slipping upon the wood pavement, and throwing the gallant officer out, who received some severe bruises on the back and limbs. [...] The regiments of Life Guards, when proceeding from Regent's-park Barracks to mount guard at the Horse Guards, have long avoided the wood pavement of Regent street, and go by Bond street, St James's street, and Pallmall.« (»Miscellaneous« 1845: 266)

Still, Colonel Cavendish came off lightly, considering the fate of the cab driver George Hurst, who received fatal injuries in an accident in the Strand when his horse slipped and he was thrown over the cab: »All the witnesses attributed the accident to the bad state of the wood pavement. The jury returned a verdict of ›Accidental death,‹ accompanied with a desire that the attention of the authorities should be directed to the dangerous state of the wood pavement in that locality« (»Coroner's Inquests« 1845: 10). At least in regard to the Strand, the authorities did eventually react, and in June they ordered the wood pavement to be replaced by granite (cf. »The Wood Pavement in the Strand« 1845: 349). In other London streets, however, the wooden pavement remained a problem, as Doyle's cartoon indicates.

In the next part of »Our Barry-eux Tapestry«, the French troops proceed to wreck havoc in London, killing off hapless citizens, pulling down Matthew Cotes Wyatt's infamous statue of Wellington – the hero of Waterloo –

on his horse Copenhagen,[4] and besieging the offices of *Punch*. Because the English guards have marched out of the wrong end of the city, the defence of London falls to Mr. Punch. The final picture of the series shows the prince defeated and the French fleeing towards the Channel with Mr. Punch and his dog in hot pursuit. This formidable duo so frightens the French army that one of the poor horses has to be carried by its owner. Thus, Mr. Punch's baton of satire triumphs over the roar of cannons, princely pamphlets and ducal predictions, while at the same time poking fun at the neo-gothic decorations of the new Houses of Parliament and the current craze for all things medieval.

## DOYLE'S ILLUSTRATIONS FOR THACKERAY

Doyle's colleague and close friend William Makepeace Thackeray shared his love for history as well as his views on the excesses of nineteenth-century medievalism. He criticised immoderate nostalgia in his novel *The Newcomes* (serialised 1853-55), illustrated by none other than Doyle. As in *Punch*, initial letters at the beginning of each chapter heighten the satire inherent in the text, and many of them depict medieval scenes or medieval fantasies. These are used in a variety of contexts. For example, the initial letter to Chapter 37 of Volume 1 emphasises Thackeray's criticism of the aristocratic ideal of gentlemanliness. It depicts the outcome of Lord Kew's

---

[4] Many Londoners considered Wyatt's equestrian statue a monstrosity (cf. also the chapter on Wellington by Ulrike Zimmermann in the present volume). The *Daily News*, for instance, called it an »atrocious violation of all artistic principle« and an »artistic eyesore« (»London, Wednesday, Sept. 16« 1846: 2). For *The Morning Chronicle* »the hideous bronze caricature« represented a »great national insult to the Duke of WELLINGTON« (»London, Wednesday, Sept. 30« 1846: 4). In *Punch* the statue became a running joke. It was a constantly recurring theme in 1846, the year in which it was erected, and *Punch* artists and writers took great delight in speculating whether it would be the cause for horrible nightmares (cf. »The Wellington Statue and the Arch«) and whether it would tear the world asunder when it fell off the arch (cf. »The Rise and Fall«). Throughout the late 1840s, the statue continued to appear in the magazine, often as a smaller joke within a larger piece such as »Our Barry-eux Tapestry«.

duel with the irascible Frenchman Castillonnes, showing a wounded knight resting in the arms of his page. In the text, Thackeray mercilessly ridicules Castillonnes, his aristocratic pretensions, and his sense of outraged honour, in which he cloaks his sexual jealousy and frustration. Both artist and writer thus censure the chivalric code of honour which demands satisfaction in form of a duel. They depict this code as outdated and not fitting for modern times.

Medieval fantasies also appear in the context of love and an excess of sentimental feeling. Sentimental emotions never sit well with Thackeray; his gentle mockery of Clive's impossible puppy-love for Ethel and of the young hero's grand, painful thoughts on leaving both Baden and girl behind in Chapter 30 of Volume 1 finds its pictorial equivalent in Doyle's initial letter with a charming, if ludicrous scene: The retreat of the lovesick Clive is echoed by a little knight taking leave of his lady-love, who sits on a rose and is so fully engrossed with her pet bird that she does not even spare him a glance (fig. 9). The artist and the writer's mockery is intensified when

*Fig. 9: Richard Doyle: Initial letter for* The Newcomes *(Thackeray 1854-55.1: 289).*

Clive loses Ethel a second time to yet another rich man in Chapter 18 of Volume 2 and once again battles with his emotions: The initial of St. George and the dragon stands for Clive's »courage and resolution« (Thackeray 1854/55.2: 169) in dealing with his disappointment. In a humorous exaggeration, the latter is represented by the ghastly monster. Ironically, in the most popular nineteenth-century version of St. George's fight with the dragon, the successful slaying of the beast wins him the love of Princess Sabra. Poor Clive, by contrast, has lost the woman he loves. Because of the constrictions of society and the dictates of money, for Clive and Ethel love, marriage, and happiness will remain out of reach until the very end of the novel – and there, their potential marriage is relegated to the realm of »fable-land« (ibid.: 373).[5]

A few years before *The Newcomes* Doyle also did the illustrations for Thackeray's *Rebecca and Rowena* (1850), a burlesque sequel to Scott's *Ivanhoe*. This short novel stands in the same tradition as »Punch's Prize Novelists«; in other words, it is part of those works in which Thackeray parodies fiction and fictional conventions of his day (cf. Salmon 2005: 24). In *Rebecca and Rowena* this intention is made clear at the very beginning when the narrator reveals that he wants to correct Scott's mistake of marrying Wilfrid off to »that vapid, flaxenheaded creature« (4), »that icy, faultless, prim, niminy-piminy Rowena« (5). What follows is a deconstruction of Scott's noble characters, which also serves to unmask clichés of the historical novel such as the protagonist's presence at all-important historical events (cf. 64-65). In addition, Thackeray disrupts the medieval setting with anachronisms. In France, for instance, Ivanhoe takes »the diligence across country to Limoges« (23), and the court of King Richard dances »quadrilles and polkas«, while Ivanhoe behaves like »a perfect wet-blanket in the midst of the festivities« (28). Such anachronisms and modern phrases hinder the readers' suspension of disbelief and further their emotional distance from the story. It soon becomes obvious that in contrast to what the narrator has told us, Thackeray's main aim is not to marry off Ivanhoe to Rebecca, but to destroy the image of chivalric heroism that was propagated by other Victorian writers and artists.

His main target is King Richard: While Scott's Lionheart might have been thoughtless, but generally merry and full of chivalric virtues, Thackeray's Lionheart is a greedy, bellowing, plagiarising fool, prone to temper tantrums and to mowing down children and women alike. His behaviour stands in direct contrast to what many Victorians thought to have been the code of conduct of the knights of old, i.e., the chivalric ideal that was described in loving detail in publications such as Kenelm Digby's *The Broad*

---

5    For a more detailed analysis of nostalgia in *The Newcomes* cf. Schwab (2009).

*Stone of Honour* (1822). Doyle's illustrations once again heighten the parody of Thackeray's text. The initial letter to Chapter 1 shows King Richard in the Holy Land with a string of severed heads wound around his horse's neck – in other words, merry King Richard is no better than a barbarous warlord. This point is also stressed in the picture which in later editions is called »King Richard in Murderous Mood« (fig. 10) and which shows the »royal butcher« (Thackeray 1850: 42) attacking the very young son of Count Chalus. Doyle's illustration visualises the contrast between the burly, giant king and the little boy, and thus emphasises the violence and brutality of Richard's actions. Instead of providing true comic relief, the caricatures in the background underline the horror of the ghastly scene.

*Fig. 10: Richard Doyle: Illustration for* Rebecca and Rowena *(Thackeray 1850: Plate between 42-43).*

King Richard's violence finds its echo in Ivanhoe, »the brave and pious knight« (75), who not only kills scores of people, but when he thinks Rebecca dead, kills for the sake of killing (cf. 87-88). While the illustration that accompanies this chapter is not as disturbing as that of King Richard about to slay the young boy, Ivanhoe's serene expression in the middle of a heap of dead or dying people is still discomfiting enough. According to the medieval worldview, his violence might be justified because it is mainly directed at »turbaned infidel[s]« (76), yet the ironising and exaggeration of his killing sprees – in Spain he kills 50.000 moors (88) – makes it clear that from a nineteenth-century point of view, such behaviour must be considered questionable at best. Ivanhoe's status as chivalric hero is further underminded by his rather feminine tendency to faint, by his ludicrous (and anachronistic) disguise as the Knight of the Spectacles, and by his numerous absurd accidents, and his equally absurd revival in a manner reminiscent of the key player in a Christmas pantomime: »Sir Wilfrid, the Harlequin of our Christmas piece, may be run through a little, or may make believe to be dead, but will assuredly rise up again when he is wanted, and show himself at the right moment« (50). Doyle's illustration on the title page (fig. 11) gives a first indication of Ivanhoe's equalisation with Harlequin, for though Ivanhoe is recognisable as a knight in chainmail, he also wears a black Harlequin mask and a diamond-patterned surcoat. His posture, too, is reminiscent of the performers in a pantomime: kneeling, he lifts up Rebecca-Columbine. Thus, Thackeray and Doyle undermine the heroic figures of Scott's novel, and the violence that is often glossed over in historical novels is both ironised and exaggerated. This way, apart from parodying their model, they challenge the idealisation of the past and point out the error of thinking of the Middle Ages as a golden time of chivalry.

*Fig. 11: Richard Doyle: Illustration on title page of* Rebecca and Rowena *(Thackeray 1850).*

## DOYLE'S LATE HISTORICAL ILLUSTRATIONS

In quite a different fashion Doyle satirises the Middle Ages and medieval trappings in his fairy paintings and drawings. Throughout his life he was attracted to the subject of fairies and fairy tales. As a young boy he illustrated various fairy tales for the family show, among them his sister Adelaide's translation of »Beauty and the Beast« (1842); as a young man, he provided the illustrations for fairy books like *The Fairy Ring* (1846), John Edward Taylor's translation of a selection of the Grimms' fairy tales, and for Anthony R. Montalba's *Fairy Tales from All Nations* (1849). By 1851 he had thus become closely associated with fairyland in the minds of his contemporaries, as the review of *Doyle's Overland Journey to the Exhibition* in *The Leader and Saturday Analyst* shows:

»Richard Doyle had a Fairy for his Godmother. This is not a myth, but a grave biographical fact, which you must accept if you study the charming and fanciful productions of his pencil; otherwise, I will thank you to explain where he, and he alone, learned those secrets of fairy land which he, indiscreetly perhaps, suffers to escape in his ›illustrations;‹ – where he, and he alone, learned that trick of fancy rioting into humour never seen before in any artist. We have known fanciful painters and humourous painters; but for the subtle combination, interpenetration, fusion of grace, fancy, and fun, no one has approached Richard Doyle.« (»The Arts« 1851: 879)

After Doyle's resignation from *Punch* in 1850, subjects from fairy and folktales increasingly dominated his work. In many of these drawings he continued to undermine the chivalric ideal. *The Knight and the Jötun* (~1865-75), for example, shows a (seemingly) friendly giant lurking among trees. Still, he so frightens a knight that the latter falls off his horse and onto his bottom. Finally, in *In Fairy Land: A Series of Pictures from the Elf-World* (1870), the crowning glory of his fairy illustrations, Doyle has shrunk the gallant knights. They are of diminutive size, and rather than on proud war horses, they ride on bugs and wasps and grasshoppers (Plate V). Just like Doyle's knights in *Punch*, the elf knights, too, wear helmets with cute decorative animals perching on top, and just like in *The Tournament*, the lowered visors of the knights are expressive and reflect their wearer's emotions.

Doyle's humorous take on history even finds expression in many of his more serious illustrations and paintings. One of the last works he exhibited in 1883, the year of his death, is the watercolour *Dame Julianna Berners Teaching her Young Pupils the Art of Fishing*. Dame Julianna Berners was allegedly Prioress of Sopwell Nunnery near St. Albans in the mid-fifteenth century and wrote a book on fishing (*Richard Doyle* 1983: 53). A facsimile edition of this book was published in 1881, and an edition with critical notes appeared in 1883. Doyle's rendering of the prioress and her impish charges is full of *joie de vivre*: The figure of the prioress herself in the middle ground exudes calm, whereas the foreground filled with children is cheerfully chaotic. The fishing rods are hanging into the river at odd angles; and while some children concentrate fiercely on their task, others are clearly bored or have even fallen asleep. To this, Doyle has added his typical whimsical touches: the little boy who has apparently slid into the river by accident; the fish nibbling at the long shoes of another boy who seems to be taking a nap; and the funny expressions of the prioress's pet dogs.

As we have seen, Doyle enjoyed caricaturing medieval (or would-be medieval) knights and ladies throughout his career. In many instances, his caricatures parody both the medieval model and Victorian medievalism. Furthermore, he used historical references to satirise issues of his day. He clearly loved history, but his view on history was humorous, and he was amused by the excesses of the gothic revival. In Doyle's opinion, reviving the days of chivalry was a bad idea, for knights had no place in Victorian England.

## WORKS CITED

Altick, Richard D. (1997): *Punch: The Lively Youth of a British Institution 1841-1851*, Columbus: Ohio State UP.

Anstruther, Ian (1963): *The Knight and the Umbrella: An Account of the Eglinton Tournament 1839*, London: Geoffrey Bles.

»The Arts« (1851): In: *The Leader and Saturday Analyst* 13 September, 879.

Barker, Joseph (1848): *The Reformer's Almanac, and Companion to the Almanacs, for 1848*, Wortley: Joseph Barker.

Bridgeford, Andrew (2006): *1066: The Hidden History in the Bayeux Tapestry*, New York: Walker.

»Coroner's Inquests« (1845): In: *Lloyd's Weekly London Newspaper* 11 May, 10.

»Death of Mr. Richard Doyle« (1883): In: *The Musical World* 15 December, 788.
»Deaths of Note« (1883): In: *The Ipswich Journal* 15 December, 10.
*The 1811 Dictionary of the Vulgar Tongue: Buckish Slang, University Wit and Pickpocket Eloquence* (1994), foreword by Max Harris, London: Senate.
Digby, Kenelm (1822): *The Broad Stone of Honour: Or, Rules for the Gentlemen of England*, London: C. & J. Rivington.
Doyle, Richard ([1840]): *The Tournament, or The Days of Chivalry Revived*, London: J. Dickinson.
Doyle, Richard (~1865-75): *The Knight and the Jötun*, Victoria and Albert Museum, London (collections.vam.ac.uk/item/O601511/the-knight-and-the-jotun-print-doyle-richard). Accessed 27 February 2013.
Doyle, Richard (1885a): *Dick Doyle's Comic Histories with* The Startling Story of Tommy and the Lion: Pall Mall Gazette *»Christmas Extra«*, London: Pall Mall Gazette.
Doyle, Richard (1885b): *A Journal Kept by Richard Doyle in the Year 1840*, introd. by J. Hungerford Pollen, London: Smith, Elder & Co.
Doyle, Richard (1981 [1870]): *In Fairy Land: A Series of Pictures from the Elf-World*, with a poem by William Allingham, facsimile edition, London: The Bodley Head.
Doyle, Richard (1983 [1883]): *Dame Julianna Berners Teaching Her Young Pupils the Art of Fishing*, private collection, *Richard Doyle and His Family*, London: Victoria and Albert Museum, inside back cover.
»Go-carts for Adults« (1848): *Punch* 14, 24.
»Imperial Parliament« (1845): In: *The Morning Chronicle* 21 February, 2-5.
»Introduction« (1885): In: Richard Doyle, *Dick Doyle's Comic Histories, with* The Startling Story of Tommy and the Lion: Pall Mall Gazette *»Christmas Extra«*, London: Pall Mall Gazette, n. pag.
»The Late Fight between the Premier and Young Ben« (1845): *Punch* 8, 163.
Leary, Patrick (2010): *The Punch Brotherhood: Table Talk and Print Culture in Mid-Victorian London*, London: The British Library.
»London, Wednesday, Sept. 16« (1846): In: *Daily News* 16 September, 2.
»London, Wednesday, Sept. 30« (1846): In: *Morning Chronicle* 30 September, 4.
Lusk, Lewis (1983 [1902]): »The Best of Richard Doyle«. *The Art Journal*, 248-252. Reprinted in Rodney Engen, *Richard Doyle*, Stroud: Catalpa Press, 183-87. [The page numbers in the text refer to the original publication.]
Martin, Robert Bernard (1962): *Enter Rumour: Four Early Victorian Scandals*, London: Faber and Faber.

»Miscellaneous« (1845): In: *The Examiner* 25 April, 266.
»One of Mr. Doyle's Bird's-Eye Views« (1883): In: *The Pall Mall Gazette* 18 December, 11.
»Our Barry-eux Tapestry« (1848): *Punch* 14, 33-38.
»Postscript« (1844): In: *The Examiner* 15 June, 378.
»Punch on the Constitution« (1848): *Punch* 15, 179.
*Punch Then and Now* (1970): London: Bradbury Agnew Press.
*Richard Doyle and His Family* (1983): London: Victoria and Albert Museum.
»The Rise and Fall of the Wellington Statue« (1846): *Punch* 11, 144.
Salmon, Richard (2005): *William Makepeace Thackeray*, Horndon: Northcote.
Samuel, Raphael (2012): *Theatres of Memory: Past and Present in Contemporary Culture*, rev. ed, London: Verso.
Saville, John (1990): *1848: The British State and the Chartist Movement*, Cambridge: CUP.
Schwab, Sandra Martina (2009): »History and Nostalgia in W.M. Thackeray's *The Newcomes*«. In: Bernhard Reitz (ed.), *»My age is as a lusty winter«: Essays in Honour of Peter Erlebach and Michael Stein*, Trier: WVT, 137-48.
Society of Antiquaries of London (n.d.): »The Art of Recording«. In: *Making History: 300 Years of Antiquaries in Britain* (http://makinghistory.sal.org.uk/page.php?cat=3). Accessed 20 February 2013.
Spielmann, M.H. (1895): *The History of* Punch, London: Cassell and Company.
»Stray Notes« (1883): In: *The Preston Guardian* 15 December, n. pag.
Thackeray, William Makepeace (1850): *Rebecca and Rowena: A Romance upon Romance*, illustr. by Richard Doyle, London: Chapman and Hall.
Thackeray, William Makepeace (1854/55): *The Newcomes*, illustr. by Richard Doyle, 2 vols., London: Bradbury & Evans.
»The Wellington Statue and the Arch« (1846): *Punch* 11, 51.
Wilson, David M. (1985): *The Bayeux Tapestry*, London: Thames & Hudson.
»The Wood Pavement in the Strand« (1845): In: *The Examiner* 14 June, 349.

# History ›from below‹
## Stanley Holloway's Monologues for the Variety Stage

STEFANIE LETHBRIDGE

## INTRODUCTION

Saki's humorous short story »The Secret Sin of Septimus Brope« (1911) describes the desperate efforts of the editor of *Cathedral Monthly* to conceal the fact that the main source of his income is the composition of fetching music-hall choruses like ›Cora with the lips of coral‹ or ›Lively little Lucie with her naughty nez retrousee‹ which prove enormously popular: »nothing else was sung and hummed in Blackpool and other popular centres« (Saki [H.H. Munro] 1988 [1911]: 213). Even though by the 1890s music halls and variety theatres were doing their best to establish themselves as respectable venues of entertainment, Saki's story captures central aspects that continued to be connected with this form: its basically questionable though highly popular status, its commercial viability and its preference for performance numbers that encouraged audiences to participate both in the hall and beyond it.

Stanley Holloway, actor, comedian and singer on the variety stage from the 1920s onwards, rose to fame with a series of monologues – rhymed sketches with minimal piano accompaniment – which he presented on the London variety stage in the early 1930s and which achieved notable cultural presence on radio and sound recordings well into the 1950s and 60s. Holloway himself denied any deep-set intention to achieve social or cultural reform with his performances:

»We would probably have shied at the word ›satire‹ as if we had been caught walking down Regent Street in our underpants, but we did our fair share of digging at pomposity, ridiculing the ridiculous and laughing at the ludicrous. But we tried to do it with good humour and without bitterness, bile or belligerence. We didn't protest or lecture.« (Holloway 1967: 40)

Nevertheless, Holloway's monologues may easily be treated as an example for the variety theatre's potential to function as »a site in which certain social, political, and moral issues and conflicts could be aired and worked through, but which ultimately tended to be resolved in the interests of dominant social groups« (Russell 1996: 74). A number of the monologues use historical settings or characters to feed the comedy of the piece. While history and historical figures become a source *for* laughter they are not normally made ridiculous. Rather, Holloway articulates a view of the past ›from below‹, from the perspective of the common soldier or sailor and the ordinary member of the working class. His monologues explore and create stereotypical forms of national self-definition; in humorous displacements and distortions they test a series of readjustments of mainstream cultural and historical narratives, but in the end the monologues confirm and support a markedly conservative position. Following an introduction to British music-hall and variety theatre, this chapter will focus on two questions: What is the source of humour – in the very general sense of provoking laughter – in Holloway's depiction of history, and what effect does this rendering have on the historical events or persons that are thus appropriated?

## CLASS TO MASS: MUSIC HALL AS A SITE OF CULTURAL NEGOTIATION

The music hall came into existence in the middle of the nineteenth century, at first merely as an extension of pub entertainment. Later forms developed into variety theatres with a mixture of songs, comical sketches or revue dancing. Initially, music halls catered mainly for the entertainment needs of workers (both male and female) in modes that combined concert performances and fair-ground attractions like animal acts or acrobatics.[1] Music-hall

---

1   Cf. Kift (1991: 10); Wilmut (1985: 15); Bailey (1982: 204).

entertainment was characterized by its variety, its comical or sensational rendering of real or fictional events and the opportunity it gave the audience for participation. Many music-hall songs or sketches were designed for the audience to sing along, provide the (repeated) catchphrase or even to perform themselves.[2] Though there were efforts to tame audience participation in the quest for respectability, these were never entirely successful (cf. Russell 1996: 71).

Music-hall and variety entertainment has an ambivalent status in cultural criticism.[3] On the one hand it has been described as an ›authentic‹ voice of the lower classes. Modernist commentary in particular celebrated the music hall as uniquely authentic heritage culture.[4] Modernists in this sense »created a discourse that connected a distinctly ›popular‹ culture to nation and history« (Faulk 2004: 24). T.S. Eliot, for instance, praised Marie Lloyd as an artiste who »represented and expressed that part of the English nation which has perhaps the greatest vitality and interest« (Eliot 1964 [1923]: 405). On the other hand, the music hall has often been condemned as the capitalized product of the culture industry, imposing established social structures on passive working-class consumers, as Laurence Senelick puts it: »the heady doses of chauvinism and caricature that passed for politics in the music hall call into question the notion of the music-hall song as the vox populi« (Senelick 1975: 149).[5] What seems to rankle with most of these critics is that music-hall audiences, instead of clamouring for a revolutionary change in their condition, vociferously support chauvinistic and conservative political attitudes. But it is obviously too simplistic to condemn all right-wing sentiment as necessarily unauthentic in a working-class environment. As Mark Philp points out, »[t]hat loyalist sentiment becomes the only acceptable script for popular politics does not mean that this sentiment is entirely manufactured« (2006: 95). The most common critical approach in recent years has been to frame music-hall and variety acts within Antonio Gramsci's notion of hegemony, casting it as a site of negotiation between dominating and dominated sections of society (cf. Kift 1991: 19;

---

2   On the importance of chorus singing in the music hall cf. also Bennett (1986).
3   A useful overview of criticism can be found in Kift (1991: 10-21).
4   Cf. Eliot (1964 [1923]); Beerbohm (1899; 1969 [1903]); Pennell (1893).
5   Similar positions are put forward for instance by Martha Vicinus (1974) and Ian Watson (1983: 49-51).

Bratton 1986: xi). By far the majority of criticism on music-hall and variety theatre focuses on their development until 1914, although the entertainment form lived on well into the inter-war years and beyond. It continued to function as a site of cultural negotiation through its specific aesthetic and use of communal laughter.

The guiding principle of ›variety‹ in these entertainments at times produced some strange bedfellows: the sentimental butted against the sensational, the boisterous jostled with the lachrymose, kings found themselves exhibited next to murderers. While the audience was asked to participate, in rapid succession, in the roles of swells, costers, working men, abandoned girls or brave soldiers, the performative nature of social roles was foregrounded and at the same time the audience was cast as co-producers: »In the music hall,« as Peter Bailey observes, »the shifts in and out of role and self, artifice and autobiography allowed the audience to see, as it were, the joins in the performance«, but the complicity in such role constructions also assert the audience's »own collective authorship/authority in the performance« (Bailey 1998: 132-133). Counting on audience background knowledge, their ability to decode language use and habitus into various social roles relied on what Bailey has termed »the knowingness of popular culture« (ibid.: Chapter 6). While variety performance thus encouraged audience participation and in many ways a shared culture of satire and song, the constant change in tone between individual numbers also fostered aesthetic distance: The audience was free to pick and choose which sentiment to identify with, it was at liberty to laugh or cry *at* a performance rather than *with* it (cf. Faulk 2004: 19). One thus needs to be wary of seeing »song and sketch as a simple reflection of a unified working-class culture«, as Russell cautions. At the same time, he considers it to be »realistic to accept that they must tell us something of contemporary attitudes among a broad span of social groups«, if only because it was »commercial common sense« to express widely popular attitudes (Russell 1992: 53).

While the music hall proved popular with an increasing number – or even because of that –, it also found many detractors: From a critical contemporary position music hall stood for vulgarity, indecency, alcohol consumption and the deleterious effects of all this on the morals of the working man (and more so, woman). Potentially disruptive elements of transgression are particularly apparent in the popular cross-dressing acts and the impersonations of upper-class ›toffs‹ which included obvious elements of social caricature (cf. for example Traies 1986: 31). Equally popular *tableaux vivants* of paintings with classical subjects simulated nakedness with nude-coloured body stockings and offered titillating appropriations of high-culture products (cf. Faulk 2004: Chapter 5; Barrow 2010). And though modernists had elevated the music hall to a quintessentially ›English‹ expression, the music hall's quest for ever new forms of entertainment led it to incorporate American influence, especially ragtime, and contemporaries began to express anxieties that this style might threaten »Englishness« (Russell 1996: 68). Operating thus on the limits of the culturally mainstream and socially acceptable, music-hall and variety performance explored boundaries of gender, class and nation. This, however, does not necessarily turn them into sites of political resistance:

»Hunters in search of ›oppositional‹ elements might glimpse one in variety's relentless pursuit of novelty, modernity (both often expressed in the absorption of non-English performers and cultural forms), and the urban. [...] To term this ›oppositional‹, in the Williamsite sense of challenging dominant culture, might be an overstatement [...].« (Ibid.: 81)

Under increasing pressure especially from middle-class positions and from the temperance movement throughout the nineteenth century, the music-hall sector attempted to turn itself into a more respectable (and sober) form of entertainment. The quest for respectability may in part have been responsible for the surge in popularity of music-hall entertainment: In 1914 about 250 English venues for variety theatre existed and a further 80 or 100 in the rest of Britain (cf. ibid.: 65).[6] The variety stage can thus be easily described as »a dominant from of cultural production in the context of a modernizing capitalist society« (Bailey 1986: viii). In this sense »music hall's particular mode of conceit, parody and innuendo constituted a second language *for all classes*, whose penetration had a powerful integrative force in English society« (ibid.: xviii; emphasis original). A growing capitalization and organization of music halls into large syndicates furthered attempts to make mu-

---

6  For changing audience composition and the growth of the middle-class sector in music-hall audiences cf. Höher (1986) and Kift (1991: 73-85).

sic-hall programmes more widely acceptable.[7] The sheer numerical presence of variety venues testifies less to a decline than to the burgeoning vitality and adaptability of the variety form which, in the long run, exercised a notable influence on the popular stage and screen. It was only in the 1950s that the variety stage was finally replaced by the cinema as major entertainment venue, and even then Dave Russell points to the resonances of variety stock devices like physical and verbal slapstick, cross-talk, puns and catchphrases for instance in the *Goon Show*, Charlie Chaplin and Laurel and Hardy (cf. Russell 1996: 65, 70). By that time, variety artistes had adapted to the new situation: »post-war holiday taste gained strength from the growth of light entertainment on radio and early television, as artistes such as Stanley Holloway, Tony Hancock, Joyce Grenfell and many more traded across the media« (Kershaw 2004: 296). The constant attempt to accommodate new forms of entertainment as well as to maintain an appeal across a fairly wide section of society contributed to a »shared experience of a typically urbanized, class-bound world seen from below« (Bailey 1998: 129).

## HISTORY ›FROM BELOW‹

Stanley Holloway's career took off with his participation in the ›concert party‹ *The Co-Optimists*, a mixture of sketches, monologues and light songs, and the only concert party ever to make the West End (cf. Wilmut 1985: 24). Holloway's monologues are a late form of the typical music-hall or variety act. They depict everyday troubles of everyday people who come into contact with historical figures, and they slot easily into discourses of patriotism and acceptance of social position of the ›respectable‹ version of late music-hall performance. They also maintain, however, vestiges of social resistance and potential elements of subversion.

As is typical of music-hall acts, Holloway's monologues focus on imaginary individuals, sometimes characters that crop up in just one monologue, but frequently across several different pieces, most famous among

---

7  By the early twentieth century large syndicates under Edward Moss or Oswald Stoll alongside some smaller circuits dominated the music-hall scene, cf. Wilmut (1985: 16) and Kift (1991: 30).

them Old Sam Small, soldier under Wellington, and Albert Ramsbottom, only son of a Lancashire working-class couple.[8] Following a suggestion by his famous colleague Gracie Fields, Holloway started touring the variety stage with his monologues in the 1930s (cf. Wilmut 1985: 29; Holloway 1967: 90); and they were successful both nationally and internationally: Harold Wilson is said to have had one of the monologues (*Yorkshire Pudding*) as his party piece and Sir Arthur Comyns Carr, QC and prosecutor at the German and Japanese War Criminals' trial, recited *Albert and the Lion* at the banquet after the trials to the particular amusement of the Russian judge (cf. Holloway 1967: 91). More importantly, Holloway's monologues regularly appeared in BBC radio programmes well into the 1960s and achieved notable sales on LPs and DVDs (cf. Wilmut 1985: 29). His major character, Sam Small, became a national icon.

Holloway's monologues cluster around two historical topics: A first group focuses on the Napoleonic Wars, a second takes up historical themes around the (modern) Tower of London. In guided tours and humorous ghost stories these pieces also offer an angle on the processes of commemoration. Both topic clusters show a strong tendency to a form of presentism that makes history an interest not mainly of the past but of the present. Holloway offers a history ›from below‹, from the perspective of ordinary people, and for current uses as entertainment and as source for (national) identification. While this perspective from below includes moments of resistance to mainstream historical narratives and occasionally to middle-class codes or the rules and regulations defended by the middling ranks of the army, it remains a culturally affirmative position that stages the ordinary man (less so, woman) as important participant in existing structures. I shall consider the two opposing strains of resistance and participation in turn.

## Moments of Resistance

Two forms of resistance re-occur in Holloway's monologues and both use humour as a central technique: The first is a deconstruction of mainstream historical narratives in the depiction of historical heroes (like Nelson, Wellington or

---

8   The Old Sam monologues come close to Senelick's category of *chanson militaire* which focuses on the experience of the individual soldier, is often comic or sentimental and has a potentially ›quizzical‹ attitude to war (cf. Senelick 1975: 173).

Napoleon) in distinctly deflationary situations or intimately connected with the shrewd or amusingly bumbling protagonists of the monologues. The second prominent form of resistance is the refusal to follow the (unjustified) rules of institutions as represented by the middling ranks of the army – or society more generally. These refusals lead to tensions which display the extraordinary pigheadedness of both sides and which are eventually resolved by the interference of the ›top brass‹ – the Duke of Wellington, Nelson or Napoleon. A few brief examples will serve to illustrate these observations.

Rendering historical personages in close contact with the ordinary soldier or struggling with the common-or-garden difficulties of life has a deflationary effect; it changes the focus of attention (from outstanding to ordinary) and turns the established hero or heroine of history into an ordinary human being, grafting the more general music-hall interest in personal experience onto the depiction of history. Thus Anne Boleyn's ghost frequently catches cold in the draughty Tower and has trouble blowing her nose »with 'er head tucked underneath 'er arm« in the song of that title. Her ghostly activities are also hampered by union regulations which restrict her appearances to Fridays (*Albert and the 'Eadman*).[9] The tour guide in the Tower asks for sympathy for the housewifely troubles that Richard Coeur de Lion's knightly armour caused: »Imagine the job 'is old woman 'ad, puttin' patches on with t'soldering iron« (*The Beefeater*). Little Albert Ramsbottom puts Lady Jane Grey's executioner out of action by slapping his toast into the ghost's face »drippin' side down« (*Albert and the 'Eadman*). King George IV casually drops in for tea at Sam's home (*Old Sam's Party*) and Wellington suffers from lumbago (*'Alt! Who Goes There?*). Such familiarity with the great and the good reduces distance, though not necessarily respect. In fact, music-hall song or sketch frequently referred to current political leaders with affectionate nicknames; thus Disraeli became ›Dizzy‹ during the Eastern crisis of the 1870s and negotiations with ›Bizzy‹ Bismarck (cf. Diamond 1990: 35); Lord Roberts turned into ›Dear old Bobs‹ during the Boer War (cf. Russell 1992: 58).

In Holloway's *Gunner Joe* (1933), the protagonist Joe is on easy terms of familiarity with the commander of the fleet: He is »boxing the compass« with Nelson »as sailor lads do« – referring to the fact that Nelson had to

---

9   Quotations from Stanley Holloway monologues are transcriptions from Stanley Holloway: *The Classic Monologues* (2000) unless otherwise stated. Transcriptions were compared to the *Stanley Holloway Monologue Index* (2005).

look for his enemy before the Battle of Trafalgar –, Joe lends him his two-headed penny when Nelson decides to toss up whether to attack or not, and when Joe falls into the water after the spectacular explosion of a powder barrel, his mates only laugh at him and it is Nelson who fishes him out.[10] The source of humour in *Gunner Joe* is not Nelson himself, but the determinedly non-heroic description of the Battle of Trafalgar which cuts across the historical myth. Trafalgar and Nelson's death furnish one of the great heroic moments in British self-definition endlessly celebrated and commemorated in both high and popular culture (cf. Philp 2006), especially in connection with Nelson's famous signal from his ship: »England expects that every man will do his duty«. In the 1941 film *That Hamilton Woman!* for instance, starring Laurence Olivier as Admiral Nelson, it is a tense moment before the start of the Battle of Trafalgar, when the sailors solemnly read Nelson's famous message. Nelson's column in Trafalgar Square gives the more peremptory »England expects every man to do his duty«. Popular songs and ballads picked up the phrase, nineteenth-century advertisements for Beecham's stomach pills earnestly exhorted the public that »England expects that every man this day will do his duty and take Beecham's Pills« (Czisnik 2006: 148), and the phrase is still used in modern film, for instance in *Jaws 2* (1978) just before a shark attack.[11] Quoted or misquoted, the phrase represents one of those cultural reference points that can be used to index a feeling of (English) community and patriotism (cf. Philp 2006; Quilley 2006). Quite different to all this earnest and solemn patriotism, *Gunner Joe* does not actually quote the message – nor does it mention Nelson's death during battle – but it does rely on the audience's knowledge both of the phrase and its solemn implications to make its joke:

»And then taking flags out o' locker,
He strung out a message on 'igh.
T'were all about England and duty.
Crew thought they was 'ung out to dry.«

---

10 Nelson was in fact known for his great compassion in helping to rescue drowning Danish sailors after the Battle of Copenhagen, cf. Philp (2006: 108).
11 Cf. the overview on »References in Popular Culture« of the phrase on *Wikipedia* (»England expects that every man will do his duty« n.d.).

The pun in the last line achieves a double entendre that makes the scene simultaneously funny and serious. It can be read as ›the crew mistook the flags for laundry‹ (the pronoun ›they‹ referring to the flags) but it also hints at the desperate and hopeless situation. If ›they‹ is taken to refer to the crew, then the line means ›the crew thought they had been deserted‹. This evocation of a patriotic moment that actually elides the patriotic phrase itself and is (mis)understood as either a very mundane action or a death sentence by the crew – who proceed to fight a heroic battle – captures the technique of Holloway's monologues: English heroism survives amidst the mundane, the ordinary, the non-heroic – in fact it survives because of the English ability to remain eminently unmoved during a crisis, however serious.

When in *Beat the Retreat on Thy Drum* (1931) Sam Small as a little drummer boy is captured by Napoleon, he steadfastly refuses Napoleon's order to »beat the retreat« despite terrible threats that he »will be shot and put underneath guill-i-otine«. Even when Josephine (»she were his Queen«) appeals to Sam's gentler feelings (»And hast thou a mother who loves thee?«), he refuses to give in, claiming English steadfastness for his mother as well as for himself:

»I said, Aye and she's Yorkshire by gum
She'll beat the retreat on me trousers,
If ah were to beat the retreat on me drum.«

Amusingly, this remark softens the stern ›Boneyparte‹: »Ah have a mother like her«, and he gives Sam a medal for heroism instead of executing him. Like Nelson, Napoleon is turned into an ordinary and non-heroic character, someone who had a strict mother and whose well-known posture with his hand in his uniform front is described in the catchphrase »Scratchin' hisself under t'arm«. Sam himself denies any heroic motivation for his refusal and insists that the reasons he could not beat the retreat were because »somebody pinched both me sticks and [...] I'd busted me drum«. Despite such deflationary treatment, neither the historical character nor the imaginary protagonists Sam Small and Gunner Joe are depicted negatively. In fact, the tone of fond familiarity, their very ordinariness, adds to their attraction. While history is depicted humorously – which resists mainstream narratives of heroic elevation – it retains its patriotic focus.

As part of middle-class code transgressions there is some tongue-in-cheek play with variety's quest for respectability. *With 'Er 'Ead Tucked Underneath 'Er Arm* for instance describes the activities of Anne Boleyn's ghost »who walks the Bloody Tower«. The Bloody Tower is the proper name for one of the prison towers in the Tower of London, but »bloody« is of course also a swear-word and thus inappropriate for respectable performance. »Surprising«, Holloway remarks in his memoirs, »how often I've had to struggle to use the word ›Bloody‹ by insisting that ›Bloody Tower‹ was the name of an historical place not just a playful oath!« (Holloway 1967: 92).[12] The ruse allowed for an unpunishable linguistic transgression and thus a dig at codes of respectability.

Probably the most widely influential moment of resistance in Holloway's monologues is Old Sam's refusal to pick up his musket. In the first Old Sam monologue (*Old Sam*, first performed 1929 and unlike most of the other monologues written by Holloway himself)[13] the soldiers stand on parade »on the evening before Waterloo«,[14] when the sergeant (»he was a terror«) accidentally knocks down Sam's musket and orders him to pick it up again. Sam, however, refuses: »Seein' as tha knocked it out of me 'and / P'rhaps tha'll pick the thing oop instead«. This piece of insubordination causes considerable excitement all the way through the ranks of lieutenant, captain, major and colonel. In each case Sam counters the order »pick oop tha musket« with the argument »he knocked it down / Reet! Then he'll pick it oop«. The mounting tension is finally resolved when the Duke of Wellington interferes – unlike the others not with an order but with a request: »he talked to Old Sam like a brother […] Sam, Sam pick oop tha musket / Come on lad, do it to please me!« This change in tone from the highest in command breaks Sam's refusal and he picks up his gun. The source of humour in this case is the helpless rage of Sam's superiors, faced with his stolid refusal to follow orders. The attitude was, in fact, adopted as a national posture for many years, as Holloway recalls:

---

12  To this day the word is blanked out on the website for Holloway monologues.
13  The majority of Holloway's monologues were written either by Marriott Edgar or R.P. Weston and Bert Lee.
14  Correct chronology is not one of Holloway's concerns: Old Sam is a grown-up soldier on the evening before Waterloo in *Old Sam* and he is a little drummer boy also at Waterloo in *Beat the Retreat on Thy Drum*.

»The cartoonists [...] used [Sam] in a lot of cartoons. My old pal the late George Strube featured him in the *Daily Express* with Lord Beaverbrook on a white horse as the Duke of Wellington in some social comment on Empire Free Trade. [...] Butterworth of the *Daily Dispatch* [...] showed a grim picture of Famine wielding a death-dealing scythe and there was the Minister of Food as Sam sitting on a horse and saying to a cigar-smoking Uncle Sam [...] ›Sam, Sam pick up tha' musket!‹ The musket was marked ›Rationing‹ and it was May, 1946.« (Holloway 1967: 84-85)

The phrase appears as late as 1971 in a cartoon by Leslie Gibbard in *The Guardian*, depicting Britain's negotiations to join the European Economic Community.[15]

While Sam's resistance to the order of his immediate superiors shows his independence – and potentially dangerous insubordination to hierarchical structures – the resolution of the problem by the Duke of Wellington re-establishes hierarchy. But while the middling ranks stubbornly insist on military obedience, Wellington shows himself a more gifted leader who asks for cooperation rather than submission. In this sense the monologue expresses a claim for a type of equality for the lower orders and participation in the nation's history, leaving hegemonic structures intact.

### Claiming Participation

After the musket incident, Wellington and Sam start a relationship of mutual support and dependence which is carried into other monologues that feature Old Sam. In *'Alt, Who Goes There?* Wellington actually picks up Sam's musket himself despite his lumbago while Sam is having tea with the King. In *Sam's Christmas Pudding* Sam – after running a-foul of his lieutenant for letting a sparrow nest in his musket – is punished by being forbidden to eat his Christmas pudding. The severity of this sentence shocks Sam (»He thought as he'd only be shot«).[16] Despite this, and only after Wellington explained that he cannot overlook such lack of discipline, Sam is instrumental in helping Wellington defeat the Spanish bastion Baradoz when he accidentally loads Wellington's canon with the forbidden pudding: »The cannon

---

15 Cf. *British Cartoon Archive* (n.d.) ref. No. 20793. The archive provides further cartoons referring to Sam and his musket.
16 Transcribed from *Stanley Holloway Monologue Index* (2005).

nigh jumped off her trunnions / And up went the bastion, sky high«. Sam and Wellington are shown to be at their most successful when they cooperate. The demand for recognition of the ordinary man becomes even more explicit in *Sam Goes To It*, when Sam decides to come out of his retirement to help out in the Second World War (after the Germans bombarded his allotment »And shelled the best part of his peas«). Once again he runs into trouble with the middling ranks, who refuse to let him join for the technical reason that his age group has not been called up. When he takes up the matter with Churchill, »Winnie« replies sententiously that »Never was there a time when so many / Came asking so much of so few«[17] and gives Sam and his musket a place in the Home Guard. This, however, does not satisfy Sam who considers it a degradation:[18]

»He said ›I come back to the Army
Expecting my country's thanks,
And the first thing I find when I get here
Is that I've been reduced to the ranks.‹«

He only accepts his new position when he discovers that Wellington (»an old chap in the corner / With a nutcracker kind of a face«) is in fact also one of the Home Guard:

»And if you should look in any evening,
You'll find them both in the canteen,
Ex-Commander-in-Chief and ex-Sergeant
Both just Home Guards – you see what I mean?«

The propaganda aspect of this monologue (written by Marriott Edgar in 1941) is blatantly obvious, encouraging every member of the public to ›do their bit‹ for the war effort. The claim for recognition neatly fits into Gareth Stedman Jones's diagnosis that music-hall culture merely offered a »culture

---

17 This puns, of course, on Churchill's famous remark on the Battle of Britain that »Never in the field of human conflict was so much owed by so many to so few« (Winston Churchill on 20 August 1940).
18 The Home Guard was frequently »mercilessly ridiculed« on the variety stage (cf. Senelick 1975: 173).

of consolation« (1983: 237). But it also makes a more general moral point: that team work is better than self-aggrandisement – a point that the Wellington character constantly makes. Sam's attitude in all the monologues does not ask for a revolutionary reorganization of existing social or political structures. While it does demand that the importance of the ordinary man be recognized, it demands this in terms of participation, of being part of the group endeavour. The same point was also made by other entertainers of the time, for instance by Gracie Fields who claimed the importance of the ordinary *woman* in her song about the factory girl and her contribution to the war effort:

»I am the girl that makes the thing
that drills the hole
that holds the ring
that drives the rod
that turns the knob
that works the thing-ummy-bob,
[...] that makes the engines roar
[...] that's going to win the war.« (Gracie Fields, »The thing-ummy-bob«, 1942)[19]

Though this is funny in its entanglement of relative clauses and the girl's naïveté, it maintains a dignified and quietly heroic position for this factory worker, a position that large numbers of the audience were likely able to relate to because it coincided with their own. She is part of the system because she is part of the group.

## HISTORY AND HUMOUR IN HOLLOWAY'S MONOLOGUES

Holloway depicts history as comically un-heroic in his monologues. Historical characters are shown as everyday people, struggling with everyday difficulties like colds, union regulations, or the memory of dominating mothers. To a large extent Holloway's history is for present use as much as for past record. Thus the tour guide in the Tower translates the Royal motto »Honi sois qui mal y pense« for his own purposes as »in Yorkshire that

---

19 Transcribed from Gracie Fields, *Looking at the Bright Side* (2002).

means beer's best« (*The Beefeater*). In logical consequence of such presentism, it is possible for Wellington and Sam to fight in the Napoleonic Wars as well as join the Home Guard in the Second World War and for Nelson to promise Gunner Joe a Victoria Cross. In fact, at times history is revealed to be a mere construction for the benefit of tourists or other consumers, for instance when the tour guide in the Tower shows off the »original« axe »that's given royal necks some hard wacks«. He concedes that »it may 'ave had a new handle and it's 'ad a new head / But it's a real old original axe!« (*The Beefeater*) Like other variety acts, such jokes about fake authenticity expose the constructedness of cultural and historical presentations, the »joins in the performance«, as Peter Bailey had it (see above).

As an element of the present rather than the past, Holloway uses history and humour to create audience cohesion. Like other variety artists, he played the audience's enjoyment in participation: »Once an audience gets over its initial shyness they like nothing better than chipping in on an act«; even the Royal Family joined in enthusiastically at a performance for the troops at Windsor in 1941 (Holloway 1967: 93). Operating in a genre that traditionally engages audience complicity, Holloway draws on audience participation in catchphrases both during the performance and, more significant for their cultural impact, across other media like cartoons. Holloway also draws on audience background knowledge of events, a version of what Peter Bailey has described as »the knowingness« of audiences: the knowledge of Nelson's solemn signal to his ships or the original version of Churchill's »Never was so much owed...« phrase which, with only minor changes is completely turned on its head in Holloway's version.

In all this Holloway plays with transgression, he tests boundaries, but he never in the end breaks them down. His history ›from below‹, from the perspective of the ordinary man, offers humorous distortions and displacements, but does not finally question established myths of community – in fact the monologues demand a participation in this community without doing away with class boundaries. Humour here functions not as criticism or deconstruction as is often assumed, but it offers consolation, another function of humour as Keith Cameron has it: »Humour has since time immemorial been a source of consolation and of defence against the unknown and the inexplicable« (Cameron 1993: 5). Holloway was perhaps himself aware of his vacillating position between resistance and social obedience; he certainly joked about it in his 1966 monologue on Magna Charta for an American television show:

»It's because of this 'ere Magna Charta
As were signed by the barons of old
That in England today we can do what we like
So long as we do what we're told.« (Holloway 1967: 93)

## WORKS CITED

Bailey, Peter (1982): »Custom, Capital and Culture in the Victorian Music Hall«. In: Robert Storch (ed.), *Popular Culture and Custom in Nineteenth-Century England*, London: Croom Helm, 180-208.
Bailey, Peter (1986): »Introduction: Making Sense of Music Hall«. In: Peter Bailey (ed.), *Music Hall: The Business of Pleasure*, Milton Keynes: Open UP, viii-xxiii.
Bailey, Peter (1998): *Popular Culture and Performance in the Victorian City*, Cambridge: CUP.
Barrow, Rosemary (2010): »Toga Plays and Tableaux Vivants: Theatre and Painting on London's Late-Victorian and Edwardian Popular Stage«. *Theatre Journal* 62.2, 209-226.
Beerbohm, Max (1899): »The Blight on the Music Halls«. In: *Works and More*, London: Bodley Head, 199-205.
Beerbohm, Max (1969 [1903]): »Demos' Mirror«. In: *More Theatres*, New York: Taplinger, 223-227.
Bennett, Anthony (1986): »Music in the Halls«. In: Jacqueline S. Bratton (ed.), *Music Hall: Performance and Style*, Milton Keynes: Open UP, 1-22.
Bratton, Jacqueline S. (1986): »Introduction«. In: Jacqueline S. Bratton (ed.), *Music Hall: Performance and Style*, Milton Keynes: Open UP, viii-xv.
*British Cartoon Archive*, University of Kent (www.cartoons.ac.uk/). Accessed 26 May 2013.
Cameron, Keith (1993): »Humour and History«. In: Keith Cameron (ed.), *Humour and History*, Oxford: Intellect, 5-9.
Czisnik, Marianne (2006): »Commemorating Trafalgar: Public Celebration and National Identity«. In: David Cannadine (ed.), *Trafalgar in History: A Battle and Its Afterlife*, Basingstoke: Palgrave Macmillan, 139-154.

Diamond, Michael (1990): »Political Heroes of the Victorian Music Hall«. *History Today* 40.1, 33-39.
Eliot, T.S. (1964 [1923]): »Marie Lloyd«. In: *Selected Essays*, New York: Harcourt, Brace & World, 405-408.
»England Expects That Every Man Will Do His Duty«. In: *Wikipedia* (en.wikipedia.org/wiki/England_expects_that_every_man_will_do_his_duty). Accessed 26 May 2013.
Faulk, Barry J. (2004): *Music Hall and Modernity: The Late-Victorian Discovery of Popular Culture*, Athens: Ohio UP.
Fields, Gracie (2002): *Looking at the Bright Side*, Audio CD, Naxos Jazz.
Höher, Dagmar (1986): »The Composition of Music Hall Audiences, 1850-1900«. In: Peter Bailey (ed.), *Music Hall: The Business of Pleasure*, Milton Keynes: Open UP, 73-92.
Holloway, Stanley (1967): *Wiv a Little Bit o' Luck: The Life Story of Stanley Holloway*, London: Leslie Frewin.
Holloway, Stanley (2000): *The Classic Monologues*, Audio CD, Avid Records.
Jones, Gareth Stedman (1983): *Languages of Class: Studies in English Working Class History, 1832-1982*, Cambridge: CUP.
Kershaw, Baz (2004): »British Theatre, 1940-2002: An Introduction«. In: Baz Kershaw (ed.), *The Cambridge History of British Theatre*, vol. 3: *Since 1895*, Cambridge: CUP, 291-325.
Kift, Dagmar (1991): *Arbeiterkultur im gesellschaftlichen Konflikt: Die Englische Music Hall im 19. Jahrhundert*, Essen: Klartext.
Pennell, Elizabeth Robins (1893): »The Pedigree of the Music Halls«. *Contemporary Review* 63, 575-583.
Philp, Mark (2006): »Politics and Memory: Nelson and Trafalgar in Popular Song«. In: David Cannadine (ed.), *Trafalgar in History: A Battle and Its Afterlife*, Basingstoke: Palgrave Macmillan, 93-120.
Quilley, Geoffrey (2006): »The Battle of the Pictures: Painting the History of Trafalgar«. In: David Cannadine (ed.), *Trafalgar in History: A Battle and Its Afterlife*, Basingstoke: Palgrave Macmillan, 121-138.
Russell, Dave (1992): »›We Carved Our Way to Glory‹: The British Soldier in Music Hall Song and Sketch, c.1880-1914«. In: John M. MacKenzie (ed.), *Popular Imperialism and the Military, 1850-1950*, Manchester: Manchester UP, 50-79.

Russell, Dave (1996): »Varieties of Life: The Making of the Edwardian Music Hall«. In: Michael R. Booth/Joel H. Kaplan (eds.), *The Edwardian Theatre: Essays on Performance and the Stage*, Cambridge: CUP, 61-85.

Russell, Dave (2004): »Popular Entertainment, 1776-1895«. In: Joseph Donohue (ed.), *The Cambridge History of British Theatre*, vol. 2: *1660-1895*, Cambridge: CUP, 369-388.

Saki [H.H. Munro] (1988 [1911]): »The Secret Sin of Septimus Brope«. In: *The Complete Works of Saki*, New York: Dorset Press, 207-214.

Senelick, Lawrence (1975): »Politics as Entertainment: Victorian Music-Hall Songs«. *Victorian Studies* 19, 149-160.

*Stanley Holloway Monologue Index* (2005) (homepage.ntlworld.com/barnacle/stanley/shindex.htm). Accessed 26 May 2013.

Traies, Jane (1986): »Jones and the Working Girl: Class Marginality in Music-Hall Song 1860-1900«. In: Jacqueline S. Bratton (ed.), *Music Hall: Performance and Style*, Milton Keynes: Open UP, 23-48.

Vicinus, Martha (1974): *The Industrial Muse: A Study of Nineteenth-Century British Working-Class Literature*, London: Croom Helm.

Watson, Ian (1983): *Song and Democratic Culture in Britain: An Approach to Popular Culture in Social Movements*, London: Croom Helm.

Wilmut, Roger (1985): *Kindly Leave the Stage! The Story of Variety 1919-1960*, London: Methuen.

# Merrying the Monarch

Charles II in Historical Comedies (1800 to the Present)

DOROTHEA FLOTHOW

> »[T]ragedy has history for plots and comedy has the fictitious.«
> (LOPE DE VAGA)[1]

> »[T]he matter consists of fictitious materials, which are called the argument. For never does actuality [*res gestae*] have a place in comedy.«
> (SERVIUS)[2]

## TRAGEDIES, COMEDIES AND ENGLISH HISTORY

It has long been a truism that comedies feature fictitious characters and events. History, it is often felt, should be confined to tragedy, as the lower genre of comedy is considered too frivolous to deal with so serious a subject.[3] Indeed, especially in the seventeenth and eighteenth centuries, under

---

1 Lope de Vaga (1991 [1609]: 186).
2 Translated by and quoted in Baldwin (1947: 66-67) from a commentary on Terence attributed to Maurus Servius Honoratus.
3 For a discussion of this issue cf. Berninger (2006: 255-262); on the status of comedy cf. Nelson (1990: Chapter 1).

the influence of neo-classical theories, writers of tragedies regularly looked to the past for inspiration (cf. Szaffkó 2008: 34). By contrast, comedy is usually set in the present. This is perhaps particularly obvious in the comedy of manners, which shows a marked awareness of contemporary fashions and morals (cf. Hirst 1979). Alternatively, comedies often remove the audience to a timeless, pastoral setting, such as Shakespeare's ›Green World‹ (Northrop Frye), where the rules of society do not apply (cf. Leggatt 1998: 75). Consequently, it has often been stated that historical comedy does not exist. For instance, while Mark Berninger shows that postmodern history plays such as Tom Stoppard's *Travesties* (1974) increasingly contain comic elements, he still asserts that comedy and historical drama have traditionally seemed two incompatible genres. According to Berninger, this is particularly true for the nineteenth century, when there were no historical comedies at all.[4]

Nineteenth-century theatre, however, is infamous for its disregard of generic boundaries and theories (cf. Booth et al. 1975: 30), and this affected its treatment of historical topics. Generally, this period was preoccupied with the past – a fascination which is evident from the period's novels, architecture and paintings. This fascination is also reflected in nineteenth-century theatre – so much so that »[s]ometimes it appears that [dramatists'] main concern was history rather than drama« (Booth 1980: 15).[5] Nineteenth-century playlists feature a remarkable number of plays set in the past, which also comprise »comic forms« (Booth 1991: 179) such as com-

---

4   »Nach gängigem Verständnis schließen sich Geschichte und Komik aus. Ebenso erscheinen Geschichtsdrama und Komödie als beinahe unvereinbare Genres. [...] Wo bei Shakespeare noch komische Elemente in den Geschichtsdramen existierten [...], fällt es im 19. Jahrhundert schwer, komische Elemente in Geschichtsdramen oder gar eine Geschichtskomödie auszumachen.« (Berninger 2006: 255). The conclusion that history and comedy are incompatible also contradicts the many comic elements in William Shakespeare's histories and those of his Elizabethan contemporaries. However, as Berninger (ibid.: 258) also points out, these have traditionally been neglected in studies of the history play. For more details on the relationship between comedy and the Elizabethan history play cf. for instance Chernaik (2007: 8) and Grant/Ravelhofer (2008: 3).

5   The theatre's fascination with the past also found a prominent outlet in antiquarian revivals of Shakespeare's histories (cf. Schoch 1998).

edy, comic drama, comic sketch, burlesque, burletta, extravaganza, comic opera, historical romance and pantomime. These include, for instance, William Brough's extravaganza *The Field of the Cloth of Gold* (1868); Francis Cowley Burnand's burlesque *E-liz-abeth; or, The Don, the Duck, and the Drake and the Invisible Armada* (1870); or E.L. Blanchard's *Harlequin Hudibras! Or, Old Dame Druden, and the Droll Days of the Merry Monarch: A New Grand Poetical, Historical, Operatical, Dramatical, Anachronismatical, Tragical, Comical, Pastoral Christmas Pantomime* (1851).[6] Many of these comic renderings of English and European history feature kings and queens such as Henry VIII or Elizabeth I – a dramatic trend which continued until well into the twentieth century.[7]

The frequent presence of Henry VIII and Elizabeth I on the English stage comes as no surprise. The Tudor monarchs are, after all, amongst the most highly esteemed English rulers and have inspired many works of popular literature and culture over the centuries (cf. String/Bull 2011). Far more surprising is the great number of comedies featuring Charles II, who ruled the British Isles between 1660 and 1685. Charles II is a much less obvious hero of English history. In academic historiography, the Stuart king often features as a dubious character and untrustworthy politician – especially if one judges his achievements by the writings of nineteenth-century Whig historians. Thomas Babington Macaulay, for instance, concluded that Charles »wished to obtain arbitrary power« (1848: 84). Similarly, Thomas Buckle referred to Charles II as »a drunkard, a libertine, and a hypocrite« (1873: 388). Of course, the assessment of the Stuart kings' political achievements is traditionally negative, and like his father and brother, Charles is accused of secret Catholic leanings, and of attempting to rule without Parliament against the interests of his people.[8] However, as Ronald Hutton points out, where Charles II's posthumous reputation is concerned, one needs to distinguish between his political actions and his private life, as well as between his image in popular culture as opposed to the reaction of ›serious‹ historians:

---

6 For further examples cf. the playlists in Nicoll (1962 and 1963).
7 However, after the Second World War, there was an increasing move away from this kind of biographical drama (cf. Berninger 2006: 60).
8 On these issues in modern studies of Charles II cf. Miller (1991) and Harris (2005).

»Other kings had inspired more respect, but perhaps only Henry VIII had endeared himself to the popular imagination as much as this one. He was the playboy monarch, naughty but nice, the hero of all who prized urbanity, tolerance, good humour, and the pursuit of pleasure above the more earnest, sober, or material virtues.« (1989: 446)

Considering that comedies traditionally rarely deal with politics, and that the Romantics and Victorians loved to see the romantic entanglements and private moments of historical characters on the stage (cf. Fricker 1940), this king's life offers rich material. Since his own times, ›The Merry Monarch‹ has been infamous for his exuberant private life, his extramarital affairs and his numerous illegitimate children – as extensively admired in Samuel Pepys's diary and satirized in the Earl of Rochester's poetry. Throughout the nineteenth and early twentieth centuries, the comic stage's fascination with Charles II continued in plays such as John Davidson's *The Knight of the Maypole* (1903); and after a gap at mid-century,[9] Charles II's affairs again offer a prolific field also for today's dramatists. This we can see for instance in Kjartan Poskitt's *Nell's Belles: The Swinging Sixteen-Sixties Show* (2002), which draws Charles as an Austin-Powers-like sex guru, stressing parallels between the 1660s and the 1960s. In this comic musical, Charles is a king who proudly proclaims:

»I don't mind admittin'
When the book of love was written
The picture on the cover – that was me.
When I encounter beauty
I respect my duty
To give myself with generosity.« (14)

Given his many affairs it is unsurprising that in Poskitt's play, Charles spends very little time ruling the country. In spite of nineteenth-century dramatists' more restrictive morality, Charles II's private life also features extensively in the comedies of this period, so much so that Ernest Reynolds identified a separate genre of the »decorous Cavalier comedy« (1936: 11).

---

9   Interestingly, during this period, Charles II was frequently to be seen in film rather than in stage comedies.

How then, is Charles II depicted in comic historical theatre from the nineteenth to the twenty-first century? How is he, an English monarch, turned into a comic figure? How can we explain Charles's great popularity? And what do the examples tell us about historical comedy?

The following observations are based on about twenty comic plays, some of which were written by the most prolific and popular dramatists of the nineteenth century: Douglas Jerrold's *Nell Gwynne; or, The Prologue* (1829) and *The Bride of Ludgate* (c.1829) and James Robinson Planché's *The Court Beauties* (1835); these comedies also include J.B. Fagan's *And So to Bed* (1926) and Paul Kester's *Sweet Nell of Old Drury* (1900) from the early twentieth century. In recent years, Charles II has returned to the comic stage in *Nell's Belles* and Liz Duffy Adams's *Or* (2010). These comedies are just a selection of the plays featuring Charles II – which also include tragedies and melodrama.[10] Altogether, in the last two hundred years, there have been more than 50 plays featuring Charles II (cf. Flothow 2012).

## CHARLES II IN NINETEENTH-CENTURY COMEDIES

While there are only few eighteenth-century plays on the Merry Monarch,[11] in the early nineteenth century he experienced a sudden popularity on the English stage. This development reached a peak in the 1820s and 1830s, when almost half of the comedies examined here were written. This trend has been explained by suggesting that the Restoration offered a picturesque ›other‹ to nineteenth-century theatre audiences (cf. Nicholl 1963: 17) – an observation which, however, probably applies to most historical periods shown on the nineteenth-century stage. With its growing pictorial realism, its interest in costumes, props and stage scenery, nineteenth-century drama generally stressed the spectacular and romantic otherness of the past and has therefore been accused of escapism (cf. Harben 1988: 22 and Meisel 1963: 349). The comedies featuring Charles II fit into this approach to-

---

10 A more extensive list of comedies featuring Charles II is available at the end of the chapter.
11 One exception is Walter Aston's silly play *The Restoration of King Charles II* (1732), which was stopped from performance by the censor.

wards history as they show the past as colourful and funny. Except for a few short references, politics is avoided; instead, the Merry Monarch is shown in pursuit of wine, women and pleasure.

The comedies featuring Charles II are formulaic, and a play like John Payne's *Charles the Second; or, The Merry Monarch* (1824) shows many of the typical elements: Here, Charles is told of a pretty young girl, Mary, who lives in a tavern at Wapping. Charles is interested at once: »A mysterious beauty! It is a case for royal scrutiny – I will investigate it myself.« (10) Disguised as sailors, he and the Earl of Rochester venture out to view the young beauty. In the tavern, they drink with the common ship mates, sing and are very popular. To the landlord Copp they are »[t]wo hearty blades – mad roysters« (15) and »good lads, though they have a little of the devil in them« (22). Charles flirts outrageously with the pretty girl, which greatly upsets Charles's page Edward, who is also in the tavern (disguised as the singing master Mr. Georgini), as he is in love with Mary: »Innocent motives bring you [Rochester] and the king, at night, to a tavern in Wapping, where there is a beautiful girl? Ah! my lord, my lord – « (23). As in many plays, Charles II loses his money (his friend Rochester steals his purse and leaves), so when asked to pay his bill, the disguised monarch looks like a common fraud:

CHAS. All I know is, that one of those honest people must have taken my purse.
COPP. Come, come, messmate – I am too old a cruiser to be taken in by so shallow a manoeuvre – I understand all this – your companion makes ail – you pretend to have been robbed – it's all a cursed privateering trick – clear as day. (39)

Charles tries to give the landlord his watch instead of money, but Copp recognizes this as the property of the king and now accuses the disguised monarch of being a common thief. He locks Charles into a bedroom and threatens to call the authorities. Charles fears detection: »Was ever monarch in such a predicament? – a prisoner in a tavern – to be presently dragged through the streets as a culprit – and to-morrow sung in lampoons, and stuck up in caricatures all through the city – what is to be done?« (41) In the end, Mary and Edward help him to escape arrest – yet Charles's escapades are revealed at court by Rochester, so that the monarch is briefly humiliated as his indecorous behaviour becomes known. Charles now discovers what the audience has known all along, namely that he had been tricked into all this by Rochester as part of a plan to convert him into a more faithful husband. The comedy ends with a festive dance. Charles's page is rewarded with the girl, while Charles, repentantly, returns to his queen: »I have pardoned you, Rochester; but my eyes are opened to the follies which I have too frequently partaken. From this night I abjure them.« (64)

Payne's play shares many features, as well as the comic moments, of countless other English comedies from at least the late seventeenth century onwards; indeed, many of the plays read like bowdlerized Restoration comedies.[12] We find for instance the typical rivalry for a young woman. Charles flirts openly with the pretty Mary: »CHAS. And as pretty a little mouth to warble a love-song. I warrant there comes none but sweet notes from these lips (*offers to kiss her.*) / MARY. (*resisting.*) Sir, give over – let me go, sir. – Mr. Georgini – help, help!« (28) As Mary, however, is already committed to Edward, Charles's attempts at flirting with her are futile from the start – and the audience, knowing this, is watching a crowned monarch making a spectacle of himself. There are stereotypical figures such as the landlord, a sailor with a heart of gold as well as the comic language of these stage types: »Thunder and lightning – what! insult Captain Copp's niece in his own house! Fire and furies!« (29) As traditional in English comedy, then, the lower-class rustic serves as a figure of fun. Edward the page, on the other hand, represents the type of the scheming servant, who serves his own purpose as well as his master's in elaborate plots (cf. Nelson 1990: Chapter 6).

Moreover, as in much eighteenth-century comedy (cf. Hare 1978: 136), there is a lot of disguising, hiding in closets and mistaking of identities. In Douglas Jerrold's *The Bride of Ludgate* (c.1829), for instance, Charles is first seen in the disguise of a Dutch wine merchant at a vintner's shop. Here, he and Sir Charles Sedley, another well-known rake, are on the lookout for the old vintner's pretty young wife. They then hear of the ›Bride of Ludgate‹, the beautiful Melissa, who is engaged to an old moneylender. In order to get near her, Charles disguises as the lawyer Dr. Inkhorn, with Sedley as his assistant Goosequill. Unsuccessfully, Charles tries to impress Melissa: »MEL. And you have the impudence to love me? / CHARLES. Very much. Ay, and the timidity to say so; and the bashfulness to make you,

---

12 On typical plots and characters of English comedy cf. Leggatt (1998); on the Restoration comedy cf. Hirst (1979).

whether you will or no, love me in return.« (34) When Melissa's jealous young lover Mapleton, a former Cromwellian, appears, Charles hides in Melissa's bedroom. Mapleton discovers him and challenges Charles to a duel; yet Charles redeems himself by saving his rival from arrest: He puts on Mapleton's cloak and hat and is arrested in his stead. »CHARLES. So here's anointed majesty, masquerading as a traitor. This were a joke for Cromwell, could he know it.« (40) Again, Charles's true identity is discovered at the end of the play, which throws his unsuspecting subjects into much confusion:

ALL. The King!
CHARLES. [*Bowing.*] The King!
[*All kneel –* [...] *in extreme confusion.*]
SHE. (R.) His Majesty! I'm ruined!
CHARLES. What! Is royalty a scarecrow, that it should strike you all so pale!! (45-46)

Finally, the young couple marry, the old moneylender – a character reminiscent of the old, duped fools of Restoration comedy[13] – receives a knighthood, and Charles – as the gracious benefactor – hosts a large celebration. »CHARLES. Now for the priest and his book; I'll give away the lady. Then for dinner, then for the dance [...].« (47) Order is restored, and all ends well.

As these examples show, much of the comedy, with its stereotypical characters and plots, would probably work without the historical setting, especially as many of the plays remain very close to the traditions of seventeenth- and eighteenth-century comedy. Yet seeing a historical king in a series of more than undignified scrapes hardly suitable for his station in life adds another layer of comedy. Unlike the characters around him, the audience would have always been aware of Charles II's real identity – and much of the comedy is derived from this dramatic irony. Moreover, the disguised king often encounters the problem that someone, unaware of his real identity, criticizes the king's loose morals to his face, resulting in an inversion of the social order:[14] Thus in Payne's play, the landlord Copp tells Charles: »He's a desperate rogue among the petticoats, they say – well I

---

13 On the stereotype of the dupe cf. Nelson (1990: Chapter 7).
14 On this comic device cf. Donaldson (1970: 7).

like a merry heart, wherever it beats. – Charley has some good points, and if I could but give him a piece of my mind – [...].« (37) Charles, however, always takes this criticism with good humour, which confirms the good opinion of the characters surrounding him.

The prefaces to several comedies reveal that presenting the Restoration period, with its well-known libertines and loose actresses, on the nineteenth-century stage posed a moral challenge. Thus, in *Rochester; or King Charles II's Merry Days* (1851 [1823]), William T. Moncrieff quotes a letter from a clergyman who admonished Moncrieff to reconsider »whether it is kind and just [...] to write, and cause to be exhibited and printed, that which may induce the loving to view the bad part of [Rochester's] character with complacency« (iv).[15] Yet if we look at Charles's and his friends' encounters with young women, we notice how harmless these rakes had become on the nineteenth-century stage. Usually, they are simply unsuccessful in seducing their prey. Even when Charles uses the full force of his charm and wealth, as in Henry Addison's *The King's Word* (1835), the heroines remain virtuous:

CHAR. [...] I would improve your fate, not injure thee, beloved one! Riches – power – rank should be yours.
KATE. I understand too well their price. No splendour can shut out the truth – gloss over the infamy [...]. No, I would sooner be the virtuous wife of an honest farmer, than the mistress of the proudest head that wears a crown. (14)

In fact, Charles and his friend Rochester only ever succeed in kissing the servant girls. Obviously, the Restoration rakes were no longer allowed to be successful on the nineteenth-century stage.[16]

The only relationship that Charles succeeds in establishing is that with Nell Gwynne, the king's most famous mistress and one of the first English actresses. Her liaison with Charles is central to John Walker's *Nell Gwynne* (1833) and Douglas Jerrold's *Nell Gwynne: The Prologue* (1829). These

---

15 Similarly, in the preface to *Nell Gwynne* (1829), Douglas Jerrold explains at length why Nell was in fact very virtuous.
16 Nevertheless, on closer inspection, Charles's position as a monarch is never in question. He is very popular with everyone he meets; moreover, when his identity is discovered, everyone accepts his rank and position at once.

remarkably similar comedies show the beginnings of Nell's career as an actress and her initial encounters with Charles II. Yet their relationship too is neatly adapted to nineteenth-century morals as well as to comic traditions: Nell is the virtuous and witty young heroine of English comedy, and in John Walker's play, she envisions the life of a wife and mother: »[...] tho we are Orange Girls now, it's no reason we should always be so. Some of us will get married, I hope.« (7-8) A virtuous heroine, she frequently escapes Charles's advances: »CHAR. By those cheeks, like blooming roses – / NELL. And as roses bear thorns, I request you'll keep your hands off, if you regard your fingers.« (10) In fact, their relationship is merely foreshadowed: As comedies traditionally concentrate on courtship and end before marriage, the plays analysed concentrate on showing Nell and Charles as a witty courting couple, thus avoiding an affront to the audience's or the censor's sensibilities.

In the stereotypical comedies of the early nineteenth century, then, Charles II is mainly shown in the pursuit of women – in most cases, however, in an unsuccessful one. The humour in the comedies arises chiefly from mistaken identities, embarrassing situations in the disguised monarch's love life, the social levelling resulting from his indecorous behaviour as well as from stock situations and types traditional of English comedies.

## THE COMEDIES OF THE TWENTIETH AND TWENTY-FIRST CENTURIES

In comedies of the early twentieth century the stereotypical characterization of Charles II continued and his funny escapades with young women were still central. Paul Kester's *Sweet Nell of Old Drury* (1928 [1900]), which was also adapted into a successful silent film (now sadly lost), stayed particularly close to its nineteenth-century predecessors, particularly Jerrold's *Nell Gwynne*:[17] It concentrates on the relationship between the king and the pretty, witty actress. Like Jerrold and Walker, Kester places much emphasis on their initial meeting (with Charles being, again, in disguise). This meet-

---

17 It can be assumed that Jerrold's play served as a pre-text, for it remained in the repertoire for a long time, and as late as 1900, it was adapted into a one-act play by E.H. Vanderfelt (cf. »Nell Gwynne« 1900: 330).

ing is full of easy banter and wit: »CHARLES. What if the King should say he loved you, Nell? / NELL. I'd box his ears! / CHARLES. Poor fellow, you don't think well of him. / NELL. I trouble myself as little with him as he troubles himself with me!« (21) Even though she does not know his true identity at first, Nell, like the characters surrounding him, likes the monarch for his easy nature: »I might have loved yon careless fellow! (*She looks after* CHARLES [...]).« (24) During the comedy's many intrigues and plots, which Charles and Nell all succeed in averting successfully, Charles has to hide in closets and is nearly arrested as a Puritan. Unlike in earlier plays, in *Sweet Nell of Old Drury* and Claude Radcliffe's *Check to the King* (1936), politics is more important. The latter is set against the background of the Treaty of Dover, about whose political implications,[18] however, remarkably little is revealed in the play. As one might expect, the comedies also become more explicit as to the true nature of Charles's and Nell's relationship; thus, in *Check to the King,* their little son actually features on the stage, suggesting that the relationship was not quite as innocent as nineteenth-century dramatists presented it.

In spite of these minor changes, however, the plays featuring Charles II remained so stereotypical that George Bernard Shaw wrote in the »Preface« to his *In Good King Charles's Golden Days*: »Let us therefore drop the popular subject of The Merry Monarch and his women. On the stage, and indeed off it, he is represented as having practically no other interest [...].« (1965 [1939]: 888) In his own play, Shaw attempts to counter these stereotypes by showing a king who is a loving husband, who is interested in science and makes astute remarks about the political situation by predicting, for instance, the Glorious Revolution as well as Monmouth's rebellion: »He [Monmouth] will try [to succeed me], poor boy; but Jamie will kill him. [...] Then the Protestants will kill Jamie; and the Dutch lad will see his chance and take it. He will be a king: a Protestant king.« (1939: 105-106)

---

18 In the secret Treaty of Dover, Charles II pledged himself to convert to Catholicism and to aid his cousin, Louis XIV, against the Netherlands. For the monarch of three predominantly Protestant nations, becoming a Catholic would have been a problematic step in the seventeenth century. In exchange, Charles received considerable sums of money from the French king – in the long run, these and other payments from Louis made Charles independent from Parliament (cf. Miller 1991: Chapter 7).

Shaw's Charles also has no longer any interest in women: »Beloved: I am done with all bodies.« (Ibid.: 103) In Shaw's play, comedy therefore arises chiefly from thwarted expectations of the audience, as Charles and the other characters do not conform to the stereotypes of earlier plays.[19] Shaw's disapproval of the superficial and stereotypical nature of previous depictions of Charles II becomes most obvious when Queen Catherine reminds her husband – tongue-in-cheek – of the most visible sign of the Merry Monarch's identity:

»No no: you have forgotten your wig. [...] Fancy your going into the Council Chamber like that! Nobody would take you for King Charles the Second without that wig. Now. [*She puts the wig on him; then the hat. A few final pats and pulls complete his toilet*]. Now you look every inch a king.« (Ibid.: 119-120)

Shaw attempted to create a different image of Charles II for the English comic stage, but judging from today's comedies, he was not successful, for Charles's sexual adventures are still a central issue. In fact, one could safely say that it is the king's seemingly modern advocacy of ›free love‹ that appears to attract comic playwrights today. In Liz Duffy Adams's *Or* (2010) we see him in a threesome with Nell and Aphra Behn in which gender is fluid and sexual preferences are put on at will. The characters' speech shifts between modern, colloquial language versus archaic blank verse and rhyming couplets, depending on the social and sexual roles which they adopt. The comedy is mainly set in Aphra's lodgings and shows her trying to finish a play. She is repeatedly interrupted by Nell and Charles, both of whom have an affair with Aphra, as well as by her former lover William Scott, who is involved in a plot to assassinate the king. Trying to keep them apart, Aphra constantly shoves them into closets and bedrooms, where they are discovered at inopportune moments, so much so that her servant remarks: »And the other one? Have you turned conjurer? It's like a disappearing act up here.« (27) The comedy uses much low, bawdy humour, which seems comically inappropriate for an historical subject, for instance when Nell calls Charles II a whore, who »with one hand [...] tickles the balls of Parliament while with the other he keeps his cousin Louis well fluffed, all to keep the money coming in« (21). Both Nell (who is in cross-dress) and

---

19 On Shaw's technique cf. also Meisel (1963).

Charles are predominantly interested in sex; as Aphra is preoccupied with her play, they happily turn to each other instead. It is the king's indecorous, unexpected behaviour which creates a comic effect:

([...] [*Charles*] *begins to carry her into the bedroom.*)
NELL. Wait. I'd better know who you are first.
CHARLES. Are you sure you want to know? It might be fun to keep the mask on.
NELL. Kinky. But yes, I need a name to cry out at the proper moment.
CHARLES. Very well. (*He removes his mask. Pause.*)
NELL. O.
CHARLES. Yes. (35)

The ›Merry Monarch‹ has obviously returned in full force.

Sex and bawdy humour are also central to Kjartan Poskitt's *Nell's Belles* (2002), a musical aimed at amateur dramatic societies. This play radically modernizes the past: In typical 1960s fashion, Charles II – Charlie – celebrates free love and has sex with everyone: »CHARLES. Hey! Who's this gorgeous creature? / IRENE. Who are you talking to? Me or my mob? / CHARLES. I'll take both.« (15) The king, the queen and his mistresses live in a palace-sharing community. Nell Gwynne is a typical working mum, she and her friends Rose, Violet and Mercy – Nell's Belles – form a girl group, who would have performed at »a giant sixties peace and love festival at this place called Woodstock« (31) if it had not been for the plague. The play abounds in bathos and bad puns. In the following quotation, for instance, comedy is caused by the fact that Helena, Nell's drunken mother, simply does not recognize a crown for what it is, and through her pedestrian interpretation of what she sees, robs it of its significance as a sign of status:

As they leave, the Queen comes on. She wears a crown but the hood of her cloak is over it. [...]
QUEEN. I'm looking for Mercy Jones.
HELENA. What's that under your hood? [...] You're wearing a spiky hat.
QUEEN. Can I see Mercy Jones?
HELENA. Maybe. Can I see your hat?
The Queen glances round nervously then lifts her hood back to reveal her crown [...].

HELENA. That's a pretty thing. I wouldn't mind one of those myself. I expect it stops the pigeons on your head when you're flat out in the gutter, doesn't it? (23)

Anachronistically, essential things, such as the relationship between the different classes, are shown to be unchangeable in English society, as the Duke of York has to experience when he is scolded by the charladies: »ELSIE. Out of the way, you. / JAMES. I could be king any day now. RITA. King? I'll flippin' crown you myself if you leave footprints on my clean tiles.« (17) In *Nell's Belles*, the past is thus constantly trivialized, and the failings of its protagonists are emphasized. Charles in particular is not taken seriously by anyone. Though the comedy features a number of political issues, such as the question of succession or the Popish Plot, all these are turned into purely personal issues which threaten to distract Charlie from the more important pleasures of life. In the course of the twentieth and twenty-first centuries then, as this short analysis shows, Charles II, with his infamous interest in women, has remained popular on the comic stage, in spite of Shaw's attempts to reform him.

## HISTORICAL COMEDY – A NEGLECTED GENRE?

There has been a lively tradition of historical comedies featuring Charles II from the early nineteenth century onwards. In particular in the 1820s and 1830s, this yielded a substantial number of plays, some of them by well-known authors of the time. Nevertheless, nineteenth-century historical comedy has been largely ignored in studies of English drama, as well as in studies of the history play.[20] There are probably two reasons for this lack of attention: Firstly, most nineteenth-century theatre has been severely criticized for its perceived poor quality.

»So ignoble has the drama of the nineteenth century been considered that only now is it emerging from that arid wasteland of indifference and contempt to which opinion has consigned it [...]. Generally, historians and critics who have bothered with the subject at all have said that the drama of about 1800 to 1890 is a formless mass

---

20 One rare exception is Szaffkó (2008), who, however, treats nineteenth-century plays very briefly and critically.

of mediocrity, dull and repetitive, lacking literary quality and thematic significance, a vast sea of theatrical trivia and down-right badness [...].« (Booth 1969: 1-2)

Similar criticism can already be found during the period itself (cf. ibid.). As part of popular culture, nineteenth-century theatre ignored the expectations of literary critics and aimed to provide entertainment.[21] Staged at a time of censorship, nineteenth-century theatre was often escapist rather than openly political; requiring mass appeal, it was formulaic rather than innovative.[22] Consequently, with a few exceptions, the nineteenth century is generally underrepresented in studies of English drama.

Secondly, historical comedies appear to have been neglected because until recently, most studies of history plays used narrow definitions of the ›proper‹ history play. As Péter Szaffkó points out, »most critics [...] have come to regard ›historical drama‹ as a value-oriented or normative category« (2008: 5). These definitions were often based on Shakespeare's histories as the »touchstone« (Wikander 1986: 7). Alternatively, they expected from the plays a certain way of dealing with the past and were based on a concept of history as serious, knowable, fact-based and objective.[23] Plays not fitting either definition were simply excluded from the genre and were often derogatorily referred to as ›costume drama‹ or ›pseudo-historical drama‹.[24] As Teresa Grant and Barbara Ravelhofer remark, however, these narrow definitions leave many plays »in search of a genre« (2008: 4).

---

21 Though a considerable number of nineteenth-century literary authors (such as Robert Browning, Alfred Tennyson or Percy Bysshe Shelley) attempted to write for the stage, they were mostly unsuccessful, as they refused to adapt their literary works to the requirements of the theatre. Plays such as Tennyson's *Queen Mary* (1876) were a success only when they were adapted by men of the theatre (cf. Watt 1983: 52 and Booth 1991: 148).

22 On Victorian theatre cf. especially Booth (1975 and 1991); Powell (2004); Donohue (2004: Part II).

23 In the following, space will only allow a brief discussion of different definitions. For two recent, extensive attempts at defining the history play, which the following takes as a basis, cf. Berninger (2006) and Szaffkó (2008).

24 Cf. for instance Booth et al. (1975: 186) and Fricker (1940: 3). Costume drama is usually criticized for merely using the past for the sake of picturesque costumes and scenery.

In these narrow definitions, characteristics of a ›proper‹ history play include a concentration on English history as well as on dynastic politics – both these aspects are of course central to definitions of Shakespeare's histories. Thus, G.K. Hunter defines the genre as »a play about English dynastic politics of the feudal and immediately post-feudal period« (1989: 15). Moreover, the events depicted are of significance for the nation and national identity. According to Dirk Niefanger (2005: 39) and other scholars, politics is the main theme of historical drama. By contrast, the private lives of individuals are considered to be irrelevant for historical drama. History plays are expected to include a sufficient number of historical characters or historical events,[25] and they should adhere closely to historical ›facts‹ (cf. Harben 1988: 4-5).[26] Other aspects prominent in these narrow definitions are an ›appropriate‹, i.e. serious treatment of the past, which is assumed to be a subject of considerable standing.[27]

Looking back on the plays discussed in this chapter, it seems obvious why they would have failed to classify as history plays: They focus on the private life of Charles II and do so in an un-heroic, comic way. Politics is of little interest; instead, the plays concentrate on Charles's extramarital affairs.[28] As comedies, the plays show stock situations and types rather than particular historical events or individuals.[29] Rather than adhering to the ›facts‹ presented by ›serious‹ historians, they depict anecdotal stories of

---

25  Cf. Peacock (1991: 5) and, for similar statements, Fricker (1940) and Hammerschmid (1972).
26  The issue of historical ›fact‹ is, as one might expect, the most widely discussed in definitions of historical drama. After the postmodern turn, the nature of historical fact has been itself called into question, as the central role of narrative and language in creating reality has been recognized. Of course, this also affects discussions of historical drama (cf. Berninger 2006).
27  For a critical discussion of this issue cf. Berninger (2006: 37-38).
28  This concentration on the private lives of monarchs and aristocrats is a general and much criticized feature of historical drama from the early seventeenth century onwards (cf. Wikander 1986) – and is perhaps also the main reason why plays from the eighteenth and nineteenth centuries are often ignored in studies of the genre.
29  Indeed, as Nicoll points out, comedy generally has a reputation of not paying attention to historical detail (1963: 44).

Charles II as they started to circulate soon after, or even during his lifetime.

A fact that points to the comedies' problematic status as history plays most clearly is that one of the plays discussed here, John Payne's *Charles the Second; or, The Merry Monarch*, was adapted from a French play featuring Henry V.[30] Moreover, the story obviously proved so popular that it was also recycled by other writers – amongst them G.A. Macfarren in his opera *King Charles II* (1849).[31] The French original tells a story from the late Middle Ages; in the English version, the plot is simply shifted to a different historical period and merely the names of the historical characters featuring are changed. In light of such practice, it is hardly surprising that nineteenth-century historical comedies have usually been excluded from the canon of the history play.

Like Charles II, however, Henry V is often credited with being a king close to his people. This is a figure which we can find in many nineteenth-century plays featuring, for instance, Peter the Great and King Alfred. The story of the king who ventures out in disguise amongst his people has of course an even longer tradition – and is used not only in Shakespeare's comedy *Measure for Measure*, but also in Elizabethan history plays (cf. Grant 2008). King Charles fitted this stage type, as he had not only a reputation for loving pleasure but was also famous for the ease with which he mixed with his people, for his well-known politeness and affability (cf. Miller 1991: 31). Charles II's frequent appearance on the nineteenth-century stage may therefore also have been a result of his easy adaptability to existing theatrical conventions. Yet the adherence to stage types again contradicts the ideal of historical detail and ›fact‹.

Nevertheless, there are several reasons why this chapter argues for an inclusion of the comedies into the definition of history: Firstly, because against the background of postmodern questioning of the canon, it would be

---

30 The adaptation of French plays, here Alexandre Duval's *La Jeunesse de Henri V* (1806), was of course common practice in the nineteenth century. Whether ›true‹ or not (cf. footnote 26), stories such as these told by the plays would not usually find a place in serious historical scholarship.

31 During most of the nineteenth century, playwrights were paid very little. Adapting a play from the French was therefore a quick way of producing ›new‹ plays (cf. Booth 1975: 50).

strange to exclude plays from the genre of the history play just because they are comic or popular – as Szaffkó points out, »a sound definition of historical drama should imply a value-neutral collective term including in itself all the possible varieties of plays that may be regarded historical whether they are ›tragic, comic, romantic or ironic‹« (2008: 6-7). Secondly, several recent studies have deliberately advocated more flexible approaches towards the history play.[32] Richard Helgerson, for instance, points out that too narrow a focus on Shakespeare's histories has considerably affected our view of even the early-modern history play. Unlike Shakespeare, other writers were less concerned with »the getting, keeping, and losing of political power« (2003: 31). Moreover, their plays are less exclusively focused on the social elite. As »forms outside the canon« (Grant/Ravelhofer 2008) are increasingly included in studies of the history play, it seems time to include the very successful comedies of the nineteenth century; for, after all, as Booth reminds us: »there is no doubt that on the whole the nineteenth century got from its dramatists the plays it wanted and refused the plays it did not want; and what it got suited it admirably.« (1980: 4)

\*

Over the last two hundred years, historical comedies featuring Charles II have made use of the king's legendary private life and his countless affairs in order to show a popular but hardly a great monarch on the English stage. While in the nineteenth century, authors still took great pains to present Charles's escapades as essentially harmless, in the late twentieth and twenty-first centuries, sex and free love have become the dominant features. Unlike the more serious, canonized history plays, the comedies largely avoid politics and events central to English history. Because of this, they hardly meet the characteristics often stated as central to the history play, and it is probable that this explains their customary exclusion from the genre. As comic depictions of history, however, tend to focus on the private, the sexual and the illegitimate (cf. Schörken 1981: 137), it seems that this exclusion is a fate shared by many comic versions of the past.

---

32 Cf. for instance Berninger (2006); Grant/Ravelhofer (2008); Szaffkó (2008).

In view of Charles II's long popularity on the English comic stage it would seem fit to inquire into the reasons for this. While several explanations have been put forward as to the origins of this trend, some of them rooted in the political situation of the 1820s and 1830s,[33] its longevity would suggest that these explanations tell only part of the story. Indeed, when looking into poems, memoirs and popular anecdotes featuring Charles II one quickly notices that the image of the affable yet licentious monarch was not only shaped by comedies and did in fact emerge prior to the 1820s and 1830s in other genres.[34] While his contemporaries were often shocked by the openness with which Charles II conducted his extramarital affairs, very soon portrayals of him, like those of Henry VIII, were also offering later generations a kind of voyeuristic pleasure at seeing an historical king's love life turn him into a very human figure.

## WORKS CITED

### Historical Comedies Featuring Charles II

Adams, Liz Duffy (2010): *Or*, New York: Dramatists' Play Service.
Addison, Henry Robert (1835): *The King's Word* (From the French), London: John Miller.
Aston, Walter (1732): *The Restoration of King Charles II, or, the Life and Death of Oliver Cromwell: An Histori-Tragi-Comi Ballad Opera*, London: R. Walker.

---

[33] Simon Shepherd and Peter Womack (1996: 183-187), for instance, suggest that the popularity of this accessible monarch should be seen against the background of the revolution in France (1830), where a distant king lost the support of his people. However, plays featuring Charles II began to emerge much earlier. For a more general discussion concentrating on the plays of the 1820s and 1830s cf. also Flothow (2012: 37-38).

[34] Richard Ollard (1993) has pointed out that Charles II's life and times were also prominent themes in the early historical novel. On the early eighteenth-century memory of the Stuart king, which has to be seen in the political context of that time, cf. also Hutton (1989: Chapter 16).

Blanchard, E.L. (1851): *Harlequin Hudibras! Or, Old Dame Druden, and the Droll Days of the Merry Monarch: A New Grand Poetical, Historical, Operatical, Dramatical, Anachronismatical, Tragical, Comical, Pastoral Christmas Pantomime*, London: T.H. Lacy.

Davidson, John (1903): *The Knight of the Maypole: A Comedy in Four Acts*, London: Grant Richards.

Fagan, J.B. (1926): *»And So to Bed«: A Comedy in Three Acts*, London: Putnam.

Hatcher, Jeffrey (2006): *Complete Female Stage Beauty*, New York: Dramatists' Play Service.

Horton, T. (1828): *Nell Gwynne, the City of the Wye; Or, The Red Lands of Herefordshire: An Historical Play*, Hereford: W.H. & J. Parker.

Jerningham, Edward (1799): *The Peckham Frolic: Or Nell Gwyn: A Comedy in Three Acts*, London: J. Hatchard.

Jerrold, Douglas ([c.1829]): *The Bride of Ludgate: A Comic Drama, in Two Acts*, London: John Cumberland.

Jerrold, Douglas ([1829]): *Nell Gwynne; or, The Prologue: A Comedy in Two Acts*, London: Thomas Hailes Lacy.

Kester, Paul (1928 [1900]): *Sweet Nell of Old Drury: A Comedy in Four Acts*, New York: Samuel French.

Macfarren, G.A. (1849): *King Charles II; An Opera*. Libretto by Desmond Ryan, London: Cramer, Beale.

Moncrieff, W.T. (1851 [1823]): »Rochester; or King Charles II's Merry Days: A Musical Comedy, in Three Acts«. In: *Selection from the Dramatic Works of William T. Moncrieff*, London: Hailes Lacy.

Payne, John Howard (1824): *Charles the Second; or, The Merry Monarch: A Comedy, in Three Acts*, London: Longman.

Planché, James Robinson (1835): *The Court Beauties: A Dramatic Sketch, in One Act*, London: John Miller.

Poskitt, Kjartan (2002): *Nell's Belles: The Swinging Sixteen-Sixties Show: A Musical*, London: Samuel French.

Radcliffe, Claude (1936): *Check to the King: A Romantic Comedy of Charles II and Nell Gwyn in Three Acts*, London: Samuel French.

Shaw, George Bernard (1939): *In Good King Charles's Golden Days*, London: Macmillan.

Walker, John ([1833]): *Nell Gwynne; An Historical Drama in Two Acts*, London: J. Duncombe.

Wilks, T.E. ([1837]): *The King's Wager; or, The Camp, the Cottage, and the Court: A Drama, in Three Parts*, London: Thomas Hailes Lacy.

## Other Works Cited

Baldwin, T.W. (1947): *Shakespeare's Five-Act Structure: Shakespeare's Early Plays on the Background of Renaissance Theories of Five-Act Structure from 1470*, Urbana: U of Illinois P.
Berninger, Mark (2006): *Neue Formen des Geschichtsdramas in Großbritannien und Irland seit 1970*, Trier: Wissenschaftlicher Verlag.
Booth, Michael R. (ed.) (1969): *English Plays of the Nineteenth Century*, Oxford: Clarendon.
Booth, Michael R. et al. (1975): *The Revels History of Drama in English*, vol. VI: *1750-1880*, London: Methuen.
Booth, Michael R. (1980): *Prefaces to English Nineteenth-Century Theatre*, Manchester: Manchester UP.
Booth, Michael R. (1991): *Theatre in the Victorian Age*, Cambridge: CUP.
Buckle, Henry Thomas (1873): *History of Civilization in England: In Three Vols*, vol. 1, London: Longmans, Green.
Chernaik, Warren L. (2007): *The Cambridge Introduction to Shakespeare's History Plays*, Cambridge: CUP.
Donaldson, Ian (1970): *The World Upside-down: Comedy from Jonson to Fielding*, Oxford: Clarendon.
Donohue, Joseph (ed.) (2004): *The Cambridge History of British Theatre*, vol. 2: *1660-1895*, Cambridge: CUP.
Duval, Alexandre (1806): *La Jeunesse de Henri V, Comédie: En Trois Actes et en Prose*, Paris (ia700301.us.archive.org/9/items/lajeunessedehenr00duvauoft/lajeunessedehenr00duvauoft.pdf). Accessed 4 December 2012.
Flothow, Dorothea (2012): »Transferring the King and the Actress to the Stage: Representations of Charles II and Nell Gwynne in Selected History Plays«. In: Sabine Coelsch-Foisner et al. (eds.), *Transfer in English Studies*, Wien: Braunmüller, 31-52.
Fricker, Robert (1940): *Das historische Drama in England von der Romantik bis zur Gegenwart*, Bern: Stämpfli.
Grant, Theresa (2008): »History in the Making: The Case of Samuel Rowley's *When You See Me You Know Me* (1604/5)«. In: Theresa Grant/Barbara

Ravelhofer (eds.), *English Historical Drama, 1500-1600: Forms Outside the Canon*, Houndmills: Palgrave Macmillan, 125-157.

Grant, Theresa/Barbara Ravelhofer (2008): »Introduction«. In: Theresa Grant /Barbara Ravelhofer (eds.), *English Historical Drama, 1500-1600: Forms Outside the Canon*, Houndmills: Palgrave Macmillan, 1-31.

Hammerschmidt, Hildegard (1972): *Das historische Drama in England (1956-1971): Erscheinungsformen und Entwicklungstendenzen*, Wiesbaden: Humanitas.

Harben, Niloufer (1988): *20th Century English History Plays: From Shaw to Bond*, London: Macmillan.

Hare, Arnold (1978): »English Comedy«. In: W.D. Howarth (ed.), *Comic Drama: The European Heritage*, London: Methuen, 122-143.

Harris, Tim (2005): *Restoration: Charles II and His Kingdoms 1660-1685*, London: Penguin.

Helgerson, Richard (2003): »Shakespeare and Contemporary Dramatists of History«. In: Richard Dutton/Jean E. Howard (eds.), *A Companion to Shakespeare's Works*, vol. II: *The Histories*, Oxford: Blackwell, 26-47.

Hirst, David L. (1979): *Comedy of Manners*, London: Methuen.

Hunter, G.K. (1989): »Truth and Art in History Plays«. *Shakespeare Survey* 42, 15-24.

Hutton, Ronald (1989): *Charles the Second: King of England, Scotland, and Ireland*, Oxford: Clarendon.

Leggatt, Alexander (1998): *English Stage Comedy, 1490-1990: Five Centuries of a Genre*, London: Routledge.

Lope de Vaga, Felix (1991 [1608]): »New Art of Making Comedies at the Present Time: Addressed to the Academy of Madrid«. In: Michael J. Sidnell (ed.), *Sources of Dramatic Theory*, vol. 1: *Plato to Congreve*, Cambridge: CUP, 184-191.

Macaulay, Thomas Babington (1889 [1848]): *The History of England: From the Accession of James the Second: Popular Edition in Two Volumes*, London: Longmans, Green.

Meisel, M. (1963): *Shaw and the Nineteenth-Century Theatre*, Princeton/NJ: Princeton UP.

Miller, John (1991): *Charles II*, London: Weidenfeld & Nicolson.

»Nell Gwynne« (1900): In: *The Penny Illustrated Paper and Illustrated Times* 26 May, 330.

Nelson, T.G.A. (1990): *Comedy: An Introduction to Comedy in Literature, Drama, and Cinema*, Oxford: OUP.
Nicoll, Allardyce (1962): *A History of English Drama, 1660-1900*, vol. V: *Late Nineteenth Century Drama 1850-1900*, Cambridge: CUP.
Nicoll, Allardyce (1963): *A History of English Drama, 1660-1900*, vol. IV: *Early Nineteenth Century Drama 1800-1850*, Cambridge: CUP.
Niefanger, Dirk (2005): *Geschichtsdrama der frühen Neuzeit, 1495-1773*, Tübingen: Niemeyer.
Ollard, Richard (1993): *The Image of the King: Charles I and Charles II*, London: Pimlico.
Peacock, D. Keith (1991): *Radical Stages: Alternative History in Modern British Drama*, New York: Greenwood.
Pepys, Samuel (1971-1983 [1660-1669]): *The Diary of Samuel Pepys: A New and Complete Transcription*, Robert Latham (ed.), vols. 1-11, London: Bell.
Powell, Kerry (ed.) (2004): *The Cambridge Companion to Victorian and Edwardian Theatre*, Cambridge: CUP.
Reynolds, Ernest (1936): *Early Victorian Drama (1830-1870)*, Cambridge: W. Heffer.
Rochester, John Wilmot of (1974): *The Complete Poems*, David M. Vieth (ed.), 2nd ed., New Haven/CT: Yale UP.
Schoch, Richard W. (1998): *Shakespeare's Victorian Stage: Performing History in the Theatre of Charles Kean*, Cambridge: CUP.
Schörken, Rolf (1981): *Geschichte in der Alltagswelt: Wie uns Geschichte begegnet und was wir mit ihr machen*, Stuttgart: Klett-Cotta.
Shaw, George Bernard (1965 [1939]): »*›In Good King Charles's Golden Days‹*«. In: *The Complete Prefaces of Bernard Shaw*, London: Paul Hamlyn, 887-890.
Shepherd, Simon/Peter Womack (1996): *English Drama: A Cultural History*, Oxford: Blackwell.
String, Tatiana C./Marcus Bull (eds.) (2011): *Tudorism: Historical Imagination and the Appropriation of the Sixteenth Century*, Oxford: OUP.
Szafkó, Péter (2008): *Under the Spell of Shakespeare's Histories: A Critical Overview of the Theory of Historical Drama*, Saarbrücken: VDM.
Watt, Stephen M. (1983): *The Making of the Modern History Play*, Ann Arbor/MI: University Microfilms.

Wikander, Matthew H. (1986): *The Play of Truth and State: Historical Drama from Shakespeare to Brecht*, Baltimore/MD: Johns Hopkins UP.

# On Boots, Beef, and *Blackadder*
The Comic Historiography of the Duke of Wellington

ULRIKE ZIMMERMANN

## A GREAT BRITON

Arthur Wellesley (1769-1852), the first Duke of Wellington, was the victor of Waterloo (1815) and Prime Minister of Britain (1828-1830). In 2002 he was voted fifteenth in the BBC ranking show *The 100 Greatest Britons*.[1] However, from a relatively early stage in his career, and certainly after reaching national fame through the defeat of Napoleon Bonaparte, Wellington was not exclusively the subject of hero worship but also the protagonist of anecdotes, the butt of jokes, and the subject of countless caricatures. In the twentieth century, he figured in popular satirical products like the *Blackadder* series of the 1980s. His appeal is obviously still strong and continues to incite cultural production, if not necessarily of a venerable sort.

Wellington as a character seems to have lent himself to comic permutations. It is worthwhile to look beyond the war hero and the politician to the comic undercurrents that became part of Wellington's image even during his lifetime. This chapter will therefore discuss the Duke, his career and his public images emphasising their comic potential, and suggest reasons for the pertinence of the comic in a character who could easily have gone down

---

1 The BBC lists only the top ten and puts the rest in alphabetical rather than numerical order (cf. BBC Press Office 2002), but there are websites retaining the ranking of the 100, for instance *Listal* (cf. ›The Flagship‹ 2009).

in history as a war hero and not much besides. Writing the history (and histories) of Wellington has apparently always been a partly comic project, with people of various times reacting to his comic qualities and keeping them alive. Most of his biographers, even if they do not explicitly address themselves to humour, seem to have sensed this kind of undercurrent as well.

In his early life, Arthur Wellesley did not promise to become much of a prominent figure. He was born in Dublin of Anglo-Irish descent, which would have implied that he was brought up with a strong sense of loyalty to the British crown. His family seemed somewhat at a loss when it came to determining his career, since the young Wellesley was an unspectacular character and did not show any signs to become anything out of the ordinary. »Faced with his languid disposition and lack of intellectual curiosity, his mother [...] and eldest brother [...] decided to place him in the army, where his shortcomings would pass unnoticed.« (James 1992: 3) This seems an inauspicious beginning to a long, eventful life and an outstanding career in the military as well as the political arena: Wellesley took part in the First Coalition War of 1792, where his active military career began. In 1796, as yet inexperienced and heavily in debt, he went to India, a decisive step for his career, military experience, and hence future employment, where he distinguished himself as a military leader and profited financially from his command. However, service in India was regarded as some kind of »sideshow« (ibid.: 103). After his return to England in 1805, Wellesley had a brief stint in politics, becoming a member of the House of Commons early in 1806 and Secretary for Ireland in 1807. Simultaneously, he pursued his military career further and was appointed for a command in the Copenhagen expedition. Later he fought in the Peninsular War against the French, winning the battle of Salamanca in 1812 and conquering Toulouse in 1814, shortly before Napoleon's abdication. Also in 1814, i.e. before his historic victory at Waterloo, Arthur Wellesley received his Dukedom.[2] At the time, he had already become a notable and feted public personality; his magnificent portrait by Goya was completed in the same year. The second phase of his career, after Waterloo, was devoted to politics, and he became Prime Minister in 1828. The Duke of Wellington reached a high age, living far

---

2 For a concise and readable account of Wellington's early life, cf. Keegan (1987: 103-113).

into the Victorian era, when he was a well-known and respected public figure who had become a household name in Britain.

## WELLINGTONIANA

Indeed, in Wellington's case, the expression household name can be understood in quite a literal sense. Wellington associations in the cultural imagination are manifold. The first thing which comes to mind would be the Battle of Waterloo and the final defeat of Napoleon. Particularly for speakers of English however, there is an additional set of associations, which has more to do with the commodities of daily life. Wellington boots are one of them, and they are indeed an original invention of the first Duke of Wellington, who improved what was known as Hessian boots, popular eighteenth-century footwear in the military. His shoemaker acted according to Wellington's practical instructions, and the result of the changes were boots which would still be ideal for horse riding, but also looked good with a uniform and could be worn in the evening as well.[3] This boot variety would become a fashionable item for men in the first half on the nineteenth century and later transform into the well-know waterproof gear of today, first made from rubber, then from PVC. The name stuck and was affectionately shortened to wellies – although it is uncertain whether this affection is for the Duke or for his functional invention. A caricature from 1827, by the printmaker William Heath,[4] published by Thomas McLean, shows Wellington's head in profile, protruding from a large boot, and bears the inscription »A Wellington Boot or the Head of the Army«. There is evidence that wellington boots were an instantly recognisable reference by 1817 already (cf. Physick 1965: Plate 2) (fig. 1). Other than clothes, Wellington can also be associated with a second necessity of life: There is no proof of a definitive relationship between Beef Wellington and the Duke, but the dish may well have been the attempt of English chefs during the Napoleonic Wars to in-

---

3   On Wellingtons in fashion history, cf. Boyle (2011) and the website on »Wellington Boot History«.
4   William Heath used the pseudonym Paul Pry between 1827 and 1829. All prints analysed here can be accessed via the British Museum's »Collection Online« (cf. Trustees of the British Museum n.d.).

vent an English name for the French recipe of *filet de boeuf en croute*. Even though the earliest recorded recipes of that name originate from the twentieth century, most of them make the suggestion that the dish was named in honour of Wellington.[5] These examples indicate that the Duke of Wellington as a public character is not solely associated with heroic deeds.[6] Their mixture of the lofty and the down-to-earth is distinctive of Wellington and can be a starting point for intrusions of the comic also in renderings of his great public achievements.

*Fig. 1: William Heath: »A Wellington Boot or the Head of the Army«, 1827.*

© The Trustees of the British Museum, Museum Number 1868,0808.8822.

---

5   Cf. Felicity Cloake (2011) for a brief overview of the history of the name. Incidentally, there is a dessert called Napoleon, or Classic French Napoleon, a *mille feuilles* construction filled with pastry cream and fruit preserves. This name, however, is not a cultural stereotype of effeminate Frenchmen, but a corruption of ›Napolitains‹, cf. Olver (2012).
6   Belinda Beaton (2005) gives an illuminating analysis of the material culture surrounding Wellington's name over time, from keepsakes commemorating Waterloo to the use of his name by the metal industry in nineteenth-century marketing to create the image of British solidity and reliability.

## THE MILITARY MAN: THE DUKE AND THE EFFECTS OF WATERLOO

Wellington took part in the Congress of Vienna, but was called back to the military field, and in 1815 he met Napoleon Bonaparte once again at the Battle of Waterloo. This battle made Wellington ultimately famous, and his name still overshadows von Blücher and the Prussian (and Allied) contribution. Wellington's ensuing fame rests largely on his strategic decisions before and during the battle, which was fought on 18 June 1815, and on his willingness to embrace personal danger, not merely overseeing the raging of the various parts of battle with his characteristic accessory, a telescope, but also getting actively involved in the action.[7]

Waterloo was also the occasion for one of the most renowned of all Wellington quotes, which, however, has never been authenticated. Allegedly, Wellington pronounced »Either night or the Prussians will come«, or alternatively, »I want night or Blucher,«[8] while his troops were holding out against the French forces and waiting for Prussian support. After the events of Waterloo, people became greatly interested in Wellington's character, and anecdotes, one-liners, sketches and reminiscences about him proliferated. Wellington himself seems to have stayed quite level-headed in the midst of his fame. When asked whether he was pleased with the enthusiastic reception he received in Brussels after his return from Waterloo, he answered, »Not in the least; if I had failed, they would have shot me« (Keegan 1987: 163). His characteristic brevity and blunt directness of speech, often paired with caustic wit, gave his contemporaries a multitude of opportunities to talk about him for and with amusement. Wellington's down-to-earth reaction to the news of Napoleon's final abdication goes along the same lines: »How, abdicated? Ay, 'tis time indeed. You don't say so, upon my honour. Hoorah!« (James 1992: 239) John Keegan refers to such utterances as »[Wellington's] clipped and utterly unambiguous style

---

7   For detailed analyses of the Battle of Waterloo, cf. for instance James (1992: Chapter 3) and Keegan (1987: 109-115).

8   Neither version found its way into the *Oxford Dictionary of Quotations* (cf. Knowles 2012). Unsurprisingly, German sources tend to make more of this quotation. In the German newspaper *Die Welt*, Seewald (2010) provides a look at Waterloo and its myth, including the quotation.

of speech« (Keegan 1987: 155), a kind of rhetoric suitable to being taken up and processed in comic forms. Indeed, a number of Wellington's sayings (of which some may be good inventions, while many were vouched for by reliable contemporaries) have the quality of punch lines in form and content.

In this context, it is noteworthy that the single meeting between Wellington and his contemporary – and British co-hero – Lord Nelson in the offices of Lord Castlereagh in 1805 did not impress Wellington. He found Nelson self-centred, vain, and a fulsome talker (cf. James 1992: 104), possibly everything that he himself thought he was not. Wellington did not have »Nelson's flamboyance and showmanship« (Cooper 1964: 102). After Nelson was made aware of the identity of his partner in conversation, he switched style and started talking politics with Wellington in a more solid manner, which finally could not fail to impress the latter. »They never met again, but at least Nelson went to his death and apotheosis knowing that owing to Lord Castlereagh's unpunctuality [he had not admitted Nelson in time, so that the two commanders were waiting together], Sir Arthur had revised his earlier opinion« (ibid.: 104). Cooper's dry remark plausibly captures the differences between the two men as well as Wellington's judgment of people who did not have his own conciseness. Cooper also points out the differences in the ways the two commanders related to their respective subordinates, which for present purposes serves as an intriguing illustration of Wellington's behaviour. While Nelson reported from the planning of his strategy for Trafalgar that some of his generals wept with enthusiasm,

»[i]t is impossible to imagine Picton, Crawford, Hill or Uxbridge [Wellington's generals] shedding tears at a tactical novelty, however startling, nor does it appear likely that such a demonstration would have been cordially received by the Commander-in-Chief. [...] They were used to curt oral orders or scribbled notes [...]. It is possible that had they assured him that he was surrounded by friends whom he inspired he would have answered with his favourite rebuke, ›Don't be a damned fool, sir.‹« (Ibid.: 109)

The latter scene is speculation on Cooper's part but the gist of it is corroborated by many of Wellington's contemporaries: He preferred brevity and down-to-earth communication to sentiment and flowery language.

Hence it does not come as a surprise that Wellington appears to have detested Napoleon Bonaparte as a person – although he appreciated his military abilities – because of the hero cult Napoleon furthered around himself. As Wellington despised poets because to his mind they did not practise what they preached with their lofty ideas, so he had an aversion to the Napoleon myth, which in reality subjected the rest of Europe by threats and extortions (cf. James 1992: 26-28). Generally, his leanings went towards the blunt, brief and direct.[9]

Celebrations after Waterloo were, despite their somewhat reticent hero, »universal, far in excess of what had followed Trafalgar ten years earlier, when the simultaneous report of Nelson's death had dulled the edge of public celebration« (ibid.: 267). The victory at Waterloo and Napoleon's ensuing final banishment ushered in a period of peace for Britain and allowed the country to expand its position as a political and economic superpower of the nineteenth century (cf. ibid.: 268-269). Wellington was credited with paving the way for this. As Lawrence James succinctly notes: »For these reasons and because Nelson had died, Wellington, the architect of victory, was assured of a position as a national hero.« (Ibid.: 269) However, this national hero, having won one of the most decisive wars in his country's history and secured stability to his native country for decades, had not died a hero's death on the battlefield. Unlike Nelson, he survived his battles to return to his country, at first in triumph, later faced with the task of forging a new career after the war. Wellington turned to politics again, a mostly unheroic and unspectacular activity compared to warfare that opened an inroad for comic representation.

---

9   Another famous Wellington quote, his »Publish and be damned« when he received a letter threatening blackmail from the publisher of Harriette Wilson's memoirs, goes along the same lines. Like the Blücher quote, it could never be authenticated, cf. Hibbert (1997: 389-390). Generally, Wellington seems to have managed to keep his relationships with women largely from the public eye. Although his marriage was not a success, there were no scandals or spectacular affairs connected to him. For the Wellington marriage, cf. for example Hibbert (1997: 54-57 and 62-63).

## THE POLITICIAN AND THE ELDER STATESMAN: COMIC INROADS

Wellington's political career had started more or less in parallel to his career as military commander, and initially this had to do with the connections of his family; later, in the years in India, he seems to have developed a genuine interest in politics. He had been a member of the House of Commons since 1806, and after the ultimate defeat of Napoleon, he was not needed as a military leader any more. Wellington became a leading figure within the Tory Party in the 1820s. In 1828, he resigned from his post as Commander-in-Chief to become Prime Minister. In that function, he was – even for a Tory – extremely conservative, one of the many people in Britain who feared nothing more than a repetition of the events of the French Revolution on British soil. »Beginning reform is beginning revolution« was Wellington's deepest conviction (Keegan 1987: 162). His return to politics (although he had never completely vanished from the political stage) proved a double-edged sword for many of his contemporaries. Lawrence James amongst other biographers points out that in British history, Wellington was the first soldier to enter a political career since Oliver Cromwell (cf. James 1992: 269-270), and this historical connection did not bode all too well. Wellington's contemporaries had issues with the fact that a Commander-in-Chief became Prime Minister, and many felt uneasy at this mingling of an army man with politics. This unease did not diminish when Wellington included two military friends into his cabinet. Perhaps naïvely, Wellington could not relate to these worries and did not do much to appease them; »ruling a country, like running an army, was best undertaken by trustworthy, hard-working men of ability and it did not matter that they happened to be soldiers« (ibid.: 270).

It is not surprising, therefore, that Wellington's political career was accompanied by a multitude of caricatures from the very beginning of his wielding power. The following discussion focuses on those by William Heath (all of which were published by Thomas McLean, Haymarket, London). Heath's caricature entitled »A Kick up Among the Wigs« (fig. 2) satirises the formation of the Tory Ministry by Wellington in 1828. Wellington is depicted in uniform on a war horse, a snorting, galloping charger – possibly the famous Copenhagen he rode at Waterloo. He is shown riding over

*Fig. 2: William Heath: »A Kick up among the Whigs«, 1828.*

© The Trustees of the British Museum, Museum Number 1868,0808.8837.

little men composed of wigs, who fall in disorder and flee in panic – a pun on the Whig party which Wellington would ride over in the process of establishing his conservative premiership. The caricature exemplifies the uneasy mixture of the military and the political for which Wellington stood in public appreciation. While Wellington is depicted as decidedly warlike and forceful, with his movement the only dynamic and purposeful element in the image, the w(h)igs do not seem to be particularly convincing in the first place, so that a lack of creditable alternatives to Wellington's Tory rule is also addressed by the caricature.

A later satirical print by William and Henry Heath, published in 1829, when Wellington's ministry was in a critical phase, takes up the warhorse theme of heroic portraiture by picturing Wellington as a horse (fig. 3). The inscription explains the image:

»To be sold with all his Trappings the splendid Charger ›Arthur‹ who served in the *Peninsular* & other *Campaigns* – must be rode without a *Curb* as he is *not used* to *restraint* & will kick at it – he comes from a notorious stock & and is *through bred* –

will not be warranted *sound* – must be taken with all his faults – & must be sold.« (Physick 1965: Plate 25, emphasis original)

Wellington was not the only contemporary politician caricatured as a horse for sale at the time (cf. Physick 1965: Plate 25, comments), but for him the image of an »old war horse« which is still impervious to attempts at curbing it, has no real use and is probably hard to sell seems particularly fitting.

*Fig. 3: William and Henry Heath: »To Be Sold with All His Trappings That Splendid Charger ›Arthur‹«, 1829.*

© The Trustees of the British Museum, Museum Number 1868,0808.9040.

Wellington was a champion for Catholic emancipation. Although the background of this attitude was probably pragmatic (after all, Ireland had to be kept under government rule), it made him unpopular, and his fierce opposition against the Reform Bill did not help to soften his opponents' hostility. His nickname ›Iron Duke‹ stems from that time, and next to the obvious metaphorical meaning of the Duke's implacability, another possible explanation is the fact that Wellington had to have boarded up the windows of his London home, Apsley House, with iron shutters because he and his possessions came under attack from the mob (cf. James 1992: 271).[10] His government had to step down in 1830, and after much political struggle, the Reform Bill was passed in 1832. Wellington remained extremely critical of its expansion of franchise and all movements to put political power on a wider, more democratic foundation. ›Mobocracy‹ was how he termed the consequences he expected from the Reform Bill. »He appeared – and his public outbursts supported this conclusion – a man who was *out of temper with his times.*« (James 1992: 271, emphasis mine) This astute observation may go some way to explain one of the comic inroads into Wellington's character, as we shall see later.

Another incident falling into Wellington's time as Prime Minister and giving rise to comic representation is a duel he fought with the 10th Earl of Winchilsea in 1829 in the context of the campaign for the Catholic Relief Bill. Winchilsea had accused Wellington of introducing »Popery into every department of the state« (Physick 1965: Plate 16), which was as good as calling Wellington's politics unconstitutional, and Wellington duly challenged him. The two opponents met on Battersea Field; Wellington's shot went wide, and Winchilsea shot in the air – presumably out of hesitation to shoot at the Prime Minister. After the event, Winchilsea apologised in a letter.[11] William Heath's caricature on this duel, »The Field of Battersea« (fig. 4), depicts the Duke of Wellington with a lobster's claw for a face as the soldiers wearing red coats would commonly have been called ›lobsters‹. The Duke wears a monk's robe and rosary to indicate his support for Roman Catholic emancipation. He says, »I used to be a good shot but have been out of practice for some years«, while the Earl of Winchilsea tries to make himself as thin as possible and stands on tip-toe to avoid being hit (and accordingly tainted with »popery«, as he fears in his speech balloon). The image digs at the Duke of Wellington's military origins and his political campaign while it also leaves no doubts about the general ludicrousness of the whole framework of the duel.

Wellington became a lover and collector of his own caricatures, and the publishers certainly gave him much to go upon. Another print by Heath of

---

10 For an alternative explanation, cf. Hibbert (1997: 326-327).
11 For a general perspective on duelling in contemporary literature and on this bloodless but nonetheless famed duel, cf. McMaster (2011).

*Fig. 4: William Heath: »The Field of Battersea«, 1829.*

© The Trustees of the British Museum, Museum Number 1868,0808.8925.

1829 called »Good Humour« (fig. 5) depicts how Wellington, surrounded by amused passers-by, looks at caricatures, some of which can be identified as caricatures of himself (cf. Physick 1965: Plate 27). He has reading glasses at the ready and wears quite a friendly expression.[12]

In the mid-1840s, Wellington retired from active political service to become an elder statesman and trusted adviser to Queen Victoria. An infirm man in his seventies,[13] he had become »a revered national institution« and »a patriarchal figure, a repository of wisdom and experience whose past po-

---

12 Mrs Arbuthnot notes in her journal of 1829 that she spent some time with Wellington laughing at caricatures about him he had brought her, cf. Physick (1965: Plate 27, comments); cf. also Foster (1984).
13 Wellington had recovered from two strokes. Still he could be seen on horseback in the streets of the capital, while people were concerned whether he would be able to keep his balance. He always did, but occasionally fell asleep on horseback (cf. Hibbert 1997: 368).

litical attitudes were forgotten or excused on account of his age« (James 1992: 273). He was much sought after and extremely occupied to the last. A well-documented quote from his later years illustrates his position:

»If a church or chapel, Glebe or School House or even Pagoda is to be built, I must patronise and subscribe for it: the same for Canals, Rail Roads, Harbours... Rest! Every other animal – even a donkey, a costermonger's donkey – is allowed some rest, but the Duke of Wellington never! There is no help for it. As long as I am able to go on, they will put the saddle upon my back and make me go ... Every Animal in the creation is allowed some relaxation from Exertion ... except for the Duke of Wellington ...« (Hibbert 1997: 357)

*Fig. 5: William Heath: »Good Humour«, 1829.*

© The Trustees of the British Museum, Museum Number 1868,0808.9063.

This is typical Wellington style. He is self-deprecating but still proud of being in demand, and he has a strong sense of public obligation. His imagery describes the feeling of being a pack animal, a donkey or mule, which he would have encountered regularly in his time in the army. »He had been an unwilling statesman, impelled to hold public office out of a sense of duty.« (James 1992: 271) The unverified and conceivably anecdotal quotation from the Duke's later life, »I am the Duke of Wellington and must do as the Duke of Wellington doth« (quoted for instance in Thompson 1990: 9), is highly suggestive in the same context. It appears that Wellington was not only aware of his public image but actively cultivated it, consciously striving to live up to his public persona and potentially even fulfilling certain expectations of his contemporaries.

In Wellington's honour, a thirty-feet equestrian statue was commissioned and finally placed on top of Constitution Arch (also known as Wellington Arch today) by Hyde Park Corner in 1846. At the time, many contemporaries felt that the statue was not just larger than life, but far too large to be aesthetically pleasing.[14] When the statue was moved to its first position, *Punch* published a caricature entitled »Awful apparition to a Gentleman whilst shaving in the Edgeware road« (cf. Hibbert 1997: illustrations section, n. pag.).[15] The statue was drawn from the workshop of its creator Matthew Cotes Wyatt to Hyde Park and would have passed many windows. In the caricature, a man with his back to the viewer stands at his dressing table underneath a window. Outside the window, a huge profile of the Duke of Wellington seems to look in on the astounded nameless gentleman, whose hair rises in fright. The statue is presented as an exaggeration, open to public ridicule. The caricature also plays upon the omnipresence of the Duke of Wellington in people's daily lives, as it conveys the idea that even while shaving any man can suddenly find himself being watched by Wellington. The statue overstretches the heroic element to the point of becoming grotesque. Wellington himself seems to have been the only person who liked it, and he was put out when he learned about plans to remove the statue from its position. Since nobody wanted to slight the Duke, the statue

---

14 Christopher Hibbert notes that the statue was »the first equestrian statue of a person other than a monarch to be erected in London« (1997: 377).

15 On *Punch*'s use of the statue in caricature cf. also the chapter by Sandra Martina Schwab in the present volume.

retained its place until 1888, when it was finally moved to Aldershot.[16] Respect for the Duke and his achievement kept his comicisation within limits during the nineteenth century, but a comic legacy survives in his representation in later times.

## LATE-TWENTIETH-CENTURY MOCKERY: *BLACKADDER*

The third part of the *Blackadder* television series – one of Britain's most famous satirical programmes and possibly its most well-known history spoof – is set in the Regency period. Here, Edmund Blackadder appears as the much-tried butler of the Prince Regent and later George IV. The episode relevant in the present context is »Duel and Duality« (BBC 1987).[17] At the very beginning, the Prince Regent, dim-witted as well as morally dubious, announces that he has made a conquest: two of Wellington's nieces. »I spent a night of ecstasy with a pair of Wellingtons and I loved it!«, he puns on the familiar association with the boots. Blackadder points out that the Duke has a reputation for challenging (and killing) anyone who takes up sexual relations with his relatives. Blackadder paints the Duke in the worst possible light and suggests to the Prince Regent that he would not stand a chance against »throat-slasher Wellington, the finest blade His Majesty commands«. When the Prince Regent realises that Wellington is no longer fighting in Spain but has returned to England in triumph, he panics. His idea of fleeing to Mongolia, however, is doomed because, as Blackadder remarks, »Wellington is a close personal friend of the chief Mongol. They were at Eton together«.

The scene plays with anachronisms: Wellington is referred to as the Iron Duke, but would not yet have acquired this nickname at the time of his engagement in Spain; there are also allusions to episodes from Wellington's later life, when he was a household character and many people claimed his acquaintance because they needed support. Also his good connections (here

---

16   A detailed account of the statue can be found in Hibbert (1997: 375-377). It may seem astonishing that Wellington should have shown a preference for the oversized statue. In fact, although he was not impressed by being worshipped as a hero, he was also extremely sensitive to (assumed) slights.

17   All following quotations are from this episode.

due to his attendance of one of the most famous public schools) are stressed. The worried Prince Regent persuades Blackadder to swap roles, so that Blackadder will have to confront the enraged Duke.

Indeed, Wellington challenges the Prince Regent to a duel. Before the duel, however, Wellington does his duty and puts in an appearance to report on the past war to his Prince Regent (whom he is bent on killing in the duel later). The »full account of the war« turns out to be a diminutive bit of paper with a note saying »We won. Signed: Wellington«. The scene is strong on physical comedy and slapstick (the Duke keeps striking the ›butler‹ of the Prince Regent and shouts commands rather than speaking), but in addition makes much of Wellington's proverbial brevity of speech. Talking over his military achievements with the false Prince Regent (i.e. Blackadder after the role swap), the acting of Stephen Fry makes the audience aware of all the Wellington clichés they might be familiar with. He shouts all the time, dismissing timid suggestions that there might be other methods of enforcing discipline in an army, such as »inspired leadership and tactical ability«, with a shouted »NO! It's all down to shouting!« When it finally comes to the duel, Wellington once again is extremely efficient, too much for Blackadder's liking. He is also a big fan of modern weaponry, confronting Blackadder with a new-fangled sophisticated cannon. While Blackadder is still desperately searching the cannon's manual for instructions, Wellington fires. The episode stresses the element of violence in Wellington; he is exclusively conceived of as a military man, and he is largely associated with fierce imagery of bloodshed, all in service of the King.[18]

Next to the rather dubious reasons for the duel (which can be easily read as an allusion to the historical, similarly ludicrous duel between Wellington and Winchilsea), the episode enlarges on Wellington's extreme efficiency, military and otherwise. He uses words sparingly and mostly barks orders, bullying all the other characters. At the same time, he appears as a narrow-minded man blindly adhering to the only code of behaviour he knows – that of the army, no matter the context. The general tendency to violence has to do with the genre of the programme and the sitcom's need

---

18 For an analysis of *Blackadder* as a product of Thatcherite Britain, see Korte (2007). Five years after the Falklands War, the »Duel and Duality« episode with its devastating image of the military would probably have had even more resonances than today.

for slapstick. But at the same time, certain expectations on the audience's part seem to be fulfilled here. Most associations with Wellington the military man are negative in this particular episode. The ridicule is produced by a great deal of physical comedy, but also by Wellington not quite fitting his surroundings. He is louder and more strident than the rest of the characters, and although he is dressed to perfection in the obligatory boots and the red coat of the soldier with all his insignia (the costume Stephen Fry wears in the episode distinctly echoes the Goya portrait), he is hopelessly out of place in the overly refined world of the court. *Blackadder* does not mock the elderly politician Wellington, but the soldier and hero, which is potentially even more subversive.

## COMIC WELLINGTON? SOME EXPLANATIONS

There are many possible reasons for the tendency towards comic deflation of the Duke of Wellington. Some of them might be rooted in the personality and the life of Wellington himself, as far as we can know them. As many of the reports on Wellington coincide, the conclusion might be safe that this is more than historical interpolation. A simple reason for comic representation is that caricaturists loved Wellington. His descendant, the 7th Duke of Wellington, contributed the foreword to Physick's edition of Wellington caricatures and noted that »Wellington was the perfect target for the caricaturist's wit. He cared nothing for popularity and was consequently an easy butt. In addition he had features which cried out to be caricatured« (Physick 1965: n. pag.).

Ever the »unwilling statesman«, Wellington seems to have been an uneasy mixture of bluntness with the somewhat overbearing behaviour of a military man's prototypical distrust against too much sentiment and exaggerated social niceties of his day. These characteristics would have come together with his sense of humour, which, although he appears to have been sensitive as to his social position and felt easily slighted, extended towards himself. His fondness for Wellington caricatures points that way and is very telling: It indicates a willingness to laugh at himself as well as a certain vanity – after all, only influential people tend to become the main subject of caricature. As we have seen, Wellington had a caustic kind of wit, a style of speech which was often perceived as unusually sparse, and he seems to have enjoyed repartee and produced punch lines where other people would produce speeches. This would have made him a good source for anecdotes and secured his popularity through all political vicissitudes.

In addition to personal features and habits, there are other explanations of Wellington's comic sides, which have less to do with his character and the speculations existing round that character. A good explanation is the fact that Wellington had two careers. All in all, Wellington's military background and resulting heroisation might have caused a particular need for comic deflation, as his presence in politics was felt as a threat by many of his contemporaries who distrusted the army man. The relationship between these careers can be seen in different ways, but it is suggested here that it is a key to Wellington's comic potential. R.E. Foster argues in »Mr Punch and the Iron Duke« that it was Wellington's work in the political rather than the military sphere which encouraged comic representation (cf. Foster 1984). It is conceivable that a war hero does not become subject of caricature as easily as a politician will. As a politician Wellington and his views offered many targets for attack. Moreover, in Wellington's later life, when he mainly concerned himself with politics, there would simply have been an increasing number of media spreading and popularising comic images. Nevertheless it seems questionable whether the two Wellingtons (or phases) can be separated from each with such certainty, or whether one should be considered without the other. Foster has a point in stressing the duality but the crucial idea is that both of Wellington's professions seen *together* constitute an important reason for him to be appreciated as comic. The dashing war hero and the elderly politician clash in the imagination; they do not fit together at all.

Wellington the soldier was powerful, energetic, and blunt. Wellington the politician would still have been blunt of speech, but was no longer (physically) powerful and seemed resistant to change compared with the impression of dynamism he gave as a soldier. Finally, he became frail, grumbling, and overly critical towards all and everything around him. The factor of age plays an important role, which should, however, not be taken as ageism on the part of Wellington's contemporaries. Since he was lucky enough to survive his military career, the public could watch him ageing, undergoing a slow transformation from a war hero into a frail old man, still esteemed for his counsel but at the same time an object of curiosity, frozen in time. Charlotte Brontë[19] came to see him in 1850, and was impressed by »a real grand old man« (quoted in James 1992: 274). Wellington would have been respected still, but was also somehow diminished, much as he kept playing down the effects of old age he was suffering. The war hero, when he stays around long enough, turns into a fossil, left over from a »heroic and by now far distant past« (James 1992: 274). In that sense, the writing of Wellington's history began in his lifetime and could be more easily conceived of as comic because it is the history of a survivor. An early death would have precluded this. One could argue that Wellington's contemporaries would not have been sensitive to these different images since they would actually see either the soldier or the politician. But both were still the same person. Also, it is highly noteworthy that the Duke's heroic past was kept present in the public eye in myriad ways:

»[A] re-enactment of Waterloo was held in the Vauxhall pleasure gardens during the summer of 1850; there was a huge model of the battlefield with thousands of model soldiers in the United Services Institute; and in the summer of 1852 visitors to the Regent Street Gallery of Illustration could see ›Dioramic Paintings‹ of all Wellington's campaigns.« (Ibid.)[20]

For present purposes, the most useful theory of the comic would therefore be that of incongruity, which goes back to Immanuel Kant. In the first part of his *Critique of the Power of Judgment* (1790), the *Critique of the Power of Aesthetic Judgment*, Kant suggests that appreciation of the comic is a matter of our perception, for instance of conceptual shifts. The comic is thus in the mind of the beholders when they encounter incongruous phe-

---

19 Charlotte Brontë was a great admirer of Wellington, who featured in her juvenilia. She also collected Wellington anecdotes from newspapers. For relatively recent findings, cf. Alexander (2007).
20 Roberts (2011) claims that Wellington »was probably Britain's greatest military commander, but he was also perhaps one of her worst prime ministers. Fortunately his premiership was only short-lived, and its failings were more than made up for by the splendour of his wartime career.« The crucial contrast, however, is not good soldier versus bad Prime Minister, as Wellington was not as black-and-white a character as this suggests. Richard W. Davis stresses Wellington's pragmatic leadership qualities as a Prime Minister (cf. Davis 2008: 252-265).

nomena which do not fit easily together. Surprising punch lines, a sudden change in expectations, reversals of anticipated orders would belong into this category. A juxtaposition of fundamentally different cognitive frames – in Wellington's case of the industrious soldier, the hero, and the old man – would cause comic irritation.[21] As time went on, Wellington would not only clash with his former selves. He would also be out of tune with the Victorians. Lawrence James recognises this when he describes the aged and irascible Wellington as »out of temper with his times«: He does not fit any more, not merely because he is old, but because he is a relic. Furthermore, Wellington's situation can be seen on a threshold between the eighteenth and the nineteenth centuries: His education and training would largely have comprised eighteenth-century politics and warfare, but he lived far into the Victorian age. Threshold positions and liminality in general are rich in comic potential because they ask for a conceptual re-framing of characters or social roles and because they produce irritation and insecurity in the beholders, which then need to be laughed off.[22] At the same time as Wellington is ridiculed, he never loses his function as an authority, an institution, or a »grand old man«; his comic facets add to the picture without destroying it. The humour Wellington attracts is not subversive, or only mildly so. The Duke of Wellington is neither solely the hero of Waterloo nor the implacable Iron Duke who is out of place and out of temper. Wellington is a literal as well as a metaphorical joker figure, and a character people could make jokes about, thus a good example of the discursivity of the comic. It is the potential of comic access to his character that contributes to his persistence in British cultural memory.

---

21 For a brief overview of incongruity theories, their development after Kant and their relevance for an understanding of the comic cf. for instance Zimmermann (2013: 34-35). Brock (2004) gives a linguistic perspective of incongruity in his analysis of British sitcoms, cf. particularly his Chapter 5. Morreall's (1987) survey on theories of the comic is also helpful in this context.

22 A convincing account of the role of liminality for comic structures is given by Little (1983). Although Little's work is on gender and her topic removed from the present one, her ideas on threshold positions and their comic drive would work very well here.

## Works Cited

Alexander, Christine (2007): »Charlotte Brontë and the Duke of Wellington: Further Evidence of Hero-Worship«. *Notes and Queries* 54.2, 142-45.
Beaton, Belinda (2005): »Materializing the Duke«. *Journal of Victorian Culture* 10.1, 100-107.
BBC Press Office (2002): »The Complete List of the Top 100 in Alphabetical Order«. In: *BBC Press Releases and Press Packs* 21 August 2002 (www.bbc.co.uk/pressoffice/pressreleases/stories/2002/08_august/21/100_list.shtml). Accessed 20 February 2013.
Brock, Alexander (2004): *Blackadder, Monty Python und Red Dwarf: Eine linguistische Untersuchung britischer Fernsehkomödien*, Tübingen: Stauffenburg.
Boyle, Laura (2011): »Shoes Make the Man: Regency Footwear«. In: *Jane Austen.co.uk* 11 June 2011 (www.janeausten.co.uk/shoes-make-the-man-regency-footwear/). Accessed 20 February 2013.
Cloake, Felicity (2011): »How to Cook Perfect Beef Wellington«. In: *The Guardian* »Life and Style« 8 December 2011 (www.guardian.co.uk/lifeandstyle/wordofmouth/2011/dec/08/how-to-cook-perfect-beef-wellington). Accessed 20 February 2013.
Cooper, Leonard (1964): *The Age of Wellington: The Life and Times of the Duke of Wellington. 1769-1852*, London: Macmillan.
*Blackadder The Third*: »Duel and Duality« (BBC, 22 October 1987).
Davis, Richard W. (2008): *A Political History of the House of Lords, 1811-1846: From the Regency to Corn Law Repeal*, Stanford/CA: Stanford UP.
›The Flagship‹ (2009): »The 100 Greatest Britons«. In: *Listal* 8 January 2009 (www.listal.com/list/the-100-greatest-britons). Accessed 20 February 2013.
Foster, R.E. (1984): »Mr Punch and the Iron Duke«. In: *History Today* 30 April 1984 (www.historytoday.com/re-foster/mr-punch-and-iron-duke). Accessed 20 February 2013.
Hibbert, Christopher (1997): *Wellington: A Personal History*, London: HarperCollins.
James, Lawrence (1992): *The Iron Duke: A Military Biography of Wellington*, London: Weidenfeld and Nicolson.
Kant, Immanuel (2003 [1790]): *Critique of the Power of Judgment*. Ed. Paul Guyer, Cambridge: CUP.

Keegan, John (1987): *The Mask of Command*, London: Jonathan Cape.

Korte, Barbara (2007): »›As cunning as a fox who's just been appointed Professor of Cunning at Oxford University.‹ *Blackadder* (1983-1989) as a Picaresque of the National Past«. In: Christoph Ehland/Robert Fajen (eds.), *Das Paradigma des Pikaresken: The Paradigm of the Picaresque*, Heidelberg: Winter, 375-387.

Knowles, Elizabeth (ed.) (2012): *The Oxford Dictionary of Quotations* (www.oxfordreference.com/view/10.1093/acref/9780199237173.001.00 01/acref-9780199237173). Accessed 20 February 2013.

Little, Judy (1983): *Comedy and the Woman Writer: Woolf, Spark and Feminism*, Lincoln: U of Nebraska P.

McMaster, Juliet (2011): »Good Punishes Bad? The Duels in Sense and Sensibility«. In: *Persuasions On-Line* 32.1 (www.jasna.org/persuasions/online/vol32no1/mcmaster.html). Accessed 20 February 2013.

Morreall, John (ed.) (1987): *The Philosophy of Laughter and Humor*, Albany: State U of New York P.

Olver, Lynne (2000) »Napoleons«. In: *The Food Timeline* (www.foodtimeline.org/foodpies.html#napoleons). Accessed 20 February 2013.

Physick, John (ed.) (1965): *The Duke of Wellington in Caricature*, London: Her Majesty's Stationery Office.

Roberts, Andrew (2011): »The Duke of Wellington: Soldiering to Glory«. In: *BBC History* 17 February 2011 (www.bbc.co.uk/history/british/empire_seapower/wellington_01.shtml). Accessed 20 February 2013.

Seewald, Berthold (2010): »Die Schlacht von Waterloo bleibt immer aktuell«. In: *Die Welt* 18 June 2010 (www.welt.de/kultur/article8072805/Die-Schlacht-von-Waterloo-bleibt-immer-aktuell.html). Accessed 20 February 2013.

Thompson, Neville (1990): »The Uses of Adversity«. In: Norman Gash (ed.), *Wellington: Studies in the Military and Political Career of the First Duke of Wellington*, Manchester: Manchester UP, 1-10.

Trustees of the British Museum (n.d.): »Collection Online«. In: *British Museum* (www.britishmuseum.org/research/collection_online/collection_search_results.aspx). Accessed 20 February 2013.

»Wellington Boot History« (n.d.): In: *Wellington Boots* (www.wellingtonboots.org.uk/wellington-boot-history.htm). Accessed 20 February 2013.

Zimmermann, Ulrike (2013): *Comic Elements in Women's Novels of Development from the 1960s to the 1980s*, Würzburg: Königshausen & Neumann.

# We ARE Amused!
The Comical Uses and Historical Abuses of
Queen Victoria's Infamous Reproach
›We are not amused‹

DUNCAN MARKS

## ›WANA‹ AND THE VICTORIAN ERA

In March 2012, Deirdre Murphy, Curator at Historic Royal Palaces, introduced a new permanent exhibition of Queen Victoria's personal artefacts at Kensington Palace. Titled »Victoria Revealed«, Murphy hoped the exhibition might make visitors reconsider the former sovereign: »Victoria was not just a fat lady in black who said, ›We are not amused‹« (Youde 2012: 12). Murphy's remark makes an association between how Victoria dressed, what she said, and how she is remembered. Scholarly attention has been given to Victoria's costume and what it tells us about her relationship to her subjects (cf. Ward 1999). Little attention, however, has been given to Queen Victoria's most famous sayings, and how they help shape how the Queen and her era are remembered.

Despite her living for eighty-two years, there is only a narrow selection of famous quotes attributed to Queen Victoria. *The Oxford Dictionary of Quotations* credits her with seven (cf. Knowles 2009: 1118-1119), *The Yale Book of Quotations* only five (cf. Shapiro 2006: 789). The cultural importance of attributed quotes comes from how they reflect the character of those being quoted as much as the quality of the quote itself. With so few popular quotes attributed to Victoria, those that are become even more telling. Aside from »We are not amused« (hereafter, WANA) – the focus of this chapter – there is Victoria's other renowned saying, »I will be good«. It is a good phrase; similar to WANA, it is short, punchy, and memorable. It invites further contextualisation: To be good at what? To whom? It also questions expectations of ›goodness‹. WANA should lead us to ask: Who were the *we*? Why were they not amused? Were they expected or expecting to be amused? Were they ever amused? The latter question becomes more pressing in view of how Queen Victoria is often seen as a symbolic figurehead for the Victorian Era and the Victorians (cf. Gardiner 2002: 141). Louisa Hadley (cf. 2010: 30-31) sees the relationship between Victoria and her subjects as interrelated, with Victoria's personal period of mourning after Prince Albert's death in 1861 becoming associated with a wider, Victorian cult of mourning. From this, Victoria's personal association with WANA potentially indicts Victorians as being collectively viewed as unamused. Therefore, only an exploration of the historical origins and reasoning behind WANA can prevent such misreading of the Victorians.

This chapter maps out the ways WANA has been interpreted and appropriated since it was first allegedly said in c.1870. Up until the Second World War, the remark was explored to resolve its factual origins: why it was said, and to whom. However, since the War, any factual context has been largely jettisoned. Instead, fictionalised accounts have been favoured and often appropriated for purposes far beyond the remit of history. Amusement has been found in using the remark to allude to Queen Victoria's entire lack of humour. What follows is not so much the study of the changing fortunes of what might be considered the standard form of humour – such as a joke, lyric, cartoon, or a comedy sketch – but rather the changing representations of how a symbolic, historic figure displayed a lack of humour.

The post-Victorian history of WANA should be seen in light of recent research that has explored the afterlife of the Victorians and their reputation.[1] The Victorian identity after 1901 is therefore an evolving construct. The twentieth century has been read as »inventing« (Sweet 2001) the Victorians to help propel its own, alternative identity. The earliest twentieth-century

---

1   Cf. Homans/Munich (1997); Gardiner (2002); Taylor/Wolff (2004); Joyce (2007); Marks (2012).

revisionist of the Victorians remains Lytton Strachey and his seminal work, *Eminent Victorians* (1918). Its debunking of the Victorians has been widely interpreted as having led to the popular belittling of Victorian style as *passé* during the interwar period. Similarly, the Victorian character was depicted as humbug and morose by comparison to the revelry and colour of the Roaring Twenties. In academia, it would not be until the 1950s that the Victorian period was re-seen in more favourable light – in wider society, a few decades longer.

The approach favoured in this chapter is primarily a traditional historical enquiry. It charts the chronological documentation of how, when, and most importantly why Queen Victoria may have said WANA. This linear approach begins in 1885; it maps out the evolution of WANA, its many contortions through the early decades of the twentieth century, and then beyond. The most immediate early references to it are literary texts – mostly hearsay accounts cited in non-Royal autobiographies and journals, and then later in biographies of Queen Victoria. They show that the origin of WANA is ambiguous, and probably a myth. Regardless, early twentieth-century interest in attributing WANA to Victoria was keen, and if she never said it then a willing audience wished and believed that she had. These literary texts are subsequently considered alongside other media, such as stage plays, films, television programmes, and finally early twentieth-century social media memes such as ›lolcats‹ and internet signatures. It will show that the arrival of each new media led to the appropriation and a novel reinterpretation of WANA.

## ›WANA‹ TIMELINES AND TRANSMUTATIONS

Before 1921, no biography of Queen Victoria includes any WANA incident. Consequently, in all likeliness Victoria never said it. However, this is not to say that there is no literary evidence made during her lifetime to link the Queen to WANA. Only these were not strictly biographical accounts. They are either purely fiction or hearsays, both of which come with reservations about their authenticity. Consequently, the timeline of WANA as a purely biographical trope must temporarily wait consideration.

In a novel of 1885, James Payn's *The Talk of the Town*, an unnamed, fictional queen is depicted saying, »We are not amused«. It is the earliest printed version of the WANA story. Payn uses the remark as an anecdotal cautionary tale about a young man trying to »make himself agreeable as a *raconteur* in the presence of royalty. When he had done his story, the Royal lips let fall these terrible words: ›We are not amused‹« (Payn 1885: 158). Beyond the vague ›Royal‹ connection, there is no direct association with Queen Victoria in this novel. If contemporaries made such an association it was because they believed it the type of remark the Queen might have said in such a scenario, and, more importantly, because humour could be found in imagining it.

Two years after Payn's novel, in *Royal Girls and Royal Courts* (1887), Mary Sherwood recounts how Queen Victoria took Sir Arthur Helps, one of her private secretaries, to task for telling a humorous story to a few ladies-in-waiting at the Windsor dining table. Overhearing Helps's tale, the Queen remarked, »What is it? We are not amused« (Sherwood 1887: 182). Sherwood's tale was substantiated in 1919 in a fleeting diary entry for 2 January 1900 by one of Victoria's former ladies-in-waiting, Caroline Holland (cf. 1919: 268-269). Unfortunately it remains unstated who is implied by *we* and in what way the joke was intended to be amusing. Holland only says that it was »a story with a spice of scandal or impropriety in it« (ibid.). In truth, these earliest accounts are unreliable. Holland did not begin her service at the court until three years after Helps's death in 1875, so at best it was a second-hand account and susceptible to the usual ›Chinese whispers‹. Mary Sherwood's version is also a second-hand account, and tellingly published only a couple of years after Payn's fictional story (cf. Shapiro 2006: 789). Offering examples of good etiquette to young American ladies – essentially how refined European Society girls act in the presence of royalty – Sherwood's book had a specific market and purpose. It makes her account of WANA a suspiciously convenient cautionary tale of what tragedy may befall a young American lady if caught speaking improperly in the presence of one's Royal betters.

The readership of these earliest accounts of WANA was always small. From which, the axiomatic association of Victoria and WANA cannot be made. The wider dispersion of WANA came from popular biographies of Victoria published between the wars – the first biographies to show any interest in the remark. In considering why this interest developed, there are two related answers. Firstly, Queen Victoria saying WANA fitted effortlessly into the supposed interwar fun to be had in Britain by debunking Victorians. The second reason is more prosaic. By 1918, the British public knew surprisingly little about Queen Victoria's private life. This is partially because of the hagiographical nature of Victorian biography. Whilst constructing the Queen's public persona as the worthiest of the Worthies, this form of biography lacked a personal, private narrative.[2] Consequently, in the early twentieth century, and propelled by a freer social code arising from experiences of the war, a popular interest developed for accounts of Victoria's private life. Until the mid-1920s, a lack of any published official documentation of Queen Victoria's later private life meant that public knowledge of it, including accounts of WANA, were based on hearsay and speculation. It was a situation made more grievous by the Queen's near total withdrawal from society following Prince Albert's death in 1861, an event that acts as a »veil« (Strachey 1921: 218) in how the Queen was represented during the interwar years. Prior to 1861, she is the Victoria of »I will be good« – youthful, active, approachable. After it she is the Widow of Windsor; a Miss Havisham figure; the Victoria of WANA – old, unseen, unapproachable. There would not be any real insight into the Queen's inner life until her diaries and correspondences were posthumously published by tranches in 1907, 1926-28, and 1930-32. Operating in this documentation vacuum, the literary fabrications of the WANA story by Payn, Holland, and Sherwood should be accepted as an understandable intrigue into the life of one of Britain's most important figures of the period.

To this list of conspirators can readily be added the name of Lytton Strachey and his seminal and popular 1921 biography of Victoria. Strachey's *Queen Victoria* was researched and written with no access to the majority of her official correspondences, and unsurprisingly his account of WANA is very similar to the one Holland had put forth only two years earlier. It involves a »transgressor shuddered into silence« at the dinner table by Queen Victoria's

---

2   Victorian biography used copious lists of facts, quotes and figures to celebrate how a subject had publicly-served society. Whilst full of platitudes, it forbade speculation on a subject's private life or subconscious impulses. The earliest biographies of Queen Victoria were written in this hagiographical style. They were published to commemorate the Jubilees of 1887 and 1897 and her death in 1901, cf. Valentine (1887); Bulley (1897); Jerrold (1901); Aitken (1901); Campbell (1901). The staid Victorian biographical approach was famously challenged by Strachey's *Eminent Victorians* in 1918, which inspired the New Biography of the interwar years.

»most crushing disapprobation«: her »awful ›We are not amused‹« (1921: 395). Strachey's account lacks titillating detail. This is surprising considering how much sardonic humour the WANA story offered. However, what is novel about Strachey's version is that he uses WANA as a conduit to a wider condemnation of Victoria's entire sense of humour (cf. ibid.: 395-396). He admits she did have a sense of humour – only it was not cultured. Strachey writes: »Her sense of humour was of a vigorous though primitive kind. She had been one of the very few persons who had always been able to appreciate the Prince Consort's jokes«; and, even after his demise, »she could still roar with laughter [...] over some small piece of fun – some oddity of an ambassador, or some ignorant Minister's *faux pas*. When the jest grew subtle she was less pleased«, and »if it approached the confines of the indecorous, the danger was serious« (ibid.: 395). Strachey uses the WANA story to offer a psychological reading of Victoria. In one way it is sympathetic; it humanises her as a complex being in ways Victorian hagiography never did. Alternatively, it undermines the subject; it makes her appear foolish. Strachey implies that Victoria's sense of humour is under-developed and childish. However, from Strachey's depiction of Victoria we can also see an analogy between her character and Lewis Carroll's fictional Queen of Hearts: especially through the abuse of power that might stem from Victoria not being amused. This abuse is revealed in Strachey's choice of language, such as »danger«, »annihilated« and »crushing disapprobation«, and in how Queen Victoria is shown as judge and jury over what constitutes acceptable humour, »a verdict from which there was no appeal« (ibid.). In Victoria's Royal Court, humour is portrayed as a deadly game, a minefield of social etiquette, and therefore no laughing matter. Whereas earlier biographies of Queen Victoria had celebrated the youthfulness of her sense of humour as one of her better inclinations (cf. Gosse 1901: 301-307), Strachey is the first to directly question the health of her sense of humour. It was not until the 1970s that scholars (e.g. Woodham-Smith 1972: 111; St Aubyn 1991: 240) would reconsider her humour more favourably.

Strachey's *Queen Victoria* also marks the final interest in the origins of WANA amongst biographers of the Queen. The two modern classic biographies of Victoria by Elizabeth Longford (1964) and Cecil Woodham-Smith (1972) resolutely distance their reading of the sovereign from how Strachey had portrayed her. Subsequently, historical scholarship no longer looks for the meaning behind Victoria's remark, »We are not amused«. It is invariably overlooked, quickly dismissed as a myth, or seen as an irrelevance in the face of more pressing revisionisms. Indeed, the desire to revise Queen Victoria as a figure worthy of study relies on portraying her in a positive and attractive light. By the twenty-first century, being humourless or, even worse, controlling of another's humour is seen as a social failing. The portrayal of former Prime Ministers John Major and Gordon Brown reflects that to be seen as grey or humourless is no longer appealing to the general public. With the demise of the biographer's interest in WANA, attention instead must be turned to visual representations of it.

The publication of collections of Queen Victoria's diaries and private correspondence during the interwar years infers a sustained interest in the former monarch, but these publications cannot compare to how visual depictions of Victoria on stage and screen during the 1930s helped shape public opinion of her in this period (cf. Gardiner 2002: 146-148). And yet, these two modes should not be seen as incongruent. Victoria's private life came under closer scrutiny after 1932 with the final publication of her correspondences. It meant that new representations of her life would have to at least pretend to be based on official sources, even if in reality popular representations rarely were. It is here that the first transmutation of the WANA tale occurs.

Laurence Housman, the English playwright, admitted to closely following the publication of the Queen's correspondences and diaries when penning *Victoria Regina* (1934), a series of thirty vignettes described as »Palace Plays« (1934: 14).[3] The popularity of *Victoria Regina* led Housman to stage it in the West End in 1937, the first permitted depiction of Queen Victoria on stage. It was a critical and commercial success. From reading across his »Palace Plays«, one can claim that Housman takes immense artistic license with factual truths about the Queen. Indeed, despite Housman's pretence to have based his vignettes on official and recently published sources (cf. ibid.: 14-15), in the case of »We Are Not Amused«, this is clearly not the case. This

---

3   Housman's »Palace Plays« were originally penned as a series of illustrated vignettes to be either read or performed in private. It was only in 1937 – the centenary of Victoria's accession and, more notably, the year in which Lord Chamberlain relaxed theatrical censorship over depictions of British sovereigns – that Housman was able to publicly stage *Victoria Regina*. Its popular success led him to publish and produce numerous other Queen Victoria-inspired vignettes.

palace play is far more likely to have been inspired by the singer, actress and former royal mistress, Lillie Langtry and her account of the WANA incident, which had appeared in her popular autobiography of 1925. Langtry (2005 [1925]: 62-63) recalls an episode she had been told by Prince Leopold about one of Queen Victoria's court attendants, a young man who had a renowned gift for mimicry, especially of the Queen. Having heard of this man's talent, one night, whilst dining at Buckingham Palace, Victoria suddenly turned on him and insisted he perform his impression of her. »The trembling victim proceeded to give a greatly modified and extremely bad imitation«; after which the Queen ordered him to rise, and »in a freezing tone« commanded, »*We* are not amused« and promptly »left the dining-room with her ladies« (ibid.: 63). Housman's play is very similar to Langtry's version of WANA, except that he gives it an all-female dynamic. Set in 1884, it centres on Queen Victoria overhearing one of her ladies-in-waiting mimicking her. The Queen then forces the woman to re-enact this impersonation in front of her. Housman's depiction of the Queen's cruel insistence to see herself impersonated by her servant, and the language used to describe the servant's discomfort, mirrors Langtry's version so closely that Housman clearly based his play on Langtry's account rather than official sources.

What is most noteworthy in Langtry's account is how she is the first to identify whom the pronoun (which she italicises) refers to in WANA. Rather than being the generally accepted belief that the Queen was employing the *pluralis maiestatis*, the »Royal We«, Langtry shows the Queen used »*We*« to refer to »her ladies«. This is surprising; a poor impersonation of the Queen is not likely to have created any gender-specific related embarrassment. In doing so, Langtry adds a gender dynamic and establishes a boundary of un/acceptable humour made by men in the presence of women that was previously missing in earlier versions of WANA. Because his entire play is composed of female characters, Housman's pronoun clearly refers to women. However, the more pressing question is whether his use of the pronoun is singular or plural? By the tone of the play it is likely to mean that the Queen considers all present in the room are not amused; thus she firmly decrees it as not an amusing impersonation, and this despite the other ladies having been previously cajoled »into squeals of laughter« (Housman 1934: 394). It makes the Queen the arbiter of humour, and a bad-tempered judge at that. To this end, Housman places more emphasis on the »NOT« (which he capitalises) part of the remark than the pronoun. It underlines how

Housman makes the play's importance – just like all his ›Palace Plays‹ – less the historical accuracy, and more to show the Queen as stern, bad-tempered and humourless. Indeed, earlier in the play the Queen is portrayed by her gossiping maids as omnipresent, hypocritical, demanding, and prone to run the rule through her »whims«, and with »an eye like a gimlet« (ibid.: 389-396). To this end, it is the first example of a new, intentionally unhistoric and fictitious depiction of WANA.

The stage production of *Victoria Regina* was not the only popular, public depiction of Queen Victoria in 1937. Herbert Wilcox also capitalised on the centenary of Queen Victoria's ascension with his film *Victoria the Great* (UK 1937). Combining British history with the splendour of Hollywood, it was a great commercial success and topped a late-1930s Mass-Observation poll of British cinemagoers' all-time favourite films (cf. Richards/Sheridan 1987: 39-40). The film depicts primarily the romance between Queen Victoria and Prince Albert. Although Victoria is shown to be far from a rounded individual, she remains an attractive character and deserves sympathy when her Albert inevitably dies. The requisite tension of the film comes from their unconventional Victorian gender roles. Albert wants to be involved with the nation's political reforms, but, since he is a foreigner, both parliament and Victoria block his ambitions. It leaves him the unfulfilled role as matron at Windsor whilst his wife operates in the traditionally male arena of *Realpolitik* with her ministers. Marital disharmony is evident and the emotional tension heightens to a crisis point midway through the film. Significantly, it is the scene in which WANA features that acts as the symbolic resolution (cf. Marks 2012: 291-294). This scene involves a dispute between Prime Minister Lord Palmerston and the royal couple. In an attempt to force Victoria to back his proposal to send an ultimatum of war to the USA, Palmerston gleefully declares Albert as the »most hated man in the country« owing to public suspicions that as a foreigner he is corrupting the Queen's political views. During the heated exchange between the two men, Victoria, who is seated between them, interjects by saying in a firm but measured voice, »Lord Palmerston, we are not amused«. What is fascinating about this scene is its provenance. The film begins by declaring that it is »[b]ased upon actual events«, with every incident founded »on historic fact«, and that »the political utterances by various statesmen are authentic«. And yet this scene is almost certainly pure hokum; there are no corroborating sources supporting it.

The depiction of the Queen in this important scene is a positive one. Albert and Victoria are shown unified once more, each supporting the other in a time of adversity. The use of the pronoun in the WANA line is evidently Victoria and Albert; the reason for not being amused is Palmerston's threat and tone. It leaves the audience very much in sympathy with the royal couple rather than Palmerston. Indeed, the analogy of the scene to contemporary events of 1936-37 should not be overlooked. Following Edward VIII's proposal to marry the American divorcée, Mrs. Wallis Simpson, the 1936 Abdication Crisis had only recently divided public opinion in Britain. It had hardened attitudes to the establishment, especially figures such as the Archbishop of Canterbury, Cosmo Lang, and the Prime Minister, Stanley Baldwin, who had forced an eventual abdication. Their establishment views of maintaining acceptable standards of conduct for the Crown were less shared amongst the middle and lower classes, which invariably sympathised with Edward VIII. *Victoria the Great*'s WANA scene shows the victory of the monarch (Victoria) standing by her unpopular foreign lover (Albert) against the bullying Establishment figure (Palmerston). These three Victorian figures could readily be analogised as Edward VIII, Simpson and Baldwin. The audience of the late 1930s was, for once, realigned to be in keeping with Queen Victoria's lack of amusement.

With the exception of Joe McGrath's *The Great McGonagall* (UK 1974) – a film so low in production values it can hardly be ranked as a feature film – Wilcox's *Victoria the Great* is the last British feature film to feature a WANA scenario. The reason for this is likely to be akin to why postwar biographers have chosen to steer away from referring to WANA – it has become a cliché. Indeed, recent films depicting Queen Victoria, such as John Madden's *Mrs Brown* (UK 1997) and Jean-Marc Vallée's *The Young Victoria* (USA 2008), have preferred to look at her reign in new ways: *Mrs Brown* focuses on the emotional relationship between Victoria and her Highland servant, John Brown; *The Young Victoria* explores the love affair between Albert and the young Victoria. Consequently, no WANA moment is entertained in either film.

Cinema aside, postwar visual media, especially television, has encouraged less formal and more purposefully comical engagements with Victoria's WANA. This was especially so during the 1970s. Against the backdrop of the Troubles in Ulster, the Three-Day Week and the Sex Pistols, authority figures were very much fair game for parody on television – Queen Victoria included. Three noticeable television depictions of Queen Victoria and her use of WANA in this decade are: Michael Palin in a 1974 episode of the BBC's *Monty Python's Flying Circus*; Peter Sellers in the film *The Great McGonagall* (1974), and an entire 1976 episode of the BBC's *It Ain't Half Hot Mum*. Reading across these depictions, two conclusions can be drawn. The first is how irreverent the depictions are. Whilst this might be expected from comedy, it undermines any possible emotional engagement with the subject. In the *Monty Python* episode, Michael Palin's Queen Victoria is portrayed as a mad, vainglorious despot. In *The Great McGonagall*, Peter Sellers' Queen Victoria is a sexually voracious imperialist – which is fortunate as she spends the whole film as the erotic obsession of the Scottish poet William McGonagall (played by Spike Milligan). The latter attempts to seduce Victoria through his abysmal poetry and general bawdiness. The requisite WANA line comes quite literally as the climax of his infamous poem, ›The Tay Bridge Disaster‹. Whilst a dead Prince Albert accompanies them on his steam organ, McGonagall embraces the Queen as he recites his poem. He gets ever more passionate until finally Albert's organ explodes in a flurry of steam and a startled Victoria cries out, »Oh shit! ... We are *not* amused!« Being so detached in its mocking, no real engagement exists in *The Great McGonagall*. Indeed, in many ways, this reflects that by the 1970s such comical depictions of Victoria were no longer expected to be realistic. No serious historical explanation is provided for WANA. Both Palin and Sellers' Queen Victorias are always no more than the comedians Michael Palin and Peter Sellers in Victorian dresses; Queen Victoria has become a vaudeville character, played in the great pantomime tradition of men showily in drag. It reduces the WANA line to a stock phrase akin to shouting out to the audience »Oh yes it is!« for a cheap laugh when the loosest Victorian connection is present.

The second conclusion to be drawn from these three comic representations of WANA is that they ask questions about British identity, especially in an era of decolonisation. The depiction of Queen Victoria in a 1976 episode of the BBC sitcom, *It Ain't Half Hot Mum*, addresses issues of Britishness, the end of empire, and the relationship between history and humour. Set in India during the Second World War, the sitcom focuses on a performing company of inept conscripts charged with entertaining troops. The episode titled »We Are Not Amused« never uses Victoria's remark in its script, but it remains fundamental to its overall message. The episode sees the company put on a special show for the visiting District Officer. Informed he is an unapologetic, English imperialist, a jingoistic pageant about British rule in India is devised. The compère for the show is the exceedingly camp character, Gunner ›Gloria‹ Beaumont, who is cast as Queen Victoria. However, the English District Officer is detained at the last minute and sends his deputy in his place. Only the deputy is both Indian and a vociferous separatist. This leads to an improvised, desperate revision of the play's content and tone. Now a counter-history of the British rule in India is offered, with the Indians civilising the British rather than *vice versa*. Although only a silly excursion for comedy, the »We Are Not Amused« episode of *It Ain't Half Hot Mum* does show how humour and history can be an odd couple. It stresses that, by the 1970s, the imperialism of Victoria's day was a complicated identity for the British. No longer masters of countries such as India, the British were in no position to dictate the history of India to Indians. Instead, it was the British who were searching for their own, new post-colonial identity. Even the acceptance of the United Kingdom into the European Economic Union in 1973 had failed to offer it a new, international mooring. This may explain why Queen Victoria is so heavily linked with Germany in both the *Monty Python* sketch and *McGonagall* film. Palin's Victoria struggles to hide her German origins and her proneness for despotism. She labours to pronounce common English words such as »ant«, and continually reverts to speaking German. This leads her to mix-up the WANA line as »*ve ar nat ... amusiert*«. Stock German comedy clichés are also ever present in the *McGonagall* film. These include a dance band of Hitler-lookalikes and the ghost of Prince Albert as a zeppelin commander. By analogising the historical zenith of British power – the Victorian era – with the then powerhouse of 1970s Europe – West Germany – these representations use humour and amusement to simultaneously reinforce and revoke Britain's newfound position in Europe. Just as the WANA line is built on the contradiction of being amused at not being amused, its use in these examples of mid-1970s popular culture acts as a befitting representation of how humour could concurrently be used to both confront and shy away from Britain's political and economic instabilities.

Since the 1970s, postmodern detachment has challenged national identities based on international standing. To this end, WANA has become detached from its historical meaning and been allotted a place in the contemporary lexicon of a British identity based on a self-referential and ironic patriotism.

For example, WANA features as one of many framed quotes, sayings, and references to material culture that are printed on the Union Jack and available to purchase as interior decorations from the online retailer Love Being British.[4] Sympathetic to the Cool Britannia style of Britpop and New Labour, this company identifies quintessential British quotes and cultural references. Besides WANA, they use Churchill's quotes, sayings such as »More Tea Vicar« and »Chin Up Old Boy«, and references to well-revered British products such as »I Love My Aga« and »Tea? I'd Prefer a G&T«. They supply a revitalised patriotic market borne out of the marriage of Duke and Duchess of Cambridge, Elizabeth II's Diamond Jubilee, and pride in hosting the 2012 Olympics. Any humour to be made from WANA is now contemporary, not historical. Queen Victoria is no longer the »butt of the joke«; her historical association is almost irrelevant. Instead, WANA has become ironic; humour is found at the idea of a national lack of humour. WANA is used to express a pride that a part of Britishness stems from the ability to laugh at itself. Debenhams, the British department store, used the WANA phrase as one of its doormat designs in 2012. Greeting a visitor with a message that you are not amused, and asking them to wipe their feet on a royal quote and the Crown, perfectly encapsulates the importance of irony to this new identity. The mat is entirely without explanatory reference, making the irony of the four-word statement more humorous than the historical reference to Victoria or Victorians.

The most recent television depiction of WANA came in an episode of the BBC's *Doctor Who* series. The episode, titled »Tooth and Claw«, attracted ten million viewers when it aired on 22 April 2006. It was the first time The Doctor and his companion, Rose Tyler, travel to the Court of Queen Victoria. The episode shows a faulty TARDIS inadvertently taking the pair of time travellers back to 1879 Scotland rather than the intended Ian Dury concert in 1979 Sheffield. The Queen is portrayed as a short-tempered, self-centred woman – perfectly suited to say WANA. Aside from the inane plotline of ninja monks eager to infect Victoria with a form of lycanthropy from the bite of an intergalactic werewolf, the narrative is driven by Rose's self-confessed ignorance of Queen Victoria's life aside from her famous remark, »We are not amused«. For their shared amusement, Rose promptly makes a bet with The Doctor that she can provoke the Queen to say »We

---

4   Cf. their web presence at www.lovebeingbritish.co.uk.

are not amused«. A significant amount of the episode is subsequently taken up with Rose's four, increasingly desperate attempts to do so. Consequently, the episode becomes a conflict between two cultures, which ultimately unsettles the balance of the drama. One culture is the twenty-first century, represented by The Doctor and Rose. They take almost nothing seriously, and act out the episode as if a comedy. The other culture is the nineteenth century, represented by the rest of the entire cast who take the story seriously, and act it out as if it were a genuine thriller. Such juxtaposition ultimately casts modern culture as not only celebrating youth, childishness, pop culture, and amusement, but one which also enjoys portraying an older, Victorian age as the opposite: aged, over-serious, studious, and lacking a sense of humour.

The way these two time periods are portrayed as opposites touches on the relationship between history – as a past, dead commodity – and humour – as a present, prescient commodity. This is seen in Rose's interactions with the Queen. At each attempt to provoke her to say WANA, Rose is increasingly embarrassed by her own conduct. By the end of the adventure, just when she finally succeeds in making the Queen say it, Rose is met with Victoria's damning declaration: »I am not amused. Not remotely amused. And henceforth I banish you«, before adding, »I don't know who you are … or where you are from, but I know that you consort with stars, and magic, and think it fun. But your world is steeped in terror, and blasphemy, and death«. Rose is clearly shaken by this outburst. It is unclear whether she is more shocked by Victoria's clear lack of humour or by the strength of the Queen's condemnation of her youthful, twenty-first century joy in finding ubiquitous amusement. However, considering that Rose had only ever known Victoria to be famous for being unamused, it suggests that Rose is more troubled by the novel notion that finding universal amusement is not necessarily a healthy trait.

## CONCLUSION: ›WANA‹ DE-HISTORICISED

Since c.1885, humour has been regularly found in contextualising, re-enacting or simply saying, »We are not amused«. A genuine interest existed amongst the earliest post-Victorian generations as to why Queen Victoria may have said it. This was not simply part of a Stracheyian snigger at that most eminent of Victorians, Queen Victoria. There was also a genuine desire to understand the private complexities of the former queen. However, owing to its likely mythical roots, attempts to historicise why Victoria said WANA were always likely to result in fictional representations, the most successful being those on the interwar stage and screen. After the Second World War, interest in Victoria and the Victorians changed. As living memory of the Victorian era diminished by the year, it was increasingly becoming purely history. Interest in contextualising why Victoria said WANA waned. It conflicted with the revisionist tendencies of biographers who were more interested in portraying Victoria as a more balanced and humane figure. By the 1970s, the new alternative comedy of Milligan, Sellers, and the Monty Python team used WANA to ridicule authority, past and present. They did so by stressing the Royal We pronoun, or by simply adopting a clipped English (or German) accent.

However, since the mid-1970s, it is unclear whether the historical roots of WANA are still central to how humour is derived from it. More pressing is how a perceived association with poshness in the WANA phrase sustains popular interest in it. Anyone who nowadays says »We are not amused« is either: genuinely posh; wants to be considered posh; or is being ironic because they do not consider themselves posh at all. Furthermore, if WANA no longer requires a British historical mooring to be humorous, nor is it solely of interest to a British audience. It has become a global comedy meme. An example of this is found in the American animated television series, *Futurama*. Despite being set in the thirty-first century, *Futurama* still draws on contemporary culture and history for humour. In an episode first aired on 2 March 2003, Bender, the anti-hero android, conveys his disapproval of a situation through appropriating WANA. He does so by putting on a crown and saying »We are not *amused*« in a higher voice register, indicating snootiness and self-importance. As *Futurama* is shown in fourteen countries outside the States, the creators of the show are apparently confident that their mostly young audience, whose first language is not always English, do not need to associate the phrase WANA with its historical reference to Queen Victoria in order to be humorous. It is, therefore, by the twenty-first century, simply a meme to express an attitude, and akin to the Californian Valley Girl's interjection, »Whatever!«

The use of the WANA clip in *Futurama* has gone on to be pirated and made viral as an image signature for people to use on the Internet, predominantly in chat rooms and forums. Whilst only one of many such signatures, it is telling that people on the Internet, a domain readily associated with anonymity, use it to define themselves as individuals. This commandeering of WANA to its most simplified root of meaning – one shorn of its historical baggage – is how it should be considered in general use today. The attention span of the modern consumer is reduced; instantaneousness and accessibility are paramount, not the weight of contextualisation and brevity of history. If WANA is used at all today, it is through irreverence. It is a sound bite for a sound-bite age of multiple and competing points of reference. Consequently, the dispersion of WANA in modern media is universal and diverse. Indeed, how Queen Victoria would feel about her most famous remark being used in such irreverent ways as a poor literary shortcut to describe a character's facial expression in a Stephen King novel (cf. 1992: 9)[5] or in becoming a staple idiosyncratic choice of that prevalent social meme, the ›lolcat‹, will always be a conjecture; however, we might suppose that in all likelihood she would be utterly, utterly bemused.

## WORKS CITED

Aitken, William F. (1901): *Victoria the Well-Beloved*, London: S.W. Partridge.
Bulley, Eleanor (1897): *Victoria the Good: Queen and Empress*, London: Gardner, Darton.
Campbell, David (1901): *Victoria, Queen and Empress*, Edinburgh: W.P. Nimmo, Hay & Mitchell.
Gardiner, John (2002): *The Victorians: An Age in Retrospect*, London: Hambledon & London.
Gosse, Edmund (1901): »The Character of Queen Victoria«. *Quarterly Review* 193, 301-337.
Hadley, Louisa (2010): *Neo-Victorian Fiction and Historical Narrative: The Victorians and Us*, Basingstoke: Palgrave Macmillan.

---

5   Stephen King's use of WANA is cited in the following passage: »Gerald had snatched the brochure out of her hand and had walked away without another word. The subject of the Porsche had not been raised since... but she had often seen it in his resentful We Are Not Amused stare«.

Holland, Caroline (1919): *Notebooks of a Spinster Lady, 1878-1903*, London: Cassell.
Homans, Margaret/Adrienne Munich (eds.) (1997): *Remaking Queen Victoria*, Cambridge: CUP.
Housman, Laurence (1934): *Victoria Regina: A Dramatic Biography*, London: Jonathan Cape.
Jerrold, Clare (1901): *Victoria the Good: True Stories of the Home Life of Queen-Empress, Wife, and Mother*, London: Jarrold & Sons.
Joyce, Simon (2007): *The Victorians in the Rearview Mirror*, Athens: Ohio UP.
King, Stephen (1992): *Gerald's Game*, New York: Viking.
Knowles, Elizabeth (ed.) (2009): *The Oxford Dictionary of Quotations*, Oxford: OUP.
Langtry, Lillie (2005 [1925]): *The Days I Knew: An Autobiography*, North Hollywood/CA: Panoply.
Longford, Elizabeth (1964): *Victoria R. I.*, London: Weidenfeld & Nicholson.
Love Being British (2012): *Love Being British: The Home of Beautifully Presented & Framed British Quotes* (www.lovebeingbritish.co.uk.). Accessed 26 June 2012.
Marks, Duncan (2012): ›*Unrepentant Victorians*‹: *Generational Identities and Tensions in Britain, c.1901-39*, Unpublished PhD thesis: University of Sheffield.
Payn, James (1885): *The Talk of the Town*, London: Chatto & Windus.
Richards, Jeffrey/Dorothy Sheridan (eds.) (1987): *Mass-Observation at the Movies*, London: Routledge.
St Aubyn, Giles (1991): *Queen Victoria: A Portrait*, London: Sceptre.
Shapiro, Fred (ed.) (2006): *The Yale Book of Quotations*, New Haven/CT: Yale UP.
Sherwood, Mary (1887): *Royal Girls and Royal Courts*, Boston/MA: D. Lothrop.
Strachey, Lytton (1918): *Eminent Victorians*, London: Chatto & Windus.
Strachey, Lytton (1921): *Queen Victoria*, London: Chatto & Windus.
Sweet, Matthew (2001): *Inventing the Victorians*, London: Faber.
Taylor, Miles/Michael Wolff (eds.) (2004): *The Victorians since 1901: Histories, Representations, and Revisions*, Manchester: Manchester UP.
Valentine, Laura (1887): *The Queen: Her Early Life and Reign*, London: Warne.
Ward, Yvonne M. (1999): »The Womanly Garb of Queen Victoria's Early Motherhood, 1840-42«. *Women's History Review* 8.2, 277-294.

Woodham-Smith, Cecil (1972): *Queen Victoria: Her Life and Times*, London: Cardinal.
Youde, Katie (2012): »Victoria's Secrets«. In: *The Independent on Sunday* 11 March, 12.

**Films:**

*The Great McGonagall* (UK 1974, Director: Joe McGrath).
*Mrs Brown* (UK 1997, Director: John Madden).
*Victoria the Great* (UK 1937, Director: Herbert Wilcox).
*The Young Victoria* (USA 2008, Director: Jean-Marc Vallée).

**TV Productions:**

*Doctor Who* (BBC, 22 April 2006).
*Futurama* (Fox, 2 March 2003).
*It Ain't Half Hot Mum* (BBC, 14 December 1976).
*Monty Python's Flying Circus* (BBC, 11 November 1974).

# The Old World and the New
## Negotiating Past, Present, and Future in Anglo-American Humour, 1880-1900

BOB NICHOLSON

### THE AMERICAN FUTURE

By the 1890s, readers of the *Newcastle Weekly Courant* would have been accustomed to a regular serving of »Yankee Snacks«. This was the name given to the paper's weekly collection of imported American jokes. Humorous clippings from the pages of US newspapers were a staple feature of the late-Victorian popular press and the *Courant* had been setting aside a dedicated column for them since the mid-1870s (cf. Nicholson 2012a). Each instalment featured a recurring cast of stereotypical American characters: unscrupulous Chicago lawyers, wise-cracking New Yorkers, verbose Bostonians, hot-tempered Texans, gun-toting, Midwestern newspaper editors, and mischievous African-Americans named »Sambo« all appeared on a regular basis. However, on the 22 July 1893, they were joined by an Englishman. He appeared in an exchange between an actor and a theatre manager:

»I tell you, said the manager of the Brimville opera House to the theatrical star, you're makin' a mistake. Yer play's no good. – Why, sir, it is one of Shakespeare's. – That's all right. But it's one of his first. I've seen it many a time. There's no use o' talkin', Shakespeare's got to hustle around and write something new or he won't be in it.« (»Yankee Snacks« 1893: 2)

This theme – that Shakespeare, one of the most illustrious figures of English history, was not *new* enough to make it on the American stage – was a recurring feature of imported Yankee jokes. A similar gag suggested that Hamlet would be livened up by the addition of skirt dancers, contortionists, boxers, and a ventriloquist. »I tell you«, concluded that particular manager, »Shakespeare won't be in it when I get started. You've [got] to hustle and keep abreast of the times« (»Wit and Humour« 1892: 2). In another joke, a jobbing Yankee journalist quipped that if the Bard were alive today his best jokes would be rejected by New York's leading comic journals – »I know«, his friend replies, »I've tried most of 'em myself« (»Yankee Snacks« 1892: 2). Finally, the *Hampshire Telegraph* printed a humorous (and allegedly true) anecdote about a senator from Colorado who insisted that his own face be painted over a local portrait of the great playwright – »Shakespeare?« he scoffed, »Don't know him; who was he? [...] What did he do for Denver?« (»Yankee Notions« 1894: 12).

We might well wonder how British audiences would have responded to these jokes. On one level, they invited readers to laugh derisively at American culture; to chuckle at the ignorance of the politician who did not recognise Shakespeare and snigger at the vulgarity of a man who wanted to add dancing girls to Hamlet. Had the jokes been published a few decades earlier, this form of anti-American laughter would have been a relatively straightforward affair. It would have offered a way for British readers to reaffirm their national superiority – both economic and cultural – over an adolescent nation that had yet to develop appropriate faculties of taste. This kind of self-confident humour was certainly in evidence in mid-Victorian culture. *Punch*, for example, took great delight in mocking the peculiarities of American slang and used exaggerated versions of the dialect to present the country's most venerable politicians as illiterate buffoons (cf. Stedman 1953). *Punch*, moreover, was not the only Victorian voice to laugh at America. The magazine's representations of the country drew upon a long tradition of exaggerated, and rather unflattering, portrayals of stage Yankees in British theatres (cf. Jortner 2005; Enkvist 1953: 20-25). On a subtler level, visions of an undeveloped America were also reinforced by the accounts of mid-century travellers, such as Charles Dickens, who returned to Britain with unflattering reports of unpaved streets, foul-mouthed newspapers, and chronic levels of public spitting (cf. Dickens 1842). Even those who viewed the egalitarian ideals of American society with admiration typically regarded the country as a work-in-progress; a social and cultural experiment that, for all of its promise, had yet to coalesce into a mature nation. In this context, with the transatlantic balance of power tipped firmly in favour of Britain, laughing *at* America and the undeveloped manners of its citizens was a relatively uncomplicated business.

However, by the final quarter of the nineteenth century, it was becoming increasingly difficult for British observers to dismiss the United States with such casual self-confidence. In 1878, William Gladstone observed that:

»The England and America of the present are probably the two strongest nations of the world. But there can hardly be a doubt as between the America and the England of the future, that the daughter [...] will [soon become] unquestionably [...] stronger than the mother.« (Gladstone 1878: 181)

The United States, he warned, was »passing [Britain] by in a canter« and would soon usurp its position on the world stage. It was essential, he concluded, that his countrymen recognise the inevitability of this impending transition and begin to address what he later termed the »paramount question of the American future« (Gladstone 1890: 26). The publication of this prophecy is important, for it marks the onset of a transitional period in Anglo-American relations. Over the next two decades, the idea of America in British culture underwent a profound transformation – one which altered the transatlantic balance of power and had significant ramifications for the reformation of British national identity.

In 1878, the response of Victorian journalists to Gladstone's warning was almost universally hostile. *The Times* concluded that his reasoning was »at once redundant and defective« and was intended only to massage the ego of its American audience (»The New Number« 1878: 7). Provincial papers, such as the *Blackburn Standard*, roundly condemned the ex-premier's »unpatriotic«, »wild«, and »sinister« prophesies (»Odious Comparisons« 1878: 5). Even the Liberal-leaning *Daily News* accused Gladstone of having »gone too far« with his »rash«, »sensational«, and »astounding« depiction of America's »unrivalled future« (»Mr Gladstone Has Addressed« 1878: 4-5). It is possible to detect an undercurrent of anxiety running beneath these protestations. The fact that the press responded to Gladstone's comments in such a defensive manner suggests that the threat posed by the

United States was felt more seriously than journalists were willing to admit. However, whether they were fuelled by bravado or genuine confidence, the fact that most papers refused to entertain the possibility of Gladstone's hypothesis suggests that the idea of an American future, in which Britain would play a subordinate role, was, at this point, regarded as culturally unspeakable.

Twenty years later, when the country mourned Gladstone's death, this taboo had been lifted. Whilst some British observers continued to deny, or at least resist, the United States' growing influence, the concept of an American future was now in widespread circulation. By the end of the Victorian period, it was commonplace for commentators such as F.A. Mackenzie to claim that an »invasion« of American products and inventions had swept the country (Mackenzie 1902), for the *Daily News* to joke that British children should be taught American English (»the language of the future«; »Americanisms« 1889: 4), or for W.T. Stead to describe the *Americanisation of the World* as the »trend of the twentieth century« (Stead 1902). No longer regarded as an unstable political experiment, or dismissed as an underdeveloped post-colonial backwater, the United States was increasingly portrayed as a land of economic and technological progress, an influential player on the international stage, and the home of a distinctive brand of social, cultural and spatial modernity. In this context, a joke about Shakespeare being *too old* to compete with the products of modern American popular culture took on an interesting new light; one that invites us to think about how the inhabitants of late-Victorian Britain came to terms with the prospect of an impending American future in the decades before it actually arrived.

It is possible to explore the changing nature of Anglo-American relations across a number of social, cultural, political and economic contexts. The importation and consumption of American foodstuffs and consumer goods; the invention and adoption of American products and technologies such as Edison's phonograph and incandescent lamp; sporting victories by American yachtsmen, boxers, jockeys and athletes; the growing presence of American popular culture in the country's bookshops, theatres and music halls; high-profile marriages between rich American heiresses and bankrupt British aristocrats all helped to signal the country's growing vitality during the last quarter of the nineteenth century. The rising fortunes of the United States stimulated discussions at all levels of British society, from the rarefied atmosphere of London clubland, where wealthy businessmen monitored the health of their transatlantic investments, to the factory floors of Sheffield and Middlesbrough where rising competition with American steel was beginning to cause alarm. It is hardly surprising, therefore, that keen-eyed humourists were alive to these developments and sought to explore them. During the 1880s, an increasing number of joke writers, caricaturists, and literary humourists on both sides of the Atlantic began to engage with the concept of an American future and what it might mean for Britain. One of the recurring tropes within this burgeoning discourse was to juxtapose images of the American future with those of an idealised British past. This chapter focuses on two particularly prominent examples: Mark Twain's *A Connecticut Yankee in King Arthur's Court* (1889) and *The Canterville Ghost* (1906 [1887]) by Oscar Wilde.[1] Both texts capture some of the key themes of Anglo-American relations in this period and demonstrate the centrality of history to British national identity at a time when the country's future was beginning to look increasingly uncertain.

## THE ALMIGHTY DOLLAR

*The Canterville Ghost* is a short story that Wilde first published in a short-lived literary magazine named *The Court and Society Review* in February 1887. It is, at heart, a comedy of manners in which English traditions clash with the forces of American modernity. In a satirical twist on the gothic ghost story, an old English spectre named Sir Simon is terrorised by an American politician and his family who move to England and buy his haunted ancestral mansion. At first, the American characters laugh-off the idea of a ghost. The head of the family, Hirem B. Otis, begins the story by brushing aside the warnings given to him by the estate's former owner:

---

1 The 1889 edition of Twain's book, published in London by Chatto & Windus, was titled *A Yankee at the Court of King Arthur*. This chapter quotes from this edition, but refers to the book using its more commonly accepted title: *A Connecticut Yankee in King Arthur's Court*. References to Wilde's story are drawn from the 1906 edition of the text published by John W. Luce and Co. Both books are currently available to view using the Internet Archive (archive.org).

»My Lord, I will take the furniture and the ghost at a valuation. I have come from a modern country, where we have everything that money can buy; and with all our spry young fellows painting the Old World red, and carrying off your best actors and prima-donnas, I reckon that if there were such a thing as a ghost in Europe, we'd have it at home in a very short time in one of our public museums [...] But there is no such thing, sir, as a ghost, and I guess the laws of Nature are not going to be suspended for the British aristocracy.« (Wilde 1906: 3)

This opening address immediately captures one of the key themes of Anglo-American relations – the growing power of what contemporaries termed the »almighty dollar«. In the half century following the Civil War the American economy industrialised and expanded rapidly until, by the 1890s, the country had surpassed Britain in terms of manufacturing output and cornered many of its markets both at home and abroad (cf. Engerman/Sokoloff 2000). This growing economic strength manifested itself across a range of social and cultural contexts. Daily updates from the New York stock exchange became a regular feature of most daily newspapers, whilst articles debating the threat of American competition were increasingly visible in the provincial papers of major industrial centres (cf. Nicholson 2012b). From the 1870s, keen readers of society gossip columns would also have noticed an increasing number of wealthy American men and women circulating among the British nobility. Some used their fortunes to host extravagant entertainments for the Prince of Wales, others bought or rented lavish country mansions, and some secured permanent positions among the social elite by marrying off their daughters (so-called »dollar princesses«) to members of the British aristocracy (cf. Montgomery 1989).

The culture-clashes that resulted from these encounters, juxtaposing modern, self-made millionaires of Gilded Age America with titled families of Europe, provided fertile ground for British humourists. Some made jokes about the transparent desperation of cash-strapped aristocrats who sought to secure their crumbling dynasties with the fortunes of a New York heiress, but the majority found humour in American visitors' peculiar accents, irregular etiquette, conspicuous consumption, and the unseemly attempts of self-proclaimed republicans to purchase the trappings of Old-World respectability. *Punch*, for example, enjoyed poking fun at the wealthy American Vanderbilt family and their attempts to secure a respected position in elite London society. Shortly after his daughter secured a high-profile marriage to Lord

Marlborough, the paper printed a humorous poem about William Kissam Vanderbilt's decision to spend £10,000 building a decorative footpath outside his London residence:

»Yes, Sir, there's a sidewalk to lick all creation;
Yes, Sir, an Amurracan did it, you bet!
Just greenbacks and dollars have done the tarnation
Consarn, there are mighty few things they cayn't get!«
(»Precious Pavement« 1896: 69)

The poem goes on to suggest that an enterprising Yankee would soon purchase the historic stonework outside of Saint Mark's Basillica in Venice in order to resurface his stable yard back home. In these jokes, the archetypal modern American appears to regard history as a commodity; something that Europe possesses and he wishes to buy, usually in bulk. The prospect of the United States establishing an official »heiress exchange« in London in order to facilitate this mass, transatlantic exchange of cash for culture was a stock jest used by the British press from the 1880s onwards (cf. »The Man About Town« 1884: 229). However, the implication in *Punch*'s poem and in Wilde's text is clear: whilst the »almighty dollar« could secure the most prized titles and artefacts of European history, one of the »mighty few things« it could not purchase was taste. The possession of an *authentic* past – and the deep cultures and traditions that stem from it – is implicitly established by these jokes as a defining feature of British national identity; something that no amount of American money could buy.

The United States' uneasy relationship with British history is a central theme of Wilde's story. Whilst the Otis family have the economic capital to purchase an aristocratic mansion, they lack the necessary cultural capital to engage appropriately with its history. Rather than succumb to the Canterville Ghost's time-honoured haunting techniques (and thereby follow the generic tropes of gothic literature), they calmly attempt to remedy the situation by using modern American products and technologies. When they first move into the property, Mrs Otis notices a large bloodstain on the Library carpet. »I don't at all care for blood-stains in a sitting room«, she remarks to the housekeeper, »it must be removed at once« (Wilde 1906: 13). She is then informed that the blood belonged to Lady Eleanore de Canterville, who was murdered by her husband in 1575; it transpires that he is the ghost. The stain, according to the housekeeper, could not be removed and had since been much admired by tourists. Washington Otis, the eldest son of the family, cries: »That is all nonsense [...]. Pinkerton's Champion Stain Remover and Paragon Detergent will clean it up in no time.« (14) He immediately gets down on his knees and, sure enough, succeeds in erasing four centuries of British history. The same joke is repeated later when Mr Otis is woken by the deliberate clanking of the ghost's chains and calmly confronts the spirit outside his bedroom door. »My dear sir«, he says,

> »I really must insist on your oiling those chains, and have brought you for that purpose a small bottle of the Tammany Rising Sun Lubricator. It is said to be completely efficacious upon one application, and there are several testimonials to that effect on the wrapper from some of our most eminent native divines.« (Wilde 1906: 22-23)

Even the family's youngest children – a pair of rambunctious twin boys who Wilde refers to as the »Stars and Stripes« – refuse to be cowed by the ghost and terrorise him into submission with their pea-shooters and traps. By the end of the story, Sir Simon is reduced to sneaking around the house late at night, terrified that he might be spotted and abused again by the American interlopers.

In an article published two months after the *Canterville Ghost*, Wilde expanded on the character of »The American Man« and his inability to appreciate the patina of history:

> »With a naivete and a nonchalance that are absolutely charming, he will gravely compare St. James' Palace to the grand central depot at Chicago, or Westminster Abbey to the Falls of Niagara. Bulk is his canon of beauty, and size his standard of excellence [...]. For him Art has no marvel, and Beauty no meaning, and the Past no message. He thinks that civilisation began with the introduction of steam, and looks with contempt upon all centuries that had no hot-water apparatuses in their houses. The ruin and decay of Time has no pathos in his eyes. He turns away from Ravenna, because the grass grows in her streets, and can see no loveliness in Verona, because there is rust on her balconies. His one desire is to get the whole of Europe into thorough repair. He is severe on the modern Romans for not covering the Colosseum with a glass roof, and utilising the building as a warehouse for dry goods. In a word, he is the Don Quixote of common sense, for he is so utilitarian that he is absolutely unpractical.« (Wilde 1887: 341-342)

Wilde's work captures two of the central qualities that British humourists considered part of American character: an irreverent attitude towards the time-honoured customs and institutions of British history, and a corresponding faith in the power of modern American ideas and technologies. Wilde, in this case, is very much an equal-opportunities satirist – he invites us to laugh at the unrefined tastes and vulgar manners of his American characters, but pokes fun too at the determination of certain sections of British society to guard their history and traditions. However, other British voices were less even-handed and focused their full attention on mocking America's appetite for new products and inventions. For example, a columnist for the *Glasgow Herald* confessed to a certain shock that:

»nothing less than an autocar will suffice [residents of Chicago] for funeral processions. The slow and stately hearse is voted to be intolerably tedious and wasteful of time, and henceforth the citizens of the metropolis [...] will be rushed right around to the cemetery by the agency of electricity and kerosene [...] A population that spends its days in hurrying hither and thither on electric railways and tramways, and being hoisted breathlessly by elevators up and down mammoth sky-scrapers [...] could hardly go to its home in the leisurely old-fashioned way that prevailed in the days before Uncle Sam woke up and woke the world along with him.« (»It Has Long Been Well Known« 1899: 6)

These responses all seek to reinterpret the driving forces of American progress and present them as essential weaknesses of character. The country's financial and industrial growth is read as a symptom of its vulgar pursuit of the almighty dollar, its go-ahead energy is dismissed as the product of youthful exuberance, and its enthusiastic pursuit of modernity is derided as an imprudent rejection of the guiding hand of history and traditional ritual. Laughing at these distorted interpretations of American identity offered British audiences a chance to ameliorate concerns over their own country's comparative lack of economic and technological progress. If Britain could no longer compete with the United States on an economic level, the only way in which it could preserve the transatlantic balance of power was to change the rules of the game; to emphasise the value of cultural capital and denigrate its economic equivalent. One of the most effective ways to accomplish this was by emphasising the value of history; by establishing the past and a society deeply rooted in its traditions as a preeminent marker of cultural authority. This was a position that no amount of economic or technological progress could threaten. As a result, despite the growing power of the almighty dollar, America still deferred to Britain when it went looking for social and cultural legitimacy. As Wilde himself concluded:

»America has never quite forgiven Europe for having been discovered somewhat earlier in history than itself. Yet how immense are its obligations to us! How enormous its debt! To gain a reputation for humour, its men have to come to London; to be famous for their toilettes, its women have to shop in Paris.« (Wilde 1887: 342)

It is to these American humourists that this chapter now turns.

## The Laughter of Good Fellowship

The works of Wilde, *Punch*, and other British humourists provide one context in which to interpret Victorian responses to America's growing power, and the newspaper jokes about Shakespeare and America's lack of historical depth appear at first glance to fit comfortably into this strain of British humour. However, this rather neat interpretation becomes muddied as soon as we recognise that most of these gags were not written by British humourists, but were produced by American joke writers for a domestic audience. They were subsequently clipped out of the American press and reprinted by British editors (cf. Nicholson 2012c). It is unlikely, therefore, that they were written in order to mock American manners and celebrate the authority of British culture. Whilst they invited American readers to laugh at the peculiar behaviour of American characters, they did not necessarily laugh at America itself. In their original publishing context, these jokes were more likely to play on regional rivalries; the gag about the Senator from Denver, for example, may well have offered New York audiences an opportunity to laugh at the ignorance of politicians from the Western frontier. Of course, it is possible that the power dynamics at work in these jokes altered as they crossed the Atlantic; that they were reinterpreted by Victorian audiences in a new, transnational context that encouraged them to judge foreign peculiarities against a British norm and laugh derisively at their American cousins.

However, an analysis of British responses to imported American humour reveals little evidence of this aggressive, self-congratulatory laughter.

In fact, Victorian commentators explained their appetite for American jokes with reference to a different kind of laughter; one which was centred on the demonstration of approval rather than condescension. *The Times*, often an outspoken critic of American culture, ended a review of a visiting American circus troupe with the following observation:

»As for the clowns, their humour is greatly of the talkative kind, and is enriched by an unmistakable Yankee accent. The American jokes excite English laughter, and as laughter is generally a *sign of good fellowship*, Messrs. Pentland, Myers, Ferdinand, and Footet may be regarded as symbols of *international cordiality*.« (»Alhambra Palace« 1858: 5; emphasis mine)

An examination of contemporary commentary and editorial strategies provides compelling evidence of this »laughter of good fellowship«. When British commentators attempted to account for the popularity of imported American gags, they reserved particular praise for the country's distinctive sense of humour. Some attempts to dissect its defining features highlighted its fondness for exaggeration, others pointed out the merits of its dry delivery, and some even remarked upon its racy irreverence towards authority figures and codes of respectability. However, across all of these accounts, British commentators invariably emphasised the *freshness* of American humour as its greatest quality (cf. Nicholson 2012a). »American jokes«, argued the *Leeds Mercury*, »are refreshing to the jaded brain that is accustomed to wade through the flavourless, six-water-grog kind of wit of the English comic journals« (»Imported Humour« 1882: 1). *The Globe* was equally unambiguous about the relative merits of British and American humour:

»The best [English humourists] are silent now [...]. We are almost compelled, therefore, to go to Yankee writers for the great bulk of our fun. But we go very willingly. And we go, mainly, because we find in the work of our lively cousins so much that is agreeably fresh and individual. It is, we say to ourselves, so unlike anything that we can get from our own people; it is so characteristic. It is like roaming about in a new world of quip and quiddity.« (clipping from *The Globe* published in »Yankee Humour« 1887: 7)

These responses suggest an interesting reversal of what we have come to expect from British commentators. Rather than voice anxiety about the way American modernity was sweeping aside British history, culture and tradition, they willingly celebrate the vitality of American popular culture and compare it favourably to British competitors. History, in this case, is presented as an encumbrance; something that prevents an older society from producing the fresh, racy, exhilaratingly culture of a country that was, in the words of one British traveller, »unfettered by the petrified conceptions of the past« (F. Herbert Stead 1893: 93).

## THE KNIGHT AND THE COWBOY

Two contradictory impulses have thus far emerged. The first, exemplified by the likes of Wilde and *Punch*, uses humour to celebrate British history and culture, and to denigrate America by highlighting its inability to honour the past. The second, captured by the popularity of imported American humour, suggests a wide-spread delight in modern American culture and its ability to cut loose from the fetters of tradition and taste. These contrasting responses were brought into direct contact in 1889 when Mark Twain, the most popular of nineteenth-century American humourists, published *A Connecticut Yankee in King Arthur's Court*. Like Wilde's narrative, this novel juxtaposes modern American manners, ideas and technologies with landscapes and characters drawn from an iconic period of British history. In this case, a wise-cracking American engineer named Hank Morgan is accidently transported back in time to the Early Middle Ages and finds himself marooned amidst the legendary trappings of King Arthur's Camelot. Throughout the text, Twain highlights a familiar range of contrasts between American and British character. Firstly, his Yankee protagonist displays the same levels of self-confidence, practicality and ›go-ahead‹ attitude that Wilde bestows on the Otis family. Shortly after coming to terms with his unexpected journey, Hank Morgan recognises that his knowledge of nineteenth-century technology makes him the smartest person on Earth and quickly sets about taking over the country. »Being a practical Connecticut man«, he recalls,

»I made up my mind to two things: if it was still the nineteenth century and I was among lunatics and couldn't get away, I would presently boss that asylum or know the reason why; and if, on the other hand, it was really the sixth century, all right, I didn't want any softer thing: I would boss the whole country inside of three months.« (Twain 1889: 20)

The narrative's chief antagonist, the wizard Merlin, attempts to foil these plans but, just like the Canterville Ghost, his traditional magic is no match for the irrepressible power of American modernity. However, unlike Wilde, who invites us to sympathise with the ghost's old fashioned ways, Twain presents Merlin as a scheming enemy of progress; a charlatan whose petty jealousy and superstitious quackery are repeatedly undermined by the scientific rationalism of his American rival.

Having secured a post as the King's chief advisor, the Yankee begins to industrialise the country. Factories are built, schools are established, a newspaper is founded, and a network of railway, telegraph and telephone lines spreads across the country. This connection between America and modern technology was another familiar trope of transatlantic humour. In 1882, for example, an American humourist who wrote under the pen name of Max Adeler published a short story called »The Fortunate Island« that bears a striking similarity to Twain's narrative (Adeler 1882). In this text, an American scientist and his daughter are marooned on a mysterious island that was separated from Britain during the medieval period and remained insulated whilst the rest of the world changed. Once again, the American visitor introduces the awe-struck natives to modern technology: Telephone, telegraph and railway lines are constructed, a Baron records his voice on a phonograph, and a paddle steamer is used to rescue a kidnapped maiden from a castle.

The fact that these technologies are introduced by Americans is significant. Whilst many of the inventions mentioned by Twain and Adeler were first pioneered in Europe, by the 1880s the United States was often depicted in British culture as the new home of technological innovation. In 1893, Victorian visitors to the Chicago World's Fair returned home with tales of electrified street-cars, high-speed elevators, and towering skyscrapers (cf. Nicholson 2012b). The modern American metropolis offered European observers »an early encounter with tomorrow« that hinted, in both exciting and alarming ways, about the shape of their own future (Lewis 1997).

However, arguably the most potent symbol of American modernity was Thomas Edison, who stood alongside Twain as one of America's leading international celebrities. News of his latest endeavours was tracked by the British press who regularly dispatched interviewers to speak with him in the hope that he would reveal details about his forthcoming inventions. An accomplished self-publicist, Edison appears to have encouraged the development of his own mythology by feeding journalists with exaggerated (or completely fabricated) information about his plans. In one instance, he claimed that he was installing an enormous phonograph in the Statue of Liberty that would perform an hourly reading of the Declaration of Independence so loud that all of New York might hear it (cf. »Mr. Edison At Home« 1878: 2). These rumours provided material for British humourists. For example, *Punch*'s »Almanack For 1879« contained several cartoons predicting what the inventor would accomplish in the coming year: The »telephonoscope« performed international video calls between Britain and Australia; the »Edison Weather-Almanack« predicted the climate months in advance; and, rather more implausibly, »Edison's Anti-Gravity Under-Clothing« allowed wearers to soar through the air like kites (»Almanack« 1878). *Punch*, as we have seen, was not the most ardent admirer of American culture, but these images did not seek to mock the country's appetite for the latest gadgets. Rather, they willingly recognised that Edison (and, by extension, America itself) had come to symbolise cutting-edge innovation.

Twain, for his part, occasionally poked fun at the excesses of American modernity. For example, his Yankee establishes a system of advertising in which knights carry advertising placards reading: »USE PETERSON'S PROPHYLACTIC TOOTH-BRUSH – ALL THE GO« (Twain 1889: 210). In a particularly satirical barb aimed at American advertising, one of these knights carries an advertisement for stove-polish and endeavours to convince the public to buy it before the stove has even been invented. However, the real targets of Twain's satire were the institutions of British history – the monarchy, the church, and the concept of chivalry. It is hardly surprising, of course, that a citizen of the Republic should champion the causes of democracy and religious freedom. These themes had loomed large in American culture for more than a century. However, it was the force of Twain's polemic that took British readers by surprise. Whilst the story includes many of the picaresque misadventures that characterised his earlier work, its mid-sections are devoted to demonstrating the evils of Monarchy and the Established Church. The politicised nature of the text divided British readers. Reactionary and conservative voices, such as a reviewer for *The Scots Observer*, condemned Twain's new taste for political soapboxing and hoped he would return to the simpler, frontier humour that had made his name (cf. »Some Yankee Notions« 1890: 246). At the other end of the spectrum, radicals and non-conformists, such as the newspaper editor W.T. Stead, appear to have championed the book's attacks on Old-World institutions. Stead, a long-term admirer of America, selected *Connecticut Yankee* as the *Review of Reviews'* book of the month for February 1890. In a characteristically uncompromising introduction to the text, he highlighted the »frigid condemnation« levelled at the book by conservative publications, but argued that these critical voices were out of step with the British public:

»Our superfine literary men of culture who pooh-pooh the rough rude vigour of the American humourist represent a small clique. Mark Twain gets ›directlier at the heart‹ of the masses than any of the blue-china set of nimminy-pimminy criticasters. In his own country [...] [the book] has been received with an enthusiasm which it has hitherto failed to evoke on this side of the Atlantic [...]. Yet I make free to say that the vote of the mass of the English people would be on the side of the American and against the English critic. For what our critical class has failed to appreciate is that the Education Act has turned out and is turning out millions of readers who are much more like the Americans in their tastes, their ideas, and their sympathies than they are to the English of the cultured, pampered, and privileged classes [...]. His [the new reader's] literary taste is not classical but popular. He prefers Longfellow to Browning, and as a humourist he enjoys Mark Twain more than all the dainty wits whose delicately flowered quips and cranks delight the boudoir and the drawing-room. This may be most deplorable from the point of view of the supercilious aesthetes, but the fact in all its brutality cannot be too frankly recognised.« (Stead 1890: 144)

Stead's predictions were borne out by the book's healthy sales figures. Chatto and Windus, Twain's British publishers, printed 40,000 copies of the book – a figure that corresponds with the print run of Twain's 1884 *Adventures of Huckleberry Finn* (cf. Welland 1978: 236). More than half of these copies were printed across four cheap editions between 1893 and 1899, suggesting that the book enjoyed an enduring popularity with the British public.

This distinction between critical condemnation and public approval prompts us to consider alternative ways of interpreting British responses to modern American culture. Rather than focus on national identity – on how new ideas about Britishness were formulated in response to a looming American future – we see the role played by class and cultural politics in separating the Old World from the New. Stead's disdain for the »dainty wits« and »delicately flowered quips« of literary humourists may well have been aimed at Wilde and his fellow aesthetes, but his attack on »superfine literary men of culture« was almost certainly directed at Matthew Arnold. The two men had enjoyed an uneasy public relationship since 1887 when the cultural critic had condemned Stead's sensationalist »new journalism« as »featherbrained« (Arnold 1887: 638). Arnold famously defined culture as »the best which has been thought and said in the world« (Arnold 1896: viii) and set it against the unrefined »anarchy« of commercialised mass culture. Whilst Arnold did not divide culture and anarchy along purely transatlantic lines, he nevertheless regarded American civilisation as an archetypal representation of the latter. At the same time as Twain was developing his ideas for *Connecticut Yankee*, Arnold made several disparaging remarks about his »Quinionian humour« (1882: 689) and described America's »addiction to the funny man« and its »glorification of the average man« as a »national misfortune« (1888: 489). Indeed, it is possible that Arnold's disparaging remarks about Twain and American culture contributed to the politicisation of *Connecticut Yankee* and its transformation from a gentle, comic burlesque into something more acerbic (cf. Lustig 2008). Arnold's disparaging remarks about American culture fit comfortably alongside the work of Wilde and *Punch* and speak for an influential strain of British opinion. However, Stead's rebuttal and the popularity of American humour amongst Britain's burgeoning reading public suggest that the authority of these »criticasters« was far from secure. And they knew it. By the 1880s, the American future (with all of its social, cultural, technological and political implications) was not something that would be imposed on an unwilling British populace by invasion. Instead, it would be welcomed by a wider public whose values and tastes mirrored those of their American cousins more closely than those of the cultural elite in Britain.

This prospect of Americanisation by choice, rather than by force, can be teased out through an examination of one of *Connectiut Yankee*'s most memorable scenes. Towards the end of the novel, Hank Morgan is compelled to fight a duel with a knight named Sir Sagramore. Rather than don the armour and lance of his chivalric opponent, the Yankee employs the weapons of a nineteenth-century American cowboy. Using a lasso and a pair of revolvers, he defeats Sir Sagramore, and a band of other Arthurian knights including the legendary Sir Launcelot. Rather than mourn their fallen heroes, the crowd applauds the Yankee:

»Unquestionably the popular thing in this world is novelty. These people had never seen anything of that cow-boy business before, and it carried them clear off their feet with delight. From all around and everywhere, the shout went up – ›Encore! Encore!‹« (Twain 1889: 456)

Whilst the people of sixth-century Britain were unfamiliar with performing cowboys, Twain's British readers were not. In 1887, Buffalo Bill's Wild West Show delighted millions of Victorians, including the Queen, as it toured London, Birmingham and Manchester. Lesser performers quickly followed in his wake, such as a frontiersman named Mexican Joe who brought a troupe of cowboys and Indians to Liverpool and took the city by storm. According to local press reports, young boys whose imaginations might once have been fired by Scott and Tennyson's depictions of chivalric adventure now wrote to an American cowboy in the hopes of returning with him to the Wild West. »I am getting tired of this town«, sighed one boy from Liverpool, »[and] should like to have a change in your country«. This, observed the *Birmingham Daily Post*, was just »one instance of the fascination which Buffalo Bill and Mexican Joe [had] exerted on the rising generation« (»Young Liverpool and the Wild West« 1887: 8).

Women were just as susceptible. Several girls proposed marriage to any cowboy that would have them (though a handsome young man named Texas Jack was particularly popular), and a group of »love-lorn virgins« followed the troupe as it toured the country. »It is melancholy«, concluded one British paper,

»how shabbily our effete manhood contrasts with that of Mexican Joe and his satellites. We are content to follow the ladies and to fall in raptures at their feet. Mexican Joe and his cowboys, on the contrary, get the ladies to follow them and to prostrate themselves in abject worship before them.« (»Mexican Joe and His Satellites« 1887: 2)

These anxieties about British masculinity tap into wider concerns about degeneration and the future of the Empire but they also capture the core dynamic explored in this chapter: the tension between American modernity and British history. By the 1880s, the inevitability of an American future was hardly in doubt. Even the most vociferous critics of American manners recognised the ability of this ›go-ahead‹ country to outpace Britain, first in economic and then in cultural terms. Literary humourists like Wilde and *Punch* responded to these developments by asserting the beauty and authority of history and the good taste that sprang from a deep historical tradition; America, in the process, was laughed at for its inability to appreciate Old-World values and institutions. Yet, in Twain's battle between a traditional knight and a modern cowboy we hear another voice. The defenders of chivalry and historical tradition are drowned out by the cheering of the crowd. It is the unmistakeable sound of an emerging mass public, ready to break free from the past and embrace a new American Century.

## WORKS CITED

Adeler, Max (1882): *The Fortunate Island and Other Stories*, Boston: Lee and Shepard.
»Alhambra Palace« (1858): In: *The Times* 11 November, 5.
»Almanack« (1878): In: *Punch* 9 December, 1-17.
»Americanisms« (1889): In: *Daily News* 31 January, 4.
Arnold, Matthew (1869): *Culture and Anarchy: An Essay in Political and Social Criticism*, London: Smith, Elder and Co.
Arnold, Matthew (1882): »A Word About America«. *The Nineteenth Century* 63, 680-696.
Arnold, Matthew (1887): »Up to Easter«. *The Nineteenth Century* 123, 629-643.
Arnold, Matthew (1888): »Civilization in the United States«. *The Nineteenth Century* 134, 481-496.
Dickens, Charles (1842): *American Notes for General Circulation*, London: Chapman and Hall.
Engerman, Stanley L./Kenneth L. Sokoloff (2000): »Technology and Industrialization, 1790-1914«. In: Stanley L. Engerman/Robert E. Gallman

(eds.), *The Cambridge Economic History of the United States*, vol. 2: *The Long Nineteenth Century*, Cambridge: CUP, 367-401.

Enkvist, Nils Erik (1953): *American Humour in England Before Mark Twain*, Åbo: Åbo Akademi.

Gladstone, William E. (1878): »Kin Beyond the Sea«. *North American Review* 127.264, 179-212.

Gladstone, William E. (1890): »A Duel«. *North American Review* 150.398, 1-27.

»Imported Humour« (1882): In: *Leeds Mercury* 29 April, 1.

»It Has Long Been Well Known« (1899): In: *Glasgow Herald* 7 September, 6.

Jortner, Maura L. (2005): »Playing America on Nineteenth-Century Stages; or, Jonathan in England and Jonathan at Home«. PhD Thesis, University of Pittsburgh.

Lewis, Arnold (1997): *An Early Encounter With Tomorrow: Europeans, Chicago's Loop, and the World's Columbian Exposition*, Chicago: U of Illinois P.

Lustig, T.J. (2008): »Twain and Modernity«. In: Peter Messent/Louis J. Budd (eds.), *A Companion to Mark Twain*, Oxford: Blackwell, 78-93.

Mackenzie, F.A. (1902): *The American Invaders*, London: Grant Richards.

»The Man About Town« (1884): In: *The County Gentleman* 23 February, 229.

»Mexican Joe and His Satellites« (1887): In: *Sheffield Independent* 18 November, 2.

Montgomery, Maureen E. (1989): *Gilded Prostitution: Status, Money, and Transatlantic Marriages, 1870-1914*, London: Routledge.

»Mr. Edison At Home« (1878): In: *Freeman's Journal* 11 October, 2.

»Mr Gladstone Has Addressed« (1878): In: *Daily News* 18 September, 4-5.

»The New Number« (1878): In: *The Times* 19 September, 7.

Nicholson, Bob (2012a): »Jonathan's Jokes: American Humour in the Late-Victorian Press«. *Media History* 18.1, 33-49.

Nicholson, Bob (2012b): »Looming Large: America and the Victorian Press, 1865-1902«. PhD Thesis. University of Manchester. (www.digitalvictorianist.com/2013/04/looming-large-america-and-the-victorian-press-1865-1902).

Nicholson, Bob (2012c): »›You Kick the Bucket; We Do the Rest!‹: Jokes and the Culture of Reprinting in the Transatlantic Press«. *Journal of Victorian Culture* 17.3, 273-286.

»Odious Comparisons« (1878): In: *Blackburn Standard* 21 September, 5.

»Precious Pavement« (1896): In: *Punch* 8 August, 69.

»Some Yankee Notions« (1890): In: *The Scots Observer* 18 January, 245-246.
Stead, F. Herbert (1893): »The Civic Life of Chicago: An Impression Left on a Guest after a Visit of a Dozen Days«. *Review of Reviews* 8, 93-96.
Stead, W.T. (1890): »Mark Twain's New Book«. *Review of Reviews* 1.2, 144-156.
Stead, W.T. (1902): *The Americanisation of the World; or, The Trend of the Twentieth Century*, London: Horace Markley.
Stedman, Jane W. (1953): »American English in *Punch*, 1841-1900«. *American Speech* 28.3, 171-180.
Twain, Mark (1889): *A Yankee at the Court of King Arthur*, London: Chatto and Windus.
Welland, Dennis (1978): *Mark Twain in England*, London: Chatto and Windus.
Wilde Oscar (1887): »The American Man«. *The Court and Society Review* 4.145, 241-343.
Wilde, Oscar (1906 [1887]): *The Canterville Ghost*, London: John W. Luce and Company.
»Wit and Humour« (1892): In: *Evening Post* [Wellington] 26 November, 2.
»Yankee Humour« (1887): In: *Belfast News-Letter* 6 January, 7.
»Yankee Notions« (1894): In: *Hampshire Telegraph* 2 June, 12.
»Yankee Snacks« (1892): In: *Newcastle Weekly Courant* 2 July, 2.
»Yankee Snacks« (1893): In: *Newcastle Weekly Courant* 22 July, 2.
»Young Liverpool and the Wild West« (1887): In: *Birmingham Daily Post* 13 October, 8.

# ›There Wont Be Inny Show Tonite‹
Humoring the Returns of Scopic Violence in
Suzan-Lori Parks's *Venus*

IRVIN J. HUNT

> »I can get more out of history if I joke with it than if I shake my finger and stomp my feet.«
> (PARKS 1994: 26)

## TRAGEDY'S COMIC REPETITION

In 1810 a Khoisan South African woman by the name of Sarah or Sartjie Bartman was smuggled to London to be exhibited as a ›freak‹.[1] Her keeper Hendrick Cezar, a slaveholding free black, entered into negotiations with Alexander Dunlop, a white doctor in the British Army stationed in South Africa, for they believed her unusually large posterior, her ›steatopygia‹, as it was categorized, would draw enough crowds in the London freak shows to bring a healthy profit. Hendrick Cezar's brother Peter, who three years earlier had captured Bartman to serve as Hendrick's nursemaid, helped finance the venture. He was highly experienced in the business of ethnographic display. To the extent that agreement was possible, Bartman agreed

---

1 The Khoisan people, the Khoekheon, »native to South Africa since prehistoric times«, were called the ›Hottentots‹ by the European colonists (Holmes 2007: 9).

to a contract which stipulated that, while carrying out some domestic duties, she would be paid part of the profits of the exhibition and be repatriated in five years. In September, under the banner of »The Hottentot Venus«, Bartman, along with other human ›wonders‹, was presented to a London crowd at 225 Picadilly Circus. A notice read: »Parties of Twelve and upwards, may be accommodated with Private Exhibition of the Hottentot [...] between Seven and Eight O'clock in the Evening« (Sharpley-Whiting 1999: 18). Bartman was either twenty-one or twenty-two at the time and would die in a mere five or six years. Yet even after her death the show continued. Because of what it ›proved‹ to comparative anatomists about the superiority of Europeans over other species in the ›great chain of being‹, her dead body was molded in wax, and her genitalia and brain were removed, then preserved in a jar.[2] This mold, together with her remains, was kept on display at the Musée de l'Homme in Paris until 1976 with a brief reinstallation in 1994.[3]

Pulitzer Prize-winning playwright Suzan-Lori Parks focuses on this history of Bartman in her 1996 production *Venus,* which opened at the Joseph Papp Public Theater in New York in May that year.[4] Co-produced with

---

2   For a detailed account of Bartman's appropriation into the scientific racism of the nineteenth century, cf. Gilman (2010). Gilman writes, »The antithesis of European sexual mores and beauty is the black, and the essential black, the lowest exemplum of mankind on the great chain of being, is the Hottentot. The physical difference of the Hottentot is, indeed, the central nineteenth-century icon for sexual difference between the European and the black« (16).

3   The reinstallation acknowledged Bartman's story as an example of institutional and continued racism, for it sought to evidence »the harsh, racist, portrayal of aboriginal peoples by nineteenth century painters and sculptors« (Raghaven 1996: A33). That same year, Nelson Mandela made a formal request to French president François Mitterand to repatriate Bartman's remains (cf. Holmes 2007: 103).

4   What to call Sarah Bartman remains a persistent question throughout the play, where she is variously named The Venus Hottentot, The Girl, Miss Saartjie Baartman and the Hottentot Venus. I will use Bartman to refer to the person beyond the play and The Venus for the figure within it. Sartjie is her Afrikaans name, which translates to ›little Sarah‹. As Susan Warner observes, »The suffix ›tjie‹ is a diminutive denoting endearment, but in the context of colonialism this form was used by whites to demean indigenous peoples and enforce racial hier-

Richard Foreman, *Venus* extends the non-naturalistic portrayal Parks became known for through such noted works as *Imperceptible Mutabilities in the Third Kingdom* (1989), *The Death of the Last Black Man in the Whole Entire World* (1992) and *The America Play* (1994), all of which meditate, at least in part, on the ethics of depicting scopic violence through absurdist humor. Indeed, Bartman might be considered the very »symbol of an era of oppression and colonialism«, especially in its scopophilic dimensions, and in the play she becomes both the target and maker of an outrageous laughter (Holmes 2007: 104). *Venus* traces Bartman's life between her arrival in England and her death and dissection in France, with the first and last scene staging her as an articulate ›haint‹, »one who haunts the present« (Hartman 2008: 5). The play within the play, a mise-en-abyme, like the comic language itself (words are spelled phonetically as in ›inny‹ for ›any‹; and grammatical links, like copulas and transitive verbs between nouns, are omitted), highlights the way we look at the colonized female body, how we watch it performed and read its traces. With this focus on seeing, Parks draws attention to the »impossibility« of recovering from the archive the »enslaved woman in the Atlantic world«, an archive that most often records not who these women were, but the imperialistic excesses that »transformed them into commodities and corpses, and identified them with names tossed-off as insults and crass jokes«, Hottentot, Venus, etc. (ibid.: 1). In the play, Parks puts further emphasis on the breach between the record of Bartman and Bartman the person by reproducing archival documents with only slight variation, like written accounts by Bartman's spectators. Like surrealist playwright Adrienne Kennedy, who inspires Parks's work, Parks extends the project of encountering the ways the colonial domination of black bodies during the era of Atlantic slavery reasserts itself in the postcolonial present.[5]

---

archies, in much the same way that black adults were (and in some cases still are) referred to as ›boys‹ and ›girls‹ by whites in America« (2008: 181). On Bartman's 1811 birth certificate appears the name Sarah, which is simply the anglicized version of her name, not the attempt to dignify her as an adult (cf. Sharpley-Whiting 1999: 19).

5   Particularly, Kennedy's *Funnyhouse of a Negro* (1964) compelled Parks, as she claims, to »take weird rifts and shifts of character« (Wetmore 2007: 8).

Despite or perhaps because of its outrageous humor, Parks's *Venus* stays true to much of the documented history up to 1996.[6] The doctor who undertook the dissection of Bartman's body, the famous French naturalist Georges Cuvier, is represented in the play as The Baron Docteur. The brothers without whom Bartman would not have gone to England, Hendrick and Peter, are staged, respectively, as The Man and the Mans Brother. The uncertainty of whether Bartman died from exposure to cold, from alcoholism or from a misdiagnosed disease, is also represented, but with this representation comes another explanation for her death: an over-exposure to a scopic violence, to »›machineries‹ and regimes of representation« (Hall 1995: 200). Nothing in Bartman's documented story comes without some scopophilic dimension. Aside from the protests that led to the final removal of Bartman's display and her celebrated return to South Africa, the sexual excitement her wax molding aroused in some of the visitors to the museum was also cited as a reason for taking her body down.[7] By referring to these facts, Parks never lets the audience forget the sexual violence entwined in Bartman's recorded history, entwined so thoroughly that any hint of pleasure in watching the performance of her story becomes problematic and ethically questionable.

To the question of what type of aesthetic form would take all this into account and force the audience to think about how to ethically enter such aestheticized violence, Parks responds with theater of the absurd. We should differentiate Parks's absurdist theater from Beckett's or Camus', only to the extent that theirs underscores a meaningless existence. In a reading of Artaud, Derrida sums theirs up nicely: »speech which is self-destructive, which once more becomes gesture or hopeless occurrence, a negative relation of speech to itself, theatrical nihilism […] is still called theater of the absurd« (Derrida 1978: 13). In Parks, the absurd describes both the repetition of racial violence

---

6   In April of 2002 Bartman's remains were delivered to a group of South African delegates at their embassy in Paris. On 9 August she was finally buried with a Khoisan cleansing ritual in the region of her birth, Hankey, Eastern Cape (cf. Warner 2008).

7   André Langaney, director of the Musée de l'Homme, claimed that the body molding aroused some visitors to such an extent that it became the object of groping and the seat of masturbatory ejaculate. Allegedly, a female tour guide was even molested during a showing of Bartman (cf. Sharpley-Whiting 1999: 29).

and the hierarchization of the value of human life. In this form, Parks critiques the characters, the audience, the structure of the theater (which necessarily facilitates a potentially dangerous gazing), the creation of the play itself, and even Bartman as complicit in the voyeuristic violence.[8]

This sweeping critique did not sit well with many theater reviewers and scholars, and the suggestion that Bartman was complicit in her own exploitation stuck out above everything else. As scholar Jean Young writes, »Baartman was a victim, not an accomplice, not a mutual participant in this demeaning objectification, and Parks's stage representation of her complicity diminishes the tragedy of her life as a nineteenth-century Black woman« (1997: 700). Young reads The Venus as »enjoying her sexual exploitation« (ibid.), a misreading of Parks's humor, but one that points out the strange relationship that the humor creates between experiences of pain and pleasure. Some theater reviewers looked at this complicity favorably, which only fueled Young's criticism. Ben Brantley of the *New York Times* »believed *Venus* to be at its ›best when it drops its sweeping condemning historical perspective [...] this woman is clearly an accomplice in her own humiliation‹« (ibid.: 702). Robert Brustein reported similarly that »Parks managed to portray the humiliation of blacks in white society without complaint or indictment« (1996: 29). When everyone is indicted, it is easy to believe no one is, and the confusion created by that sweeping critique being couched in an absurd humor might have helped to push a large swathe of the audience to the exits midway through the play. According to Brustein, in the showing at the Yale Repertory Theater in New Haven one-third of the audience »decamped« (ibid.). Some critics saw Bartman's complicity as extending to the audience and cutting across racial lines; they read a dramatization of the divide between perpetuator and victim. Thus to William Triplett of the *Washington Post* »Parks deplores the exploitation of Venus, but is not above exploiting her to lecture whites on their need to feel ashamed and blacks on their duty to feel used« (Triplett 1998: C07). It is obvious that missing from all these readings is serious attention to Parks's comedy. Young significantly considers the play »fictitious melodrama« (1997: 699).

Interestingly enough, those who have turned to the humor to defend the ethics of the play turn out to push it toward the form of tragedy. Greg

---

8   For a comprehensive definition of the Theater of the Absurd, cf. »The Significance of the Absurd« in Esslin (2001).

Miller reconsiders what many deemed to be ›trivializing‹ of the real Bartman's dilemma. As mentioned above, according to some historical records Bartman died an alcoholic. Yet instead of alcohol, Parks shows her addicted to chocolates. Miller rightly states that »the history of chocolate suggests a history of colonization«, but then takes the insight a step away from the humor towards a tragic heaviness: »Parks imbues the scene with [...] poignant *weight*« (Miller 2002: 134).[9]

My argument is that Parks's aim is precisely to trivialize and remove the »weight« surrounding Bartman's story. This is not so that we may look at it without being crushed under its tragedy, not, in other words, to provide some comic distance. Rather, lightening the tragic underscores its everydayness. The risk of constructing history as tragedy is that such a construction might separate the past from our historical moment: We become the survivors with greater insight and the possibility of transcendence. And this tragedy turns Bartman into an exception, »a special case«, even as she symbolizes the sexual commodification of the black female (Holmes 2007: 104). It is important to note that the French government agreed to repatriate Bartman's mold and remains largely because South African anthropologist Phillip Tobias, French archaeologist Henry de Lumley, and others negotiating on behalf of South Africa »made it clear that [they] regarded Saartjie's case as unique, not as the forerunner of similar requests« (ibid.). As these negotiations continued (begun in 1995), Parks, by contrast, achieved the effect of making Bartman's story feel purely like an everyday part of today's reality, notably through the technique of repetition. The play's structure, the citations from the historical archive, and the dialogue of the characters are repeated to show Bartman as imbuing the present. This concurs with Alenka Zupancic's remarks in one of the most insightful philosophical readings of comedy:

»[The repetition of tragedy] involves the recognition of the fact that the tragic itself (with all its epic splendor) is ultimately but a mask of the really miserable, a mask that cannot survive its own repetition. The repetition of tragic events deprives the

---

9   For an alternative reading of the humor that focuses on the incongruities particular to the perspective of tragicomedy, which views opposites as similar, cf. Carpio (2008).

latter of their aura and transforms them into something common, unexceptional.« (2008: 175)

The normativity of the violence Bartman endured is signaled by the unbearable lightness of Parks's humor.

## »ARRIVING ON THE SCENE«: COMIC AFFECTS AND THE DENIAL OF DISTANCE

The denial of tragic pathos is announced from the very start of Parks's play, when Venus's death is denied all finality. In place of this is an abounding uncertainty about what to feel towards the (non-)event of her death. The Negro Resurrectionist, a character who functions as both an archivist digging up the past and the narrator commenting on the scenes, states matter-of-factly, »I regret to inform you that thuh Venus Hottentot iz dead« (Parks 1997: 3). Then others add, »There wont be inny show tonite« (ibid.). The irony compounds when Venus herself makes the same statement. Not only is the fact of her death emptied of its tragic weight (it is no more significant than a »regret«), but the singularity of its event is undermined as well. In none of the productions of the play is Venus presented as a ghost, which would preserve a sense of some divide between the temporal levels of then and now. But if she is not a ghost, what does speaking of herself as dead make her? The contradiction of how she occupies the present (as both fully dead and fully alive) is never resolved, keeping her presence a question and in turn opening up the possibilities of different types of affect. Furthermore, in the »list of scenes«, the scenes are written in reverse order, from 31 to 1, as if by the end of the play, the audience will experience a climactic revelation explaining why Venus died. This revelation would bring about an emotional purging, a climax of affect, tantamount to, if not greater than, witnessing the death of the hero. However, nothing of the sort happens. Venus simply repeats the same words with which she ironically begins (cf. 160-161). This denial of pathos surrounding her quasi-death, the unending demise and continued exploitation, is foreshadowed in the play's »overture«. There she responds to an explanation of why she died with a strange emotional expression, something she will repeat throughout the play:

THE MAN, LATER THE BARON DOCTEUR.
I say:
Perhaps,
she died of drink.

THE NEGRO RESURRECTIONIST.
It was the cold I think.

THE VENUS.
Uhhhh! (3-4)

How should one read this? What is Venus expressing here? Is it sadness, pain, frustration? Whatever it is she feels, it is couched in the conventional expression of impatience. In other words, Parks does not indicate exactly the emotion she is impatient with, but she does suggest that there is no end to it in sight.

The uncertainty – indeed, the general distance from tragic pathos – unsettles the typical orientation towards the death or abjection of blacks. Black suffering is typically met with pity and fear, compassion and terror, but there is a danger in this conventional reaction. As Saidiya Hartman claims, »rather than inciting indignation, too often [tragic scenes of blacks in subjection] immure us to pain by virtue of their familiarity« (1997: 3). In this light, Ann Cvetkovich's commentary on the humor in Lisa Kron's *2.5 Minute Ride*, applies equally to Parks. She »wants to jolt her audience out of its customary responses, including not only the numbness of no response but also the dutiful feelings of sympathy and horror, in order to confront them with other affects such as humor« (2003: 23). Yet aside from the sheer reiteration of tragic affect, the affects themselves are dangerous for the inter-subjective divides they create. As Ann Cheng notes, »the path connecting injury to pity and then to contempt can be very brief [...]. It can be damaging to say how damaging racism has been.« (2000: 14) In the speculative reading that Fred Moten gives to a photograph of a lynched body, there is a way the tortured body communicates that creates neither absolute divides nor undivided identification, but a range of affects in between. Venus's »Uhhhh!« brings to mind what Moten calls a situation in which »the looker is in danger of slipping not away, but into something less comfortable than horror – aesthetic judgment, denial, laughter« (2002: 65).

The »Uhhhh« could be any of these last three. Whatever it is, it falls short of the intensity of horror. In looking at herself dead either by cold or drink, dead by two quotidian realities, Venus emits an emotion that is comic not only in its designation of something akin to laughter, but also in the range of things it could be outside of the tragic affect we expect (Moten's asyndeton connotes this indeterminate range nicely). Among the many things that the affects of Parks's humor do is that they refuse to bring any closure to Bartman's life and death. Horror and fascination, pity and terror, by themselves are emotions that would close off the meaning of her experience and the person she became – i.e. a woman seemingly so abject horror cannot be separated from fascination. The affect of Parks's humor keeps Bartman and her history present as we question what it was.

There is a certain immediacy that Parks's comic affects create as well. To again think of them in relation to the pathos of tragedy is helpful. Tragedy's evocation of awe, along with its kindred emotions mentioned above, effects a distance between the audience and the hero. This is not to say that an identification does not also occur (i.e. sympathy or compassion), but that the exceptionality of it – by its sheer intensity – renders it distant from quotidian experience. Humor is usually thought of as creating a different type of distance, a necessary one from the pain that inspires it. In traditional interpretations of humor, whether it is laughter evoked or generally comic feeling, the humored affect separates one from the ache. Even the wit employed to respond to that ache contributes to the distancing, rendering the witty »indestructible«, as Freud remarked famously in his late essay on »Humor« (1928). However, the humor in Parks's play, particularly its comic affect, achieves neither a distance nor the opposite, a closeness. It achieves an immersion. When a member of the chorus repeats what some of the actual nineteenth-century apologists for the exhibition said to its protestors, Venus responds with a humor that expresses not a distance, but a feeling of being immersed.

A CHORUS MEMBER.
Thuh gals got bottoms like hot air balloons.
Bottom and bottoms and bottoms pilin up like
like 2 mountains. Magnificent. And endless.
An ass to write home about.
Well worth the admission price.

A spectacle a debacle a priceless prize, thuh filthy slut.
Coco candy colored and dressed all in *au naturel*
she likes when people peek and poke.

THE VENUS.
Hum drum hum drum. (7-8)

The way Venus expresses »hum drum hum drum«, glibly repeating it, in the face of her molestation (molestation because she adamantly does not like the »peek and poke«, as she says later) is uncomfortably comic. The words are comic because on their own they are meaningless, a nonsensical response. But what they sound out communicates the meaning of their comic feeling: humdrum, the commonplace. In other words, what ought to be exceptional, a voyeurism and a physical violation, are so normal they attract a degree of funniness.

When Venus laughs she expresses an even deeper sense of immersion. Consider the scene in which she seems to be given a choice to leave for England or remain in South Africa as a servant. The Brother and The Man, representing Hendrick Cezar and Peter Cezar, Bartman's keeper, encourage her to go.

THE GIRL [VENUS].
Do I have a choice? Id like to think on it.

THE BROTHER.
Whats there to think on? Think of it as a vacation!
2 years of work take half the take.
Come back here rich. Its settled then.

THE MAN.
Think it over, Girl. Go on.
Think it all over. (17)

After a very long pause, The Girl/Venus guffaws, »Hahahaha!« (18) To this The Man says, »What an odd laugh« (ibid.) – a rejoinder that unsettles what the laughter means. Is Venus laughing because she knows she has no choice, because the choices are almost equally terrible, or because she believes she will return superior in status to where she is now? The point in separating the laughter from its cause, making it linger in open space, is less to suggest it could be expressing any one of those thoughts than to suggest it is expressing all of them. That the laughter is described as »odd«, which also means »surplus«, reinforces the idea that it designates a complex of affects. There is no safe-space from which Venus looks on contemplatively and laughs: The laughter itself is bound within her circumstance, effecting no change to it or her disposition within it.

This surplus laughter withholds the futurity of catharsis. As Glenda Carpio remarks, whatever it expresses, it is not cathartic since Venus does not »release [...] anger and pathos« (2008: 228). »The denial of her own catharsis«, Carpio continues, »leaves the black body to suffer with no guarantee that the ritual of reinstantiation [restaging the exhibition of Bartman's body] will lead audiences to deep exploration and change« (ibid.). Because Bartman does not move beyond her predicament or transcend it, neither does the audience, as the conventional logic of spectator psychology goes. Parks places audience members inside, not beyond Bartman's circumstance. The continual wrestling with a complex of affects, a complex that denies the purity of catharsis, might be the closest thing to a guarantee that the audience might change and alter, if necessary, their orientation to black suffering. Nonetheless, Carpio's point that »deep [...] change« is hardly guaranteed is well taken, for transformation, a movement beyond the painful present, is hardly provided through Venus's laughter. The humor, then, enacts what Parks calls »arriving on the scene«:

»A playwright should pack all five, all six – all 7 senses. The $6^{th}$ helps you feel another's pulse at great distances; the $7^{th}$ is the sense of humor. Playwrights can come from the most difficult circumstances, but having a sense of humor is what happens when you ›get out of the way‹. It's sort of Zen. Laughter is very powerful – it's not a way of escaping anything but a way of arriving on the scene.« (Parks 1995: 15)

Zen is the practice of immersing oneself in the historical present. And to »get out of the way« is to refuse to impose one's own »difficult circumstances« on those of another. It is to see them as inseparable.

## Comic Self-Consciousness and the Merging of Selves

The erasure of absolute divisions between past and present also occurs between people of different sexual, racial and economic backgrounds, between, that is, Self and Other. The comic conflation of egos appears in the overture to *Venus* when characters deliberately confuse the audience about who they are. At first the characters each announce themselves. The Negro Resurrectionist calls out, »The Negro Resurrectionist!« (1) The Chorus exclaims, »The Chorus of the 8 Anatomists!« (2) But then the »The Man, later the Baron Docteur« states, »The Negro Resurrectionist!« and so on (ibid.). While in some productions the Resurrectionist was played by a black actor, he could easily be of any race. He could have that name because he is a Negro or because he resurrects Negroes. Furthermore, as a gravedigger he does not belong to the same economic class as the doctor. In fact, this point is emphasized at the end of the play, when the doctor's colleague and friend, The Grade-School Chum, pressures the Resurrectionist through money and influence to release Venus into his custody (151). In addition to these confusing announcements of character, the list of characters (cf. »The Roles«) is equally playful. Consider the gender transformation stated in »The Mans Brother, later the Mother-Showman, later the Grade School Chum«. To reinforce the notion of intersecting identities, Parks also employs the comic device of mimicry. Characters will repeat with slight variation the lines already said by others in such a way as if they are their own. For example, the Resurrectionist says of Venus, »When Death met her Death deathd her and left her to rot« (9), and she repeats this statement at the end, except that she substitutes »love« for »her« (161).

The effect of these mergings, what Ben-Zvi calls »the play between discourses«, is to interrogate binary thinking (quoted in Geis 2008: 191). It is the thinking of identities, selves, or others within binaries that Patricia Hill Collins considers a leading cause behind racial, sexual and class discrimination. »The foundations of intersecting oppressions«, writes Collins, »become grounded in interdependent concepts of binary thinking, oppositional difference, objectification, and social hierarchy« (2000: 71). The insight recalls the postmodernist Foucauldian thesis of the »Death of Man«, a summary of which elucidates how she addresses binary thinking. Foucault posits that the discursive constitution of the subject spells »the disappearance of man« and the »possibility of knowing him empirically«, knowing him as autonomous and at least partially beyond language, a thesis that certainly dismantles conceptual binaries (Foucault 1970: 385-386). But rather than endorsing what Seyla Benhabib (1995: 20) calls the »strong« version of this theory, endorsing, that is, the impossibility of agency, self-reflexivity, identity and so on, Parks preserves the notion that one can speak within a discourse without already being spoken.[10] She does this by adding a new word within a character's mimicry of another's speech, like »love« replacing »her«, as we saw above. Indeed, she goes as far as to offer this repetition with a difference as an epistemological frame through which to interpret her plays. She states, »›Repetition and Revision‹ is a concept integral to the Jazz esthetic in which the composer or performer will write or play a musical phrase once and again and again; etc. – with each revisit the phrase is slightly revised. ›Rep & Rev‹ as I call it is a central element in my work« (Parks 1995: 8-9). By abbreviating the phrase Parks does more than create a humorous reference. The humor itself suggests that revisions are minor, the space for agency there, but small.

It is in this light we should interpret Venus's complicity. When The Baron Docteur wants to move the exhibit from London to Paris, Venus tries to negotiate a greater remuneration than her current pittance. »100 a week« and »My own room«, she demands. But »Yll sleep with me«, he says. »Say ›yes‹«. There is a long pause and then The Mother-Showman returns rattling »a stick along the bars of the cage« (89). In the face of her abusive ›mother‹ and the lascivious Baron, Venus says »(yes.)« The parentheses underscore that her agreement is bound, compressed by two options, neither one of which allow for much freedom, an »interregnum space where true choice becomes impossible« (Wright 2002: 79). Yet the parentheses also show her attempt to find a freedom in an interstice, however unsuccessful that turns out to be. Parks turns to a comic form because, as Suzan Langer remarks in her foundational study on comedy, the comic character understands the radical contingency of everyday life (cf. 1979: 333). As opposed

---

10 Seyla Benhabib makes a valuable distinction between »strong« and »weak« versions of postmodernist theories. The strong versions dissolve the ability to think of an emancipatory project, while the weak preserve them. The weak version of the »Death of Man« thesis is a »radical situatedness«, where the subject is situated in not only language but »various social linguistic and discursive practices« (1995: 20).

to romance, a form that figures a »self-indentified« subject who defeats a blocking character or society (cf. White 1973: 8), comedy imagines the limitation of choice and one's awareness of chance. Venus's awareness is intimated in her being the very embodiment of a life-after-death (»The Venus Hottentot iz dead«). Parks might contend that the Venus she conveys is »complicit«, though on closer inspection complicity alone hardly describes her involvement in her state of coercion.[11] In a world where the self is wrapped in the other's language – and where Venus's conception of herself is largely informed by the oppressive language in which she speaks, the manipulation of her keepers, a manipulative complicity, is not only a more accurate description but may also be the necessary precondition towards emancipation.

While Venus does not have unencumbered agency, she performs a multiplicity of roles with many skills. She moves between the professional positions of lawyer, historian, poet and merchant. She speaks multiple languages (French, English, Dutch, along with her native Khoisan tongue). During the trial, she speaks as her own attorney and offers information about herself in comic understatement. One witness testifies that she poses a danger to people viewing her, for the witness's husband died two days later – died, Venus says, from the »shock« of her »butts« (69). The witness implies that the death might have also happened because of a feather she wore that was supposed to »bring good luck« (ibid.). Venus responds by speaking of herself in the third person, a speech-act noticeable especially here since the witness referred to herself in the form of the »I«.

VENUS.
Exhibit B:
A feather from the head of the
so-called Venus H.
The feathers were said to bring good luck—

---

11 Michele Wallace points out that »exhibitees [at world fairs] were not enslaved or dragged unwillingly to fairgrounds or forcibly bound. A more accurate way to describe their relative position to their keepers is to say that they were coerced. They were not fully appraised of their rights in the situation. They were often promised a great deal more money and comfort than they received« (2010: 152).

when stroked such feathers cured infertility.
When ground and ingested these same feathers proved
a brilliant aphrodisiac. (70)

She recognizes the difference between the Venus her spectators refer to (the »so-called«) and who she is in truth. But more, she subtly mocks the death of the witness's husband. Whereas the witness believes he died of shock, she suggests he died from desire that he could not excite himself. Such desire having been dead for so long, she gave him an »aphrodisiac« to bring it back to life, to »cure« its »infertility«. It was brilliant in its ability to rid her of his demeaning presence. The mockery of the witness and her husband is subtle enough to intimate that Venus's trickery is nothing out of the ordinary, for it characterizes daily living in a world of normative violence. But without making the trickster techniques extraordinary, Parks also refuses to make much of the binary opposition between an empowered and disempowered subject.

Therefore, while Venus's talents are many, Parks makes a point of portraying them as normal. Consider, for instance, her adoption of French. She is tested by the doctor's colleagues, the 8 Anatomists, to see how much French she has acquired. They ask her to translate phrases from English, which she does accordingly: »Et maintenant, le livre est / sur ma tete!« They reply: »Thats excellent! And shes only been here / what, Sir, 6 months?« (112). To have learned similar sentences, along with other colloquial phrases, in the span of half a year indicates intelligence, but not genius. One of the traps that await a romantic view of an historically oppressed person's achievements is the fatuous concept of exceptionalism. The Docteur implies such when he adds: »We study a people as a group / and dont throw away our years of labor / because of one most glorious exception« (ibid.). Parks once said in an interview: »I could have written a two-hour saga with Venus being the victim. But she's multifaceted. She's vain, beautiful, intelligent, and, yes, complicit« (Elam/Ryaner 2008: 279). By making her multifaceted without making her various skills extraordinary, she returns Venus the myth, the »so-called Venus H«, to a full humanity. Her normal weaknesses, like vanity, and her normal strengths, like intelligence, refuse the opposite of her reduction to a »creature« – her inflation to a romanticized demigod. Nothing better communicates the equivalence of these two poles than her show-time moniker, the Hottentot

Venus, the beast goddess, a name Venus, I am claiming, persistently interrogates.

In the same way that the audience is prohibited from exalting her, they are prohibited from exalting themselves. In no place is this leveling between the audience and the characters more explicit than in the intermission. While the audience is encouraged to walk out of the theatre, The Baron Docteur enunciates one of the most damaging effects of the dissection and examination of Bartman's body, the invention of scientific racism. The Baron speaks from his journal, which is a close translation of Cuvier's. Most of what he reads are notes on the measurements of Bartman's body. He begins, »the height, measured after death, was 4 feet 11 and ½ inches« (91). He proceeds to give descriptions of her pubic region, her steatopygia, her labia minora and majora, and many other parts of her anatomy. He speaks directly to the audience compounding their discomfort:

I do invite you, Distinguished Gentlemen,
Colleagues and yr Distinguished Guests,
if you need *relief*
please take yourselves uh breather in thuh lobby.
My voice will surely carry beyond these walls and if not
my finds are published. (92)

The emphasis on »relief« is ironic in that it is the very thing disallowed by his deliberation about the erotic way and the heinous reason he dismembered Bartman's body. To make matters worse, he puts the audience in two double binds. First, if they leave his voice will carry beyond the walls, he will spread its influence beyond the theatre, but if they stay they are accepting the position of his »distinguished gentlemen« and indulging, like the 8 Anatomists, in Bartman's posthumous oppression. Ilka Saal spells out the second double bind nicely: »to leave means to ignore the reality of the text, to shrug it off as yet another commodity offered up to use for consumption, while to stay means willingly to submit to and participate in a discourse of blatant biological racism« (2005: 61). In a word, any righteousness or moral superiority felt among the members of the audience is unsettled, if not expunged. Through The Baron's twisted humor, they are forced to question their own complicity in the erection of the scopic regime surrounding

Bartman, for complicity lies in something as simply and seemingly innocent as exiting the theatre, leaving a past event behind.

The ultimate effect of this imposed sense of entwinement with those one wishes to scorn is temporal. Simply put, one takes the play with oneself after it is over. What Parks calls the »strange relationship between theatre and real-life« persists. She hardly could have devised a better way of not only joining, but also imbedding history into the present. In so doing, she evades the critique that Roland Barthes (1974) directed at parodic texts or plays: that they strengthen the very norm they undermine by positing themselves as temporary. Because parody legitimizes official law, Barthes called it a »classic« discourse (1974: 45). As the »temporary liberation from prevailing truth and from established order«, parodies provide relief precisely so that the audience can return to their regular lives (Bakhtin 1984: 10). A fifteenth-century theological tract that Bakhtin quotes in his meditation on carnivalesque parody supports Barthes's point succinctly: »we permit folly on certain days so that we may later return with greater zeal to the service of God« (ibid.: 75). Parks's humor promises to work longer on its recipients and thereby becomes more effective as a mode of critique. Indeed, one could consider the intermission the climax, as it is the dramatic accumulation of multiple lines that implicate the audience as scopophilic voyeurs. Earlier The Mother-Showman speaks to the paying spectator of the freak show in a way that recalls the paying audience: »take a look at one for just a penny and a half / you can gawk as long as you like« (31). She reiterates the message a few scenes later: »Stand up thats it let Mother help ya. Lets give these folks their moneys worth« (46). These sorts of veiled references to the audience recur, and to the extent that their implication is at the highest point of tension in the middle of the play when the audience is asked to leave, the actual leave-taking when the play is over becomes climactic as well. The play is extended beyond ›the walls‹ of the theater.

Embroiling the audience in Bartman's history calls them to take responsibility for her continued violation and that of the other women her figure symbolizes – a collective culpability that Parks applies to herself. Parks does not allow her audience to forget that in the same way Cezar, Cuvier and others profited from Bartman's exhibition, so, too, do the play's makers. Thinly veiled references link the staging of Bartman to that of Parks's version. We see this most bitingly in a scene where Venus counts the money accrued from the freak show (cf. 50-52). The Mother-Showman interjects by numbering the batches of cash, until she reaches batch number 31, which is also the total amount of scenes in the play. That her chronological numbering opposes the reverse numbering of the play's scenes is suggestive. Deborah Geis remarks that the »counting down of scenes underscores the inevitability of Venus's demise« (2008: 80). To the extent this is true, the Mother's counting up counters Venus's death, as well as the forces that led to it. The implication is that even while the play in some ways reifies Bartman's oppression it also reverses it, an opposition that ultimately underscores the ethical riskiness but possible productivity of dramatizing Bartman's life, however fabulated. A question emerges here that lingers unanswered and is perhaps unanswerable: »is the cost, the reinstantiation of black suffering, too high?« (Carpio 2008: 228)

The notions of culpability that underlie the play are no black and white matter. »The main thing folks misunderstand in *Venus*«, Parks claims in an interview, »is not so much the ›race‹ issue, but the ›blame‹ or ›responsibility‹ issue« (Wetmore 2007: 137). There is a distinction the play underlines between being blamed and being culpable, a distinction that has everything to do with its comic form, which, like modern comedies, imagines an interactive, social world. Blame creates a moral hierarchy, the blamed person being placed lower, or morally inferior to the one exacting the charge. Responsibility, however, is less damning. As Kenneth Burke remarks in *Attitudes Toward History*, »[c]omedy deals with *man in society*, tragedy with *cosmic man*« (1937: 52-53). Burke claims that comedies are inclusive in the way they ultimately treat those responsible for wrongs, reincorporating them within the social fold:

»Like tragedy, comedy warns against the dangers of pride, but its emphasis shifts from *crime* to *stupidity* […]. The progress of humane enlightenment can go no further than in picturing people not as *vicious*, but as *mistaken*. When you add that people are *necessarily* mistaken, that *all* people are exposed to situations in which they must act as fools […] you complete the comic circle.« (Ibid.: 52)

The difference between Burke's definition of comedy and the comic world Parks imagines is not that everyone is ›foolish‹ in equal measure or that the wrongs were unintentional, but that no one can be free of blame, that all are responsible. To again cite Burke, one of the greatest effects the comedy achieves, and Parks's comic play particularly, is »enabl[ing] people to observe themselves while acting. It's ultimate would not be passiveness but maximum consciousness« (ibid.: 171). This conscious and collectively culpable community is precisely what is inspired by Park's treatment of the voyeurism Bartman endured.

If the humor in Parks points to the ways in which the past is embroiled in the present and ways in which that past repeats itself, where does this leave the future? How does the play imagine progress? Let us turn to a comment Parks makes about one of her previous works that equally applies to *Venus*:

»Rep & Rev texts create a real challenge for the actor and director as they create a physical life appropriate to that text. In such plays we are not moving from A → B but rather, for example, from A → A → A → B → A. Through such movement we refigure A. And if we continue to call this movement FORWARD PROGRESSION, which I think it is, then we refigure the idea of forward progression.« (Parks 1995: 9-10)

The humor in *Venus* does not move back in order to move forward; it moves back as a way of moving forward. Staging the repetition of a repetition, repeating on stage what is already being played out again and again, is an avenue towards a new confrontation with what emerged in the nineteenth century as a racially inflected voyeurism. Because Parks renders Venus as the synechdochal figure for »hundreds of thousands of other girls who *share* her circumstances«, ultimately the play compels us to think of the historically traumatic nature of scopic violence in opposition to the singularity, the ›special case‹, that ›trauma‹ usually denotes (Hartman 2008: 2, emphasis mine). But more importantly, rather than the play imagining an end to the exploitation of the black female body it asks the audience to enact that end. Reiterating what one would wish to bury incites indignation, the precursor to action, and pointing out the ways one is implicated in that reiteration inspires a self-consciousness: As we look to stop quotidian acts of voyeuristic violence we must simultaneously look at ourselves.

## Works Cited

Bakhtin, Mikhail (1984): *Rabelais and His World*, Bloomington: Indiana UP.
Barthes, Roland (1974): *S/Z*, trans. Richard Miller, New York: Hill & Wang.
Benhabib, Seyla (1995): *Feminist Contentions: A Philosophical Exchange*, New York: Routledge.
Burke, Kenneth (1937): *Attitudes Toward History*, vol. 1, New York: New Republic.
Brustein, Robert (1996): »Robert Brustein on Theatre«. In: *New Republic* 20 May, 29.
Carpio, Glenda R. (2008): *Laughing Fit to Kill: Black Humor in the Fictions of Slavery*, New York: OUP.
Cheng, Ann (2000): *The Melancholy of Race: Psychoanalysis, Assimilation, and Hidden Grief*, Oxford: OUP.
Collins, Patricia-Hill (2000): *Black Feminist Thought: Knowledge, Consciousness, and the Politics of Empowerment*, New York: Routledge.
Cvetkovich, Ann (2003): *An Archive of Feelings: Trauma, Sexuality, and Lesbian Public Cultures*, Durham/NC: Duke UP.
Derrida, Jacques (1978): »The Theater of Cruelty and the Closure of Representation«. *Theater* 9.3, 6-19.
Elam, Harry/Alice Rayner (2008): »Body Parts: Between Story and Spectacle in *Venus* by Suzan-Lori Parks«. In: Jeanne Colleran/Jenny Spencer (eds.), *Staging Resistance: Essays on Political Theater*, Ann Arbor: U of Michigan P, 265-282.
Esslin, Martin (2001): *The Theatre of the Absurd*, London: Methuen.
Foucault, Michel (1970): *The Order of Things: An Archeology of the Human Sciences*, New York: Vintage.
Freud, Sigmund (1927): »Humor«. In: James Strachey (trans.), *Standard Edition of the Complete Psychological Works of Sigmund Freud*, vol. 21, London: Hogarth, 160-166.
Geis, Deborah (2008): *Suzan-Lori Parks*, Ann Arbor: U of Michigan P.
Gilman, Sander (2010): »The Hottentot and the Prostitute«. In: Deborah Willis (ed.), *Black Venus 2010: They Called Her »Hottentot«*, Philadelphia/PA: Temple UP, 15-31.
Hall, Stuart (1995): »New Ethnicities«. In: Bill Ashcroft/Gareth Griffiths/Helen Tiffin (eds.), *The Post-Colonial Reader*, London: Routledge, 199-202.

Hartman, Saidiya (1997): *Scenes of Subjection: Terror, Slavery, and Self-Making in Nineteenth Century America*, Oxford: OUP.
Hartman, Saidiya (2008): »Venus in Two Acts«. *Small Axe* 12.2, 1-14.
Holmes, Rachel (2007): *African Queen: The Real Life of the Hottentot Venus*, New York: Random House.
Langer, Suzan (1979): *Feeling and Form*, New York: Routledge.
Miller, Greg (2002): »The Bottom of Desire in Suzan-Lori Parks's *Venus*«. *Modern Drama* 45.1, 125-137.
Moten, Fred (2002): »Black Mo'nin«. In: David L. Eng/David Kazanjian (eds.), *Loss: The Politics of Mourning*, Berkeley: U of California P, 59-76.
Parks, Suzan-Lori (1994): »Alien Nation: An Interview with the Playwright by Michele Pearce«. *American Theatre* 13, 26.
Parks, Suzan-Lori (1995): »From Elements of Style«. In: *The America Play and Other Works*, New York: Theatre Communications Group, 6-18.
Parks, Suzan-Lori (1997): *Venus*, New York: Theatre Communications Group.
Raghaven, Sudarsan (1996): »Body Becomes Symbol of Oppression«. In: *Houston Chronicle* 11 February, A33.
Saal, Ilka (2005): »The Politics of Mimicry: The Minor Theater of Suzan-Lori Parks«. *South Atlantic Review* 20.2, 57-71.
Sharpley-Whiting, Denean (1999): *Black Venus: Sexualized Savages, Primal Fears and Primitive Narratives in French*, Durham/NC: Duke UP.
Triplett, William (1998): »London Derriere: Studio's Poignant ›Venus‹«. In: *The Washington Post* 13 March, C07.
Young, Jean (1997): »The Re-Objectification and Re-Commodification of Saartjie Baartman in Suzan-Lori Parks's *Venus*«. *African American Review* 31.4, 699-708.
Warner, Sara L. (2008): »Suzan-Lori Parks's Drama of Disinterment: A Transnational Exploration of *Venus*«. *Theatre Journal* 60, 188-199.
Wallace, Michele (2010): »The Imperial Gaze: Venus Hottentot, Human Display, and World's Fairs«. In: Deborah Willis (ed.), *The Black Venus 2010: They Called Her ›Hottentot‹*, Philadelphia/PA: Temple UP, 149-154.
Wetmore, Kevin (2007): »It's an Oberammergau Thing: An Interview with Suzan-Lori Parks«. In: Kevin Wetmore/Alycia Smith-Howard (eds.), *Suzan-Lori Parks: A Casebook*, New York: Routledge, 124-140.
White, Hayden (1973): *Metahistory: The Historical Imagination in Nineteenth-Century Europe*, Baltimore/MD: Johns Hopkins UP.

Wright, Laura (2002): »›Macerations'‹ French for ›Lunch‹: Reading the Vampire in Suzan-Lori Parks's *Venus*«. *Journal of Dramatic Theory and Criticism* 17.1, 69-86.

Zupancic, Alenka (2008): *The Odd One In: On Comedy*, Cambridge/MA: MIT.

# Geoff Hurst's Ball

Popular Tabloids and Humour on the Dark Side

MARTIN CONBOY

## HUMOUR IN THE BRITISH TABLOID PRESS

This chapter will explore the ways in which humour can be used as part of an editorial strategy in the British tabloid press when referring to historical events which conform to reader expectations of the representation of outsiders. Its main focus will be on the account published in two popular tabloid newspapers of the return of a football to England from Germany in 1996. The football was significant to English football fans as it was the ball that had been used in the World Cup final victory of England over West Germany in 1966. The scorer of a hat-trick in that victory, Geoff Hurst, should, according to tradition, have kept the ball after the game. Instead it disappeared and was only returned to Hurst after campaigns by the two newspapers brought the matter to the attention of the public. The fact that this chapter focuses on a story concerning football does not diminish its relevance for a study of the serious potential of humour in styling the acceptable face of prejudice. Humour has long been a staple within the editorially »imagined community« (Anderson 1987) of the British popular tabloid press. It may seem strange, at first sight, to highlight a humorous approach to the past within the discourse of a genre so closely associated with the present yet increasingly our traditional news media are moving from information provision towards greater contextualizations of news (cf. Pöttker 2012), and this includes historical contextualization.

Theorists on humour have claimed that it serves a range of important and identifiable functions such as the reassurance of superiority, the exposure of incongruity, demonstrating a levelling or distancing effect or else performing a relief function (cf. Morreall 1983). Most often humour can perform several of these functions simultaneously. Most importantly, humour as a whole is underpinned by social significance (cf. Bergson 2008 [1900] and Zijderveld 1983). In certain circumstances, these functions can combine to provide a challenge to authority while in others they can be employed to reinforce structures of dominance. Bakhtin (1984 [1940] and 1996 [1975]) is a renowned proponent of the destablilizing potential of comedy from below in his analyses of the dynamics of carnival, while in contrast the British tabloids appropriate this style of irreverent, populist humour often to disguise their reactionary tendencies with regard to issues of ethnicity, nation and gender (cf. Conboy 2002 and 2006).

Amusing the audience had become a core expectation in much of the press as newspapers turned increasingly to profitable mass markets towards the end of the nineteenth century in Britain. Within the press, humour became located in special subsections or, as markets for print grew, as standalone publications (cf. Nicholson 2012). Cartoons had been a part of print culture for centuries but their incorporation into regular periodicals, especially weekly or daily publications, had to wait until print and reprographic technologies had advanced sufficiently to incorporate topical material within the print cycle. By the 1880s the boundaries of the generic conventions were being drawn up. George Newnes's *Tit-Bits* was published from 1881 in the first example of a kind of weekly journalism which combined humorous writing with copious illustration, closely followed by *Ally Sloper's Half-Holiday* which was the first regular British comic weekly from 1884. In the United States, comic illustrations became a common feature of the burgeoning popular newspapers and from the1890s a key part of the rivalry and competition between Hearst and Pulitzer as they produced what became known as the Yellow Press. In fact, it was the appearance of a gangly, gormless mischievous character tinted with yellow called »The Yellow Kid« that this American version of the popular mass press was named after. Comics and cartoons provided both inter-newspaper competition and humour at each other's expense. The audience from the start was in on the jokes. This influence spread to popular newspapers in Britain with Harmsworth's *Daily Mail* (1896) and Pearson's *Daily Express* (1900) vying for popularity.

Beyond the explicit humour of the cartoon in popular newspapers, the inclusion of humorous angles into news reporting became both more prevalent and more generalized through the nineteenth century. This had been an occasional element in much popular periodical production down the centuries but it had been mainly confined to periodicals of a serious political intent such as the radical unstamped press of the first two decades of the nineteenth century and elements of the Chartist press from 1838 and more mainstream publications such as the satirical weekly *Punch* from 1841. It became more of a central feature in popular daily newspapers from the turn of the twentieth century. Its inclusion moves from sketches to commentary and leading articles with an increasing emphasis on irony as a tool of the editorial trade. This sort of approach to the news of the day was very much in keeping with several of the popular press's main characteristics. Its stance of sceptical and mocking authority enabled readers to identify as a community on a slightly different level in stark contrast to the traditional political constituencies beloved of the elite press. It allowed for an editorial distancing through bringing to the attention of a readership certain incongruities in the behaviour of those in public life. As popular newspapers became more nationalistic in their focus they could also deploy humour as a means to denigrate outsider groups or foreigners. Newspapers used xenophobia as a means to construct a sense of insider community (cf. McWilliam 1998). Particular victims of this popular prejudice were Indians, Boers, the French and the Jews.

The use of humour as an editorial device comes to full prominence in a British context as part of the rivalry between the *Sun* and the *Daily Mirror*. The *Daily Mirror* had been the best-selling popular tabloid newspaper in Britain from the late 1940s and had achieved an unprecedented circulation and reach. When Rupert Murdoch purchased the *Sun* in 1969 he decided that he could make it a more popular paper than the *Daily Mirror* by foregrounding ›fun‹, not taking things too seriously and, as the *Daily Mirror* had from the mid-1930s, appealing to a younger readership. The cross-over between comic culture and news media fitted well within the hybrid tradition of the popular press which the *Sun* set out to exploit. The competition between the two newspapers, still very much alive in the 1990s, was part of traditional tabloid rivalry. On the occasion focused on in this chapter we see the combination of the comic with another perennial of journalism and especially popular journalism: the scoop – one newspaper first with a particularly fresh news item.

In this case, the scoop was the return, from Germany to Britain, of the ball with which Geoff Hurst had scored the hat-trick in the 1966 World Cup Final. In the intervening years, this victory acquired heroic status amongst the nation's sporting memories, while the ball was in the possession of former German player Helmut Haller, who had taken it after the match in Wembley and kept it as a souvenir, against tradition. Thirty years later, both the *Sun* and the *Daily Mirror* revisited this event in a witty and populist engagement with popular history to win back this relic of modern sporting achievement. Both newspapers sought to persuade Haller to return the ball but eventually it was the *Daily Mirror* which succeeded. The *Sun* reported that money had been demanded for its return and although it was not explicitly admitted that the *Daily Mirror* had paid anything, the appearance of millionaire Richard Branson as a facilitator in the process photographed with the ball and Geoff Hurst in the *Daily Mirror* led one to conclude that Haller's demands had been met. In the reporting of this aftermath to a historic sports event, and in anticipation of a new one, the newspapers drew upon a lexicon of familiar stereotypes in a humorous vein to vie for popular legitimacy.

## THE TALE OF GEOFF HURST'S BALL

On 25, 26 and 27 April 1996, in the run-up to the European Football Championships which were to be held in England later that year, both the *Sun* and the *Daily Mirror* ran stories which laid claim to harnessing patriotic pride through retrieving the actual football with which England had won the World Cup in 1966. The rivalry bristled between the two newspapers, one boastful and the other dismissive of the coup which returned the ball to Geoff Hurst. A significant range of the tabloid repertoire is deployed: puns, populist association with the people's game, heroic personification, and the inscribing of history in the present for new readers.

On the second day of the mini-campaign, we have a fine example of the intertextual popular cultural orchestration so beloved of the British tabloids. A special edition of the *Sun*'s popular football strip *Striker* appeared on the *Sun*'s news pages for 26 April, drawn by Nash, the illustrator renowned for this popular cartoon series.[1] This special edition of *Striker* on 26 April provided a brief account of how Helmut Haller had made off with the ball from the 1966 World Cup Final. The story of the retrieval is summarized from start to finish in *Striker* without mention of the rival *Daily Mirror*'s decisive involvement. The dialogue bubbles feature a grumpy Helmut Haller, scorer of the first goal for West Germany, saying: »Enjoy your triumph, Hurst […] soon you will be more upset than if I had taken ze last sunbed« (Nash 1996: 4). Here we see two regular features of characterization in comic form. First, the transcription of the German's accent and second, an anachronistic allusion to the alleged practice often invoked in the tabloids, of the Germans stealing sunbeds from other tourists on holiday. Later in the strip cartoon we see another common intertextual feature in the echo of a stereotypically militaristic command mixed with an English vernacular expression: »On my head, son […]. zat is an order«. The role of the *Sun* is prominently proclaimed with a cartoon version of the paper's front page announcing: »SUN FINDS GEOFF HURST'S LOST BALL«. The strip depicts the decisive meeting in a traditional German Bierkeller as the *Sun* reporter confronts the ex-footballer with the words: »Come on, Helmut, give Geoff his ball back«.

At first the story is reported optimistically in the *Sun* on 25 April (cf. Kay 1996: 1). The tone is one of celebration on the location and promised return of the ball. However, on the 26th there is a marked shift as in addition to Nash's *Striker*-cartoon it is reported that far from being willing to hand over the ball, the Germans want £80,000 just for a photograph, under the front-page headline: »THE GREEDIEST KRAUTS ON EARTH« – a *Sun*

---

1   This strip cartoon itself had an unusually long run in its own right over twenty-four years from 1985 to 2009 and has just recently been relaunched in the paper. *Striker* was an imitation of *Roy of the Rovers* which had run as a football story in strip cartoon form in a boys' comic called *Tiger* from 1954. Roy of the Rovers has been described as »[t]he definitive comic-strip sporting hero 1954-1976 during« the heyday of British children's comic culture« (Chapman 2012: 93-95). The character was a storming centre-forward with a remarkable knack of scoring late winning goals for his team, Melchester Rovers, and only a knee injury kept him out of the 1966 World Cup squad itself. The use of a traditionally children's form in a newspaper is as old as the modern popular newspaper with roots back to the Yellow Press of Pulitzer and Hearst in the late nineteenth century.

»world exclusive« (Wooding 1996: 1). The *Sun* sets out a range of anti-German nicknames with resonances of militaristic stereotypes referring to Haller as: »Sour Kraut«, »crafty Kraut«. Inside the newspaper, an English comedian, Stan Boardman, famous for his anti-German, World War II stereotypes of the Germans, is drawn in for a couple of quotations which are used to amplify the paper's approach: »Comedian Stan Boardman declared war on the ›Jeermans‹ last night and said: ›They should've done what comes naturally – and just surrendered the ball‹« (Rae 1996: 4). Furthermore, the *Sun* opens a dedicated phone line on page five of this edition for readers to record their own views in time-honoured tabloid fashion: »TELL KRAUTS WHERE TO STICK THEIR BALL – are they kraut of order?«

On 27 April, in response to the phone line, the *Sun* reports that both Haller and their popular newspaper rivals at the *Daily Mirror* have received negative responses from their readers and introduce another stereotypical nickname in punning fashion: »Helmut's ball deal blasted [...] *Daily Mirror* panned. Sun readers last night blitzed German Helmut Haller [...]. [C]ash hun-gry Hallers« (Pyatt 1996: 11). The density of puns deployed as a humorous device is one of the features of popular tabloids which continues to distinguish them from their elite counterparts. This has been identified as a stylistic misdirection intended to deflect anxieties about some of the actual content:

»Interestingly, the *Sun* indulges in ›poetic‹ structures in places where it is being at its most outrageous about politics or sex. Cues are foregrounded to the point of self-parody. Deplorable values are openly displayed, pointedly highlighted; even a critical reader can be disarmed by pleasure in the awfulness of the discourse.« (Fowler 1991: 45)

One of the more obvious rhetorical strategies through which the tabloids attempt to reinforce their relationship with their readership is by employing colloquial expressions and slang in relation to the nation and its manifestations, both historical and contemporary. This appears to allow the newspapers to talk to their readers in their own, informal manner and further extends the claim of these papers to be on the side of the people, leading discussion in a highly constructed version of the vernacular. The implication of this language is that the tabloids are on the side of the people and opposed to the interests of the power-bloc (cf. Fiske 1994). It is a deliberate strategy to cement that ideological bond with a readership which sees itself as sceptical of the establishment and, by implication, the formalities of its language.

Not only is humour deployed more often in the tabloids but it is the irreverence and the coarseness of the humour which is alien to the more traditional newspapers even in their contemporary web manifestations. Compared to the elite press and the heavily regulated content of broadcast journalism in the UK, it is one example of how the popular press carves out a distinct territory where it can operate seemingly without intrusion from legislation or good taste. The mockery implicit in much of the tabloids' approach fits well within the patterns of popular culture down the centuries. It may have an anti-establishment tone to it but there is often little beyond this rhetoric as it seems to align with the outsider, the little person (Little Englander) but nearly always in terms of compliance with longer-term chauvinistic accounts of a lost Golden Age of the British nation. This is why the symbolism of World War II is so interesting: The range of reference is narrow enough to imply an insistence on an ethno-centric view of Britain and its identification of a particular version of the past as a key component of the present.

In contrast to the *Sun*'s coverage, the *Daily Mirror*'s account is more literal in claiming the major role in securing the return of Geoff Hurst's ball. The story first breaks, on 25 April 1996, accompanied by a photograph of Hurst scoring the third goal in the final in 1966 and plays on the rhythm of a famous phrase from the commentary of that day: »GIVE ME MY BALL BACK. ENGLAND'S 1966 World Cup hero Geoff Hurst wants his ball back – and it won't all be over until he gets it« (Oliver 1996: 11).[2] The following day the story is elevated to the front page emphasizing the nationalist context here which is especially important for sporting rivalry and even more so for one with such military significance:

»WORLD EXCLUSIVE SNATCH OF THE DAY I GET MY HANS ON HURST'S BALL
back in British hands [...]. The *Daily Mirror* tracked it down [...]. We persuaded him [Haller] that, following an appeal by hat-trick hero Hurst, it must be returned.« (Allen 1996: 1)

---

2  »Some people are on the pitch. They think it's all over. It is now.« Kenneth Wolstenholme, BBC commentator World Cup Final 1966.

On page two the national significance of the ball as sporting symbol for the present is reinforced by supporting quotes from a collection of managers, players and commentators from that era beneath the headline: »The supreme symbol of English football glory was on its way home last night – thanks to the *Mirror*«. (Ibid.: 2) On 27 April the *Daily Mirror* rounds off the tale in a celebratory tone continuing the same story from the front page on page three: Haller and Hurst are pictured holding the ball in *Daily Mirror* tee shirts with magnate Richard Branson who seems to have played an undefined financial role in enabling it all to happen (cf. Anon. 1996c).

These events were to become merely prologue to the controversy surrounding the actual coverage in the tabloids, particularly the *Daily Mirror*, when in June, the European championship duly got underway. England's team progressed well on home territory to reach the semi-finals where they were drawn against Germany. The tone of the humour took on a darker complexion as the build-up to this game has become one of the most notorious expressions of chauvinism in the British popular press. It is worth noting that the coverage of the European football championships took place in the midst of the ›Beef War‹ caused by the outbreak of BSE in Britain which provided, in its own way, a fertile backdrop of chauvinistic vocabulary and a continuous drum-beat of stereotypical references to a range of European countries and their past relationships to Britain mapped onto the contemporary. An anonymous editorial in the *Sun* on 24 June 1996 blends football, war and politics in a potent populist brew:

»THE BEEF WAR WITH EUROPE IS OVER – AND BRITAIN BLINKED FIRST [...].
But let's hope Whitehall and Brussels now act to free our herds of BSE and get the beef trucks rolling again.
If they do, this Italian job may turn out a score draw [...]
RATHER THAN THE CAVE-IN IT LOOKS LIKE.« (Anon. 1996a: 7)

The *Daily Mirror* immediately went for the sensational on 24 June as England prepared to play Germany with its now notorious headline on its front page, complete with images of England players Pearce and Gascoigne with World War II tin helmets on: »ACHTUNG SURRENDER. For you Fritz, ze Euro 96 Championship is over« (Wallace 1996: 1). The dates in the top corner of this front page may state 66/96, but it is an older and more literal conflict that the piece is resting on for its impact as well as its humour. As if to confirm this, the side of the front page on this day has a column headlined »Mirror declares football war on Germany« (ibid.). There is additionally a cut-out scissor line around the front page illustrations of the headline and the players in their helmets exhorting readers to »cut out and stick in your window« as a literal request for manifestation of support akin to putting out bunting or waving flags. On page two there is a declaration that »THE MIRROR INVADES BERLIN«, and in a sign that the Germans at least are joining in with the joke the German ambassador is reported to have claimed »it will be victory or else« (Dunn 1996: 2). This main article is in full wartime pastiche and is worth quoting in some detail:

»THE MIRROR INVADES BERLIN
CALLING LONDON [...] THIS IS AGENT DUNN REPORTING. THE FIRST STAGE OF OUR MISSION IS COMPLETE. WE HAVE REACHED THE GERMAN CITY OF BERLIN, DEEP IN ENEMY TERRITORY [...].
We have decided to teach the Hun a lesson. We have to put the wind up these chaps – warn them of the terrible danger that awaits them at Wembley [...]
There is a strange smell in Berlin [...]. and it's not just their funny sausages.
*The smell of fear*
It's the smell of fear – because they know, deep down, that we're going to beat them again.
This is why the Daily Mirror has penetrated the Fatherland. To shake the nerves of the so-called indomitable Jerries.
We have come fully armed with a special St George's flag and thousands of leaflets bearing the warning: ›Achtung! Surrender! Remember 1966.‹
The Germans hate being reminded of their failures. Like eating well-matured cheese for breakfast. Or nicking all the sun loungers in the Mediterranean. But what they hate most is being reminded of that glorious day in 1966 when England made them the sourest of sour-krauts.« (Ibid.)

The whole piece is characteristically tabloid in style. The newspaper takes on the guise of a wartime infiltrator as it makes inroads into enemy territory. Dunn, senior staff reporter for the *Daily Mirror*, presents himself here as their secret agent-in-chief. The narrative is replete with archaic stereotypes of the Germans at war but the piece shifts quickly to a teasing mode to maintain its humorous intent. The verb »reminded« is used twice but the call to memory is of 1966 while the narrative is shaped by allusions to

1939-45. In this way the sporting victory which the paper predicts will come is described in terms of the historical victory in war.

The *Daily Mirror* also calls on readers to fax messages answering the leading question whether the Germans should go into battle or make an honourable retreat. On page four the paper fans another popular stereotype by claiming that the Germans have been »beaten at their national game – when we bagged the best spots by the pool with a cache of Mirror towels« (Anon. 1996b, 4).

This coverage did not go unremarked. In the liberal *Guardian*, Matthew Engel rebuked the *Daily Mirror* for its second-world-war-style German-baiting edition and referred to it as: »A coarse and demented newspaper [...]. There is a strong case for saying that the *Mirror* should be prosecuted [...]. It is obscenely irresponsible journalism. [...] a desperate newspaper« (Engel 1996: 17). Engel was using a phrase, »coarse and demented newspaper«, that the *Daily Mirror* itself had used to condemn the *Sun* during its jingoistic coverage of the Falklands in 1982 (cf. Chippendale/Horrie 1992: 124).[3] The British Press Complaints Commission (PCC) received more than 300 complaints about the *Daily Mirror*'s coverage but did not uphold any, claiming that the newspaper articles were mostly concerned with standards of taste rather than articulating discrimination or incitement to hatred. The PCC has guidelines to ensure that robust comment is protected but that it does not bleed into racism (cf. Ahmed 1998: 7).

## THE DARK SIDE OF HUMOUR

It may have started with a joke and in fact it may have continued within a familiar pattern of humorous tradition but such a revisiting of a particular

---

[3] It is instructive to dwell for a moment on the specifics of Engel's tirade given the traditional editorial identity of the *Daily Mirror* in the context of real, as opposed to symbolic, military conflict. Through many military episodes from World War II to Suez or the Falklands War, the *Daily Mirror* had always represented a moderate and restraining voice within the British mass media, often opposed to what it considered jingoism and military opportunism and always on the side of the British soldier as a fundamentally decent character (cf. Tulloch 2007 and Chippendale/Horrie 1992).

British version of the past can have implications which are far from positive for the present. Against positive readings of the deflationary potential of humour, this chapter argues that within popular culture there is also a dark side to humour which feeds into a wide range of socially regressive tendencies which persist very much to the fore of contemporary British popular culture. Anderson and Weymouth (1999) studied the general tone of the content of political coverage of the EU and the ways in which such negativity and even hostility fuels a democratic deficit which leaves the British public woefully underinformed about the reality of European politics. Ours is an example of how tabloid humour, incorporating historical references, may contribute at a more populist level to reinforcing stereotypes and associations of other nations which are rooted in out-dated realities rather than using history as a means of educating a public.

The tabloids allow the past and the popular to come together, drawing upon a version of what Williams might have called a »structure of feeling« (1966: 47). The *Daily Mirror* and the *Sun* are highly effective in constructing an interpretation of English identity with resonance from lived experience and longer historical narratives. They do so for the enjoyment of their readers but also for the political purpose of maintaining a national identification among those same readers. Carey has argued that journalism is »a particular symbolic form, a highly particular type of consciousness, a particular organization of social experience« (1989: 25). This implies that newspapers have always been more concerned with rituals of identity formation rather than acting as vehicles which contribute to our knowledge of events in the world. In the case of tabloid representations of Germany, we could argue that the organization of social experience involves a reconstruction of a sense of a shared past. The reconfiguration of this particular national past draws upon a wide repertoire of mnemonic devices to effect the continuity and coherence of that community through time. The symbolic construction of community highlighted by Carey is all the stronger for it being narrated from a position of national superiority and it is disarming to the extent that it operates through humorous devices. By 1996 generations familiar with the symbolism and direct narratives of World War II were dying out and even 1966 was three decades past. But a powerfully populist set of rhetorical claims for national identification could not be left to drift into discursive disuse. The popular press is here flagging them vigorously for both commercial and political purposes.

Horst Pöttker has contributed to discussions of this tradition of journalism and has linked it specifically to contemporary historical representations. Drawing upon Bonfadelli's observation that journalism is now more involved with its »orientation function« (Bonfadelli et al. 2005: 308) as opposed to the older tradition of its »news function« which is increasingly displaced by social media and non-journalistic forms of electronic and digital transmission, Pöttker states:

»In a more general way, if it is the special duty of the journalistic profession to cater for publicness in modern, functionally differentiated societies, that is, to assure the optimal transparency of important occurrences and unsolved problems so that social self-regulation can function, then history is part of its thematic field because such occurrences and problems as require publicness result from the past.« (Pöttker 2012: 521)

Pöttker sees the sort of connections between the past and the contemporary as key to the effectiveness of this aspect of journalism:

»Because historical journalism – as opposed to the study of history – must be topical, its own logic of quality spurs it on not to deal with the past as a subject in its own right, as a certain positivist branch of historical studies would like, but to connect the past with the present.« (Ibid.: 525)

There is the liberal aspect to Pöttker's perspective but there is also the aspect provided by the popular tabloids which fits more within atavistic traditions of popular laughter. The discourse emanating from World War II could be seen as an attempt to maintain a patriotic pride in a core ›white‹ British identity – an example of a sort of inferential racism described by Stuart Hall (1981: 36-37).

Krishan Kumar (2003) has emphasized that despite a general toning down of strident expressions of national identity and explicit racism within the context of an increasingly multi-cultural reality, British or English identity is still predicated to a large extent on an exclusivity based on ethnicity. This reinforces the point made some years earlier by Stuart Hall that »a culturally-contrasted sense of Englishness and a particularly closed and exclusive form of English national identity […] is one of the core characteristics of British racism today« (Hall 1996: 446). Ethnic exclusivity is certainly one of the discourses in play within these humorous traditions of the popular tabloid press. Moreover it is worth noting that they operate, as I have argued elsewhere, very much within a pedagogic mode (cf. Conboy 2008).

In the humorous mode of expression discussed in this chapter, the nation can be articulated explicitly as providing a symbolic expression of the reality of that community for the readers of these newspapers confirming the observation of Seton-Watson that »a nation exists when a significant number of people in a community consider themselves to form a nation, or behave as if they form one« (1977: 5). The newspaper is expressing this symbolic reality in its representation of the present of the nation as intrinsically bound up within the achievements in the past with a double attraction, combining sporting with military memories. Through these mechanisms the readership in being addressed within a long-term version of their collective self-identity. It is of course a key component of the audience design (cf. Bell 1991) of these national and nationalist newspapers.

Football is significant in this construction of a popular variety of national identity, even more so since the embourgeoisement of football from Italia 90 through the founding of the Premier League in 1992. It is often deployed as a general metaphor for the well-being of the nation. The militarization of the vocabulary is already in place so that when the newspapers need to press this a little further it is discursively unproblematic. It is also a key part of the strategy of »personalization« so characteristic in drawing readers closer to the institutional discourse of the newspaper (cf. Landert/ Jucker 2011) – a vital tool in the tabloid box.

Especially in terms of events beyond the lived experience of readers, the tabloids play a part as popular educators (cf. Hall 1975: 11) within whose discourses Renan's (1990 [1882]) »daily plebiscite« on the validity of the nation is very much in play. The tabloids continue to ›normalize‹ national identification as a white, male and predominantly working-class mode of behaviour, drawing upon football as a central part of their myth-making. Their combination of linguistic style and narrative selection places their operations firmly within what one could claim is a popular-hegemonic *modus operandi*. The language which they use is deliberately constructed to fit within the personalized and intimate approach which has for so long been part of the appeal of the popular press (cf. Jackson 2001). The public idiom (cf. Hall 1978) for which they are renowned enables them to link with the everyday lives of their readers, and in extending this experience to fit historical allusions they extend their reach from the contemporary to the construction of an everyday version of selected parts of the national narrative of the past. Indeed this bridging of the tabloids brings the past very much within the scope of the »social semiotic« of Halliday (1978: 109): an idealized approximation of the language and the social identification of the target audience.

Narratives of nation are particularly easy for the popular tabloids to shape to meet these ends, and it is particularly perceptive of McGuigan to point out that the narratives are most often located on »fertile chauvinistic ground« (1993: 184), meaning that the tabloid tales of national memory are almost always rooted in a chauvinistic context. Their version of national identity is also one which is, at least rhetorically, styled as being on the side of the little people and opposed to the interests and tastes of the powerful elite, adding credence to the tabloids' assertion that the nation belongs to the common people. Their irreverent approach fits well within a tradition of plain talking – ›telling it as it is‹ – and attempts to reconstruct the past in terms belonging to the same idiom. Not only is this an example of a nation put to daily use (cf. Billig 1995: 95) but also increasingly its past, in terms of its tabloid iconography at the centre of which is World War II and the World Cup of 1966. Such constructed memories assist in the maintenance of simultaneity which is of such importance in Anderson's (1987) view of nation construction.

One country – two histories: In the coverage in the two tabloids discussed above 1966 is the historical referent but the iconography is from a different history. The history of World War II has particular relevance in the tabloids' coverage of a game against Germany but this range of reference and imagery is not restricted to England-Germany games and has not diminished over time as can be seen during coverage of the football World Cup in South Africa in 2010 (cf. Conboy 2012). The deployment of historical events as context to contemporary stories is, perhaps surprisingly, a regular feature of tabloid representation. These historical contexts are often highly nationalistic and use a style of abbreviated and stereotypical reference to Britain/England and the outside world. For many they are part and parcel of the British tabloid view of the world, and humour – entertaining a readership which is in on the joke – is never far down the list of reasons why historical references are framed in this way. Humour in the British tabloids based on historical references is rarely a discourse of liberation or contestation and more regularly a reminder of core nationalistic claims based on chauvinism and national stereotypes. Humour is not the key to unlocking the past; more likely it is an acceptable way of maintaining populist prejudices in the present. – Only having a laugh! Possibly the oldest excuse for behaving badly.

## WORKS CITED

Ahmed, Kamal (1998): »Press Warned to Watch Language in Covering World Cup«. In: *Guardian* 14 May, 7.
Allen, Peter (1996): »I Get My Hans on Hurst's Ball«. In: *Daily Mirror* 26 April, 1-3.
Anderson, Benedict (1987): *Imagined Communities*, London: Verso.
Anderson, P.J./T.A. Weymouth (1999): *Insulting the Public? The British Press and the European Union*, London: Longman.
Anon. (1996a): »We Need to Let Cattle Commence«. In: *Sun* 24 June, 7.
Anon. (1996b): »JURGEN THROWS [...] and Mirror Captures Their Sunloungers«. In: *Daily Mirror* 24 June, 4.
Anon. (1996c): »They Think It's All Over. It's His Now«. In: *Daily Mirror* 27 April, 1 and 3.
Bakhtin, Mikhail M. (1984 [1940]): *Rabelais and His World*, Bloomington: Indiana UP.
Bakhtin, Mikhail M. (1996 [1975]): *The Dialogic Imagination*, ed. Michael Holquist, Austin: U of Texas P.
Bell, Allan (1991): *The Language of News Media*, Oxford: Blackwell.
Bergson, Henri (2008 [1900]): *Laughter: An Essay on the Meaning of the Comic*, Rockville/MD: Arc Manor. [*Le Rire: Essai sur la signification du comique*, Paris: Presses Universitaires de France, 1900.]
Billig, Michael (1995): *Banal Nationalism*, London: Sage.
Bonfadelli, Heinz/Otfried Jarren/Gabrielle Siegert (eds.) (2005): *Einführung in die Publizistikwissenschaft*, Bern: Haupt.
Carey, James W. (1989): *Communication as Culture: Essays on Media and Society*, Boston: Hyman Publishers.
Chapman, James (2012): *British Comics: A Cultural History*, London: Reaktion Books.
Chippendale, Peter/Chris Horrie (1992): *Stick It Up Your Punter: The Rise and Fall of the* Sun, London: Mandarin.

Conboy, Martin (2002): *The Press and Popular Culture*, London: Sage.
Conboy, Martin (2006): *Tabloid Britain: Constructing a Community Through Language*, London: Routledge.
Conboy, Martin (2008): »A Tale of Two Battles: History in the Popular Press«. In: Siân Nicholas/Tom O'Malley/Kevin Williams (eds.), *Reconstructing the Past: History in the Mass Media 1890-2005*, London: Routledge, 137-152.
Conboy, Martin (2012): »How Journalism Uses History«. In: Martin Conboy (ed.), *How Journalism Uses History*, London: Routledge, 1-14.
Conboy, Martin (ed.) (2012): *How Journalism Uses History*, London: Routledge.
Dunn, Justin (1996): »The Mirror Invades Berlin«. In: *Daily Mirror* 24 June, 2.
Engel, Matthew (1996): »A Coarse and Demented Newspaper«. In: *Guardian* 25 June, 17.
Fiske, John (1994): *Reading the Popular*, London: Routledge.
Fowler, Roger (1991): *Language in the News: Discourse and Ideology in the Press*, London: Routledge.
Hall, Stuart (1975): »Introduction«. In: Anthony Smith, *Paper Voices: The Popular Press and Social Change, 1935–1965*, London: Chatto and Windus, 11-24.
Hall, Stuart (1978): »The Social Production of News«. In: Stuart Hall/Chas Critcher/T. Jefferson/J. Clarke/B. Roberts (eds.), *Policing the Crisis: Mugging, the State and Law and Order*, London: Macmillan, 53-77.
Hall, Stuart (1981): »The Whites of Their Eyes: Racist Ideologies and the Media«. In: George Bridges/Rosalind Brunt (eds.), *Silver Linings: Some Strategies for the Eighties*, London: Lawrence and Wishart, 28-52.
Halliday, Michael A.K. (1978): *Language as Social Semiotic: The Social Interpretation of Language and Meaning*, London: Arnold.
Jackson, Kate (2001): *George Newnes and the New Journalism in Britain, 1880-1910: Culture and Profit*, Aldershot: Ashgate.
Kay, John (1996): »Geoff Hurst Gets His Ball Back«. In: *Sun* 25 April, 1.
Kumar, Krishan (2003): *The Making of English National Identity*, Cambridge: CUP.
Landert, Daniela/Andreas H. Jucker (2011): »Private and Public in Mass Communication: From Letters to the Editor to Online Commentaries«. *Journal of Pragmatics* 43.5, 1422-1434.

MacWilliam, Rohan (1998): *Popular Politics in Nineteenth Century England*, London: Routledge.
McGuigan, Jim (1993): *Cultural Populism*, London: Routledge.
Morreall, John (1983): *Taking Laughter Seriously*, Albany: State U of New York P.
Nash, Pete (1996): »All Action Story of the Lost Ball«. In: *Sun* 26 April, 4.
Nicholson, Bob (2012): »Jonathan's Jokes«. *Media History* 18.1, 33-49.
Oliver, Ted (1996): »Give Me My Ball Back«. In: *Daily Mirror* 25 April, 11.
Pöttker, Horst (2012): »A Reservoir of Understanding: Why Journalism Needs History as a Thematic Field«. In: Martin Conboy (ed.), *How Journalism Uses History*, London: Routledge, 15-32.
Pyatt, Jamie (1996): »Helmut Ball Deal Blasted«. In: *Sun* 27 April, 1 & 11.
Rae, Charles (1996): »Hans Off My Ball, Helmut«. In: *Sun* 26 April, 4.
Renan, Ernest (1990 [1882]): »What Is a Nation?«. In: Homi K. Bhabha (ed.), *Nations and Narration*, London: Routledge, 8-22.
Seton-Watson, Hugh (1977): *Nations and States: An Enquiry Into the Origins of Nations and the Politics of Nationalism*, Boulder/CO: Westview.
Tulloch, John (2007): »The *Daily Mirror* and the Invasions of Egypt (1956) and Iraq (2003)«. *Journalism Studies* 8.1, 42-60.
Wallace, Richard (1996): »Achtung! Surrender. For You Fritz, ze Euro 96 Championship Is Over«. In: *Daily Mirror* 24 June, 1.
Williams, Raymond (1966): *The Long Revolution*, Harmondsworth: Penguin.
Wooding, David (1996): »The Greediest Krauts on Earth«. In: *Sun* 26 April, 1.
Zijderveld, Anton C. (1983): *The Sociology of Humour and Laughter*, London: Sage.

# List of Contributors

**Martin Conboy** is Professor of Journalism History and Director of Research in the Department of Journalism Studies at the University of Sheffield. He is also the co-director of the Centre for the Study of Journalism and History based in Sheffield. His research interests include the representation of national identity, popular journalism and celebrity culture. He is the author of seven single-authored books on the language and history of journalism and is on the editorial boards of *Journalism Studies: Media History; Journalism: Theory, Practice and Criticism*; and *Memory Studies*. He is also co-editor of the book series *Journalism Studies: Key Texts*.

**Dorothea Flothow** is a lecturer at the Department of English and American Studies at Salzburg University. She studied English Literature and Modern History at the Universities of Tübingen (Germany) and Reading (UK). While employed at the Collaborative Research Centre »Kriegserfahrungen«, University of Tübingen, she completed her PhD on war imagery in British children's novels (1870 to 1939). Her research interests include historical drama and fiction, British children's fiction, and the First World War. She is currently working on a project on rewritings of the Restoration period in English historical drama.

**Irvin J. Hunt** is a doctoral candidate in the Department of English and Comparative Literature at Columbia University. In 2007 he received an M.A. in English from the University of California, Berkeley. In 2008, he received an M.A. in English from Columbia, and in 2009 an M.Phil from Columbia's Institute of Comparative Literature. In May of 2014 he will be defending his dissertation, *Humoring Racism: Comic Forms of Resistance* *in 20th Century African American Literature*. It is a study of Zora Neale Hurston, Ralph Ellison, Charles Wright, and Suzan-Lori Parks.

**Barbara Korte** is Professor of English Literature at the University of Freiburg, and co-speaker of the DFG-funded research group *History in Popular Cultures of Knowledge*. Recent publications include work on the British short story, English travel writing, Black and Asian British culture and the cultural reception of the First World War in Britain. Her current research focuses on British periodicals of the nineteenth century.

**Doris Lechner** received her MA in European Literatures and Cultures at the University of Freiburg with a thesis on Marina Lewycka's *Popular Novels about Eastern Europe:* Tractors, Caravans *and the Mechanics of the British Book Market* in 2010. She is currently working towards her PhD on representations of history in nineteenth-century British family magazines as part of the research group *History in Popular Cultures of Knowledge*. She is co-founder of www.bookhistorynetwork.wordpress.com.

**Stefanie Lethbridge** is a lecturer in English Literature and Cultural Studies at the University of Freiburg. Her major research interests are in eighteenth- and nineteenth-century book history and popular culture. She is the author of *James Thomson's Defence of Poetry* (2003) and has recently completed an extensive study of British poetry anthologies 1557 to 2007. As part of a DFG-supported research programme she has recently started a project on concepts of the heroic in eighteenth-century periodicals and prints.

**Brian Maidment** has recently been appointed as Professor of the History of Print Culture at Liverpool John Moores University. He has written widely on nineteenth-century literature, especially periodicals, writing by working men and women, and mass circulation publishing. More recent work has focused on down market visual culture, especially illustrated comic publications. His new book, *Comedy, Caricature and the Social Order 1820-1850* was published by Manchester University Press early in 2013.

**Duncan Marks** is a researcher of Modern British History at Sheffield University. He has recently successfully defended his AHRC-sponsored doctoral thesis, ›*Unrepentant Victorians*‹: *Generational Identities and Tensions in Britain, c.1901-39*. This research explores generational identities and tensions in Britain in the earlier decades of the twentieth century, with a particular focus given to those who continued to identify themselves as a ›Victorian‹ long after the death of Queen Victoria in 1901.

**Bob Nicholson** is a lecturer in History at Edge Hill University. His research interests center on the history of transatlantic cultural relations, jokes, slang, journalism history, and the digital humanities. He blogs at www.digitalvictorianist.com.

**Sandra Martina Schwab** received her PhD from the University of Mainz, where she is currently a lecturer for British Literature at the Department of English & Linguistics. In 2010 she was Visiting Professor at York University, Toronto. Her research interests include Victorian periodicals, Richard Doyle, popular literature, folk literature, as well as British society and culture in the 1800s. Her study on the history of the dragonslayer story, *Of Dragons, Knights and Virgin Maidens: Dragonslaying and Gender Roles from Richard Johnson to Modern Popular Fiction*, will be released in 2013. Her post-doctoral project deals with travel and transport in *Punch*, 1841-91. For further information visit www.SandraMartinaSchwab.com.

**Ulrike Zimmermann** studied English and German in Freiburg and Newcastle-upon-Tyne and did a PhD at the University of Freiburg on humour in contemporary novels of development by women writers, where she is a lecturer for British Literature and Cultural Studies at the English Department. Her current research project deals with popularisations of the 18th century. Research interests include metaphysical poetry, literature and the supernatural, as well as the contemporary British novel.

# Index

absurd 38, 64, 173, 175
   theatre of the a. 18, 173-177
Adams, Liz Duffy (*Or*) 91, 98, 105
Addison, Henry Robert (*The King's Word*) 95, 105
Adeler, Max (»The Fortunate Island«) 163, 168
affect (see emotion)
Albert, Prince Consort 134, 137, 141-144
Alfred the Great 103
Americanisation 154, 166
Americanness 159-160, 162
Anderson, Benedict 193, 203, 206
anecdote, anecdotal 37, 102, 105, 111, 115, 124, 128, 129, 136, 152
Anglo-American relations 151-168 (see also Americanisation)
Arnold, Matthew 166
Arthur, King 162
attitude 9, 17, 23, 36, 37, 71, 72, 75, 79, 82, 120, 123, 142, 147, 159, 162

authenticity, authentic 71, 83, 115, 117, 135, 141, 157

Bakhtin, Mikhail 10, 13, 187, 190, 194, 207
Barry, Charles 55-56
Barthes, Roland 187, 190
Bartman, Sarah 18, 171-189
Battle of Britain 81
Bayeux Tapestry 55-58
Benhabib, Seyla 183, 190
Bentley, Frederick (*Seymour's Humorous Sketches*) 32-33, 44
Bergson, Henri 10, 12, 194
biography, biographical writings 32, 40, 135-142
Bismarck, Otto von 76
*Blackadder* 8, 111, 125-127
body 23, 172-174, 178, 181, 186, 189
Bohn, Henry (*Sketches by Seymour*) 32, 40, 44
Boleyn, Anne 76, 79
book history 21, 23
boundary 12, 13, 73, 83, 88, 140, 194

Britishness 17, 77, 143-145, 166 (see also Englishness, identity)
British Press Complaints Commission (PCC) 202
Buckle, Henry Thomas 89
Burke, Kenneth 188-190
burlesque 22, 52, 62, 89, 166

caricature 10, 15-17, 21-44, 47-66, 71-72, 111, 113, 118-125, 127-128
carnival, carnivalesque 10, 13, 17, 23, 44, 187, 194
cartoon 13, 22-23, 48, 59, 80, 83, 134, 164, 194-195, 197
Catholic Relief Bill 121
censorship 101, 139
Charles II 16, 87-105
chauvinism 71, 200, 207
Churchill, Winston 81, 83, 145
class 16, 27, 32-34, 36-37, 39, 42, 70-75, 79, 83, 93, 100, 142, 165-166, 182, 205
colonialism, colonial 18, 172-173
comedy 10, 13-14, 22-23, 27, 38, 40, 41, 70, 87-105, 134, 143-144, 146, 147, 171-189, 194
   c. of manners 88, 155
   historical c. 91, 100
   physical c. 126-127
comic (see cartoon)
commemoration 55, 75, 77, 114, 137 (see also remembrance)
community, imagined community 12-13, 70, 72, 77, 82-83, 187-189, 193, 195, 203, 205 (see also Anderson, Benedict)

compassion (see emotion)
consumer, consumption 23, 29, 33, 40-41, 71, 83, 148, 154, 156, 186
Crowquill, Alfred (*Seymour's Humorous Sketches*) 31-33, 37-40, 45
Cruikshank, George 24, 25, 29, 42-43
culture industry 71
custom 159 (see also tradition)

*Daily Mirror* 195-203
debunking 8, 12-13, 135, 136
deflation 14, 17, 53, 76, 78, 127-128, 203
democracy 23, 41, 43, 121, 164, 203
Derrida, Jacques 174, 190
Dickens, Charles 24, 27, 29, 152
disempowerment 185 (see also empowerment)
displacement 70, 83
Disraeli, Benjamin 53-54, 76
distortion 13, 70, 83, 159
*Doctor Who* 145, 150
Doyle, Richard 16, 47-66
   *Comic English Histories* 52
   *Dame Julianna Berners* 66, 67
   fairy paintings and drawings by D. 65
   *The Newcomes* (William Makepeace Thackeray) 60-62, 68
   »Our Barry-eux Tapestry« 55-60, 68

*Rebecca and Rowena* (William Makepeace Thackeray) 62-64, 68
*The Tournament* 50-51, 65, 67
drama 88-91, 100-104, 175, 187-188

Edward I 52-53
Edward VIII 142
Egan, Pierce (*Life in London*) 24-27, 31, 44
Eglinton Tournament 50-52
Elizabeth I 89
emotion 11-12, 51, 61-62, 65, 143, 177-179
  affect 177-181
  compassion 77, 178-179
  horror 8, 60, 63, 178-179
  pity 178-179, 183
  sympathy 76, 138, 141-142, 163, 165, 178-179
Empire 48, 143, 168
empowerment 185 (see also disempowerment)
England 18, 56, 66, 77, 84, 112, 125, 153, 155, 173-174, 180, 193, 196, 200-201, 206
Englishness 73, 77-78, 203-204 (see also Britishness, identity)
everyday 7, 15, 17, 74, 82, 176, 183, 205-206
exaggeration 51, 56, 61, 64, 124, 127, 152, 161, 164

Fields, Gracie 75, 82

film 8, 14, 17, 77, 90, 96, 135, 141-144
Fiske, John 198, 208
Foucault, Michel 182-183, 190
France, French 8, 16, 55-62, 92, 103, 105, 112, 114-115, 118, 172-174, 176, 184-185, 195
freak show 18, 171, 187-188
Freud, Sigmund 10, 19, 179, 190
*Futurama* 147, 150

gender 10, 43, 73, 98, 130, 140-141, 182, 194
George IV 76, 125
Germany 14, 18, 144, 193, 196-197, 200-201, 203, 206
Gladstone, William E. 153-154
Glorious Revolution 97
Gramsci, Antonio (see hegemony)
*The Great McGonagall* 142-143, 150
Grey, Lady Jane 76

hagiography 137-138
Hall, Stuart 174, 190, 204-205, 208
Haller, Helmut 196-200
Heath, William 42, 113-114, 118-123
hegemony 71, 80
Helps, Sir Arthur 136
Henry V 103
Henry VIII 89-90, 105
heritage 71
heroisation 17, 111-112, 114, 117, 128-130

heroism 59, 62, 64, 75-78, 82, 89-90, 124-125, 127, 167, 196-197, 199
  national h. 117
  unheroic 16, 77-78, 82, 102, 117, 147
history
  academic h. 89
  h. from below 16, 69-84
  historians 10, 22, 89, 100, 102, 184
  value of h. 159
Holland, Caroline 136-137
Holloway, Stanley 16, 69-70, 74-84
Hood, Thomas 29-30
horror (see emotion)
Houses of Parliament 55-56, 60
Housman, Laurence (*Victoria Regina: A Dramatic Biography*) 139-141, 149
humour (see also incongruity, superiority)
  h. as editorial device 194-195
  lack of h. 17, 134, 139, 141, 145, 146
Hurst, Geoff 193, 196-197, 199, 200

idealisation 14, 17, 54, 60-66, 88, 155
identity 11-13, 15-17, 93-98, 116, 134-135, 173, 179, 182-183, 195
  national i. 16, 17, 75, 102, 143-145, 153, 155, 157, 159, 166, 203-206 (see also Britishness, Englishness, nation)
imagined community (see community, Anderson, Benedict)
incongruity 11-12, 16, 38, 129-130, 176, 194-195
innovation (see progress)
irony 17, 61-62, 64, 144-145, 147, 177, 186, 195
  dramatic i. 16, 94
*It Ain't Half Hot Mum* 143-144, 150

Jerrold, Douglas (*The Bride of Ludgate*) 91, 93-94, 106
  (*Nell Gwynne*) 91, 95-96, 106
  (see also Meadows, Kenny)
joke 8, 13, 17, 27, 37, 59-60, 77, 83, 94, 111, 130, 134, 136, 138, 145, 151-152, 154-158, 160-161, 171, 173, 194, 201-202, 206

Kant, Immanuel 129-131
Kester, Paul (*Sweet Nell of Old Drury*) 91, 96-97, 106

Langer, Suzan 183, 191
Langtry, Lillie (*The Days I Knew*) 140, 149
lightness 18, 176-177
Love Being British 145, 149

Macaulay, Thomas Babington 89, 108
Macfarren, G.A. (*King Charles II*) 103, 106

*Rebecca and Rowena* (William Makepeace Thackeray) 62-64, 68
*The Tournament* 50-51, 65, 67
drama 88-91, 100-104, 175, 187-188

Edward I 52-53
Edward VIII 142
Egan, Pierce (*Life in London*) 24-27, 31, 44
Eglinton Tournament 50-52
Elizabeth I 89
emotion 11-12, 51, 61-62, 65, 143, 177-179
  affect 177-181
  compassion 77, 178-179
  horror 8, 60, 63, 178-179
  pity 178-179, 183
  sympathy 76, 138, 141-142, 163, 165, 178-179
Empire 48, 143, 168
empowerment 185 (see also disempowerment)
England 18, 56, 66, 77, 84, 112, 125, 153, 155, 173-174, 180, 193, 196, 200-201, 206
Englishness 73, 77-78, 203-204 (see also Britishness, identity)
everyday 7, 15, 17, 74, 82, 176, 183, 205-206
exaggeration 51, 56, 61, 64, 124, 127, 152, 161, 164

Fields, Gracie 75, 82

film 8, 14, 17, 77, 90, 96, 135, 141-144
Fiske, John 198, 208
Foucault, Michel 182-183, 190
France, French 8, 16, 55-62, 92, 103, 105, 112, 114-115, 118, 172-174, 176, 184-185, 195
freak show 18, 171, 187-188
Freud, Sigmund 10, 19, 179, 190
*Futurama* 147, 150

gender 10, 43, 73, 98, 130, 140-141, 182, 194
George IV 76, 125
Germany 14, 18, 144, 193, 196-197, 200-201, 203, 206
Gladstone, William E. 153-154
Glorious Revolution 97
Gramsci, Antonio (see hegemony)
*The Great McGonagall* 142-143, 150
Grey, Lady Jane 76

hagiography 137-138
Hall, Stuart 174, 190, 204-205, 208
Haller, Helmut 196-200
Heath, William 42, 113-114, 118-123
hegemony 71, 80
Helps, Sir Arthur 136
Henry V 103
Henry VIII 89-90, 105
heritage 71
heroisation 17, 111-112, 114, 117, 128-130

heroism 59, 62, 64, 75-78, 82, 89-90, 124-125, 127, 167, 196-197, 199
national h. 117
unheroic 16, 77-78, 82, 102, 117, 147
history
academic h. 89
h. from below 16, 69-84
historians 10, 22, 89, 100, 102, 184
value of h. 159
Holland, Caroline 136-137
Holloway, Stanley 16, 69-70, 74-84
Hood, Thomas 29-30
horror (see emotion)
Houses of Parliament 55-56, 60
Housman, Laurence (*Victoria Regina: A Dramatic Biography*) 139-141, 149
humour (see also incongruity, superiority)
h. as editorial device 194-195
lack of h. 17, 134, 139, 141, 145, 146
Hurst, Geoff 193, 196-197, 199, 200

idealisation 14, 17, 54, 60-66, 88, 155
identity 11-13, 15-17, 93-98, 116, 134-135, 173, 179, 182-183, 195
national i. 16, 17, 75, 102, 143-145, 153, 155, 157, 159, 166, 203-206 (see also Britishness, Englishness, nation)
imagined community (see community, Anderson, Benedict)
incongruity 11-12, 16, 38, 129-130, 176, 194-195
innovation (see progress)
irony 17, 61-62, 64, 144-145, 147, 177, 186, 195
dramatic i. 16, 94
*It Ain't Half Hot Mum* 143-144, 150

Jerrold, Douglas (*The Bride of Ludgate*) 91, 93-94, 106
(*Nell Gwynne*) 91, 95-96, 106
(see also Meadows, Kenny)
joke 8, 13, 17, 27, 37, 59-60, 77, 83, 94, 111, 130, 134, 136, 138, 145, 151-152, 154-158, 160-161, 171, 173, 194, 201-202, 206

Kant, Immanuel 129-131
Kester, Paul (*Sweet Nell of Old Drury*) 91, 96-97, 106

Langer, Suzan 183, 191
Langtry, Lillie (*The Days I Knew*) 140, 149
lightness 18, 176-177
Love Being British 145, 149

Macaulay, Thomas Babington 89, 108
Macfarren, G.A. (*King Charles II*) 103, 106

Magna Carta 83-84
mainstream 16, 29, 70, 73, 75, 78, 195, 203, 206
›march of intellect‹ 27, 33-40
mass culture 22-31, 33, 41-43
master narrative 9, 14
material culture 17, 25, 113-114, 145
Meadows, Kenny (*Heads of the People*) 27-28
medievalism 16, 49-66
Middle Ages 16, 47-66, 103, 162-168
military 16-17, 57-60, 75-83, 111-130, 197-202, 205, 143-144
modernity 17, 71, 73, 154-159, 162-164, 166, 168
monarchy 16-17, 87-105, 133-148, 164
Moncrieff, W.T. (»Rochester«) 95, 106
Monmouth Rebellion 97
*Monty Python's Flying Circus* 143-144, 147, 150
Morreall, John 10-11, 19, 130, 132, 194, 209
*Mrs Brown* 142, 150
Murdoch, Rupert 195
music hall 16, 69-86, 154
myth 14, 30, 77, 83, 115, 117, 135, 139, 147, 164, 185, 205

Napoleon I 9, 55-56, 76, 78, 111-115, 117-118
Napoleonic Wars 16, 75, 83 (see also Waterloo, Trafalgar)

nation, national 13, 15-18, 70-71, 73, 75, 79-80, 102, 111, 117, 122, 141, 144-145, 152-155, 157, 160-161, 166, 194-196, 198-200, 202-207 (see also identity)
Nelson, Horatio 9, 75-78, 83, 116-117
newspaper 17, 47, 129, 151-154, 156-157, 160,163, 165, 193-207

ordinary man/woman 69-84
other, othering 12, 14, 17, 42, 91, 172-173, 182

Palmerston, Lord (Henry John Temple) 141-142
Parks, Suzan-Lori (*Venus*) 18, 171-192
parody 9, 15, 49, 51, 53-60, 62-64, 66, 73, 142, 187, 198
participation (cultural) 69, 75, 80-83
patriotism 74, 77-78, 144-145, 153, 196, 204
Payn, James (*The Talk of the Town*) 135-137, 149
Payne, John Howard (*Charles the Second*) 92-94, 106
Peake, R.B. (*Seymour's Humorous Sketches*) 32-37, 39, 45
Peel, Robert 53-54
performance 3, 69-70, 72-74, 79, 83, 173-174, 183-184
Peter the Great 103

picaresque 23, 30-31, 34, 36-37, 39, 41, 44, 164
pity (see emotion)
popular culture 25, 27, 42, 71-72, 77, 89, 101, 144, 154, 162, 199, 203
popularisation 10, 128
populism 18, 194, 196, 200, 203, 207
Poskitt, Kjartan (*Nell's Belles*) 90, 99, 106
postwar 15, 74, 142
Pöttker, Horst 193, 204, 209
power 8, 14, 73, 117, 121, 138, 144, 153, 159-160, 163, 198, 203, 206 (see also empowerment, disempowerment)
prejudice 18, 193, 195, 207
presentism 75
private life 89-90, 102, 104, 137, 139 (see also everyday)
progress 33, 36, 154, 159-160, 163-164, 188-189 163-164
pun 78, 119
*Punch* 9, 24, 47-68, 124, 152, 156-157, 160, 162, 164, 166, 168, 195

racism 172, 174-175, 178, 182, 186, 188-189, 202, 204
Radcliffe, Claude (*Check to the King*) 97, 106
Reform Bill (1832) 120-121
Regency 16, 21-46, 125
remembrance 133 (see also commemoration)

resistance (cultural) 13, 75-80, 83
Richard I 62-63, 76
ridicule 12-13, 16, 50, 57, 61, 70, 81, 124, 127, 130, 147

satire 8-11, 14, 16-17, 22, 34, 37, 41, 43-44, 53, 55-56, 59-60, 65-66, 70, 72, 90, 111, 118-119, 125, 155, 159, 164, 195
Scott, Sir Walter 49, 62-64, 167
Seymour, Robert 22, 29-40, 42, 44
Shakespeare, William 88, 101-104, 151-152, 154, 160
Shaw, George Bernard (*In Good King Charles's Golden Days*) 97-100, 106
Sherwood, Mary (*Royal Girls and Royal Courts*) 136-137, 149
slapstick 8, 74, 126-127
slavery 171, 173, 184
social media 17, 135, 148, 204
stage 16, 27, 69-86, 87-110, 135, 139, 141, 147, 152, 171-192 (see also theatre)
Stead, W.T. 154, 165-166
stereotype 16, 18, 70, 93-94, 96-98, 114, 151, 196-198, 200-203, 206-207
Strachey, Lytton 135, 137-138
*Striker* 196-197
*Sun* 195-200, 202-203
superiority 17, 152, 172, 181, 186, 194, 203
sympathy (see emotion)

tabloid press 18, 193-208
technology 33, 154, 157, 159-160, 162-163, 166, 194
television 8, 74, 83, 125-127, 135, 142-143, 145, 147
Thackeray, William Makepeace 42-44, 60-64
theatre 69-86, 87-110, 152, 154, 171-192
Tower of London 75-76, 79, 82-83
tradition 8-9, 13, 15-16, 22-23, 27, 31, 33-34, 36, 38-39, 41, 43, 62, 83, 88-90, 93-94, 96, 100, 103, 135, 141, 143, 152, 155, 157, 159, 162-163, 168, 193, 195-197, 199, 202, 204, 206 (see also custom)
Trafalgar 77, 116-117
tragedy, tragic 7-8, 87-91, 104, 136, 171-179, 188
tragicomedy 8, 176
transcultural 14-15
transgression 12, 39-40, 42, 72, 79, 83, 137
trauma 14, 17-18, 189
Treaty of Dover 97
trivialisation 23, 100, 176
Twain, Mark (*A Connecticut Yankee in King Arthur's Court*) 155, 162-168

variety stage 69-86
Victoria, Queen 16-17, 122, 129-150, 167
*Victoria the Great* 141-142

Victorian 10, 16-18, 21-46, 47-68, 90, 113, 130, 133-150, 147-170
violence 18, 63-64, 126, 171-192
visual culture 10, 15-16, 21-44, 47-66, 113-114, 118-125, 139, 142, 194, 196-197, 201
voyeurism 105, 175, 180, 187, 189

Waterloo 59, 79, 111-118, 129-130
Wellington, Arthur Wellesley, Duke of 16-17, 55-56, 58-59, 75-76, 79-83, 111-132
Wilde, Oscar (*The Canterville Ghost*) 155-160, 166, 168
working class (see class)
World War II 14, 18, 198-200, 202-204, 206

xenophobia 141-142, 195

*Young Victoria, The* 142

Zijderveld, Anton C. 11-14, 20, 194, 209